LANCASTER COUNTY
The Best Fun, Food, Lodging, Shopping, and Sights

Alonna F. Smith

For additional copies write or call:

Food Companion Press
P.O. Box 27266
Philadelphia, PA 19118-0266
(215) 844-3850

Printed in the United States of America

Editor: Louise Stoltzfus
Text and cover design: Bob Hires
Front cover photograph: Robert Leahy
Back cover photographs:
Two Amishmen: Roger L. Berger
Mother and daughter: Ron Bowman Visual Communications
Maps: Eric Lee Smith
Photographs unless otherwise noted are copyright 1997 by Alonna F. Smith.

Smith, Alonna F.

Lancaster County: the best fun, food, lodging, shopping and sights /
by Alonna F. Smith. -- 1st ed.
p. cm.

Includes Index

1. Lancaster County (Pa.)--Guidebooks. 2. Amish and Mennonites (Pa.)--Guidebooks
3. Pennnsylvania Germans (Pa.)--Guidebooks I. Title

ISBN 0-9644975-1-4

Library of Congress Catalog Card Number: 96-062098

| F157.L21997 | QB197-40569 | 95-067116 |
| 917.481504'043 | | CIP |

First Printing

10 9 8 7 6 5 4 3 2 1

FOR
MY GRANDMOTHER
RUTH MOYER DERSTINE

ACKNOWLEDGEMENTS

An author inevitably relies on a whole host of people in order to produce a book. I am grateful to my paternal grandparents for their patience in taking their oldest of many grandchildren to explore their favorite corners of Lancaster County.

I was assisted on a day-to-day basis by my editor Louise Stoltzfus, who gave me much encouragement, invaluable feedback, and kept me on course. Bob Hires, as graphic designer was appreciated as much for his calming influence as his creativity.

I am especially grateful to my Aunt Geri Sell, who generously invited me to stay with her in her Lancaster County home while I did my research.

Thanks also goes to Tim Ardinger and Beth Oberholtzer who aided me many ways including sharing information about the food of Lancaster County, collecting newspapers, and aiding me in my data collection.

Finally, I'm indebted to the following friends for their enthusiasm for this project and their encouragement, advice, and moral support: Donna Antony, Paul Antony, Rick Bunker, Ruth Harvey, Dana Jacobi, Marilyn Odesser-Torpey, Adrienne Redd, and Tami Sherman.

Last, but most of all, I want to thank my husband whose encouragement and faith in me is the only reason I weathered this project.

TABLE OF CONTENTS

Acknowledgements 7
Introduction 12
Visitors' Centers 15
Calendar of Events 16
How This Book Works 23
Maps 23, 226

CHAPTER ONE: A BRIEF HISTORY
Lancaster County: Past and Present 30
Who Are the Pennsylvania Dutch? 32
Visitors' Centers 39

CHAPTER TWO: LODGING
Bed and Breakfasts 44
Inns 61
Farms and Guest Houses 69
Camping 74
Resorts, Hotels, Motels, and Travel Lodges 78
Lodging Outside Lancaster County 82

CHAPTER THREE: FOOD
Restaurants 89
American and Continental 89
Breakfast 95
Ethnic 96
Family and Pennsylvania Dutch Food 102
Fine Dining 108
Lunch 113
Pub Grub 114
Restaurants Outside Lancaster County 118
Purveyors 121
Bakeries 121
Butchers 124
Candy 126
Coffee and Tea 127
Country Stores 128
Farm Stands 129
Farmers' Markets 133

Flour 135
Honey 136
Herbs 136
Ice Cream 137
Imported Foods 138
Jams and Jellies 139
Natural Food Stores 140
Pretzels 141
Trout 143
Wine and Beer 144

CHAPTER FOUR:
PLACES TO SEE AND THINGS TO DO

Buggy Rides 149
Covered Bridges 150
Especially for Children 151
For Train Lovers 152
Getting to Know Amish and Mennonites 155
Museums and Historic Sights 157
Recreation 165
That's Entertainment 173
Tours 175
Things to See and Do Outside Lancaster County 176

CHAPTER FIVE: SHOPPING

Antiques 186
Auctions 189
Books 191
Country Stores 194
Galleries 196
General 196
Handcrafted Furniture 198
Handcrafted Gifts 204
Knives 212
Outlets 212
Quilts 217
Quilting Materials 220
Consignment Shops 221

CHAPTER SIX:
THE INTRIGUING TOWNS
OF LANCASTER COUNTY

Map 226
Ephrata 227
Intercourse 227
Lancaster City 228
Lititz 229
Marietta and Columbia 229
Strasburg 230
Trips Outside Lancaster County 231

RESOURCES

Airport 233
Auto Rental 233
Medical Services 233
Pet Lodging 234
Pharmacies 234
Service Stations 234
Transportation 234

RECOMMENDED READING
..............................235

INDEX
....238

INTRODUCTION

Trips to Lancaster County were a special treat for me when I was a child. My grandmother, a Mennonite farmer's wife from Montgomery County, would pack up several of her many grandchildren and take us to her favorite haunts. Lancaster County was where she handpicked a quilt when her grandchildren got married, bought material for her dresses, and picked up various and sundry household goods. Her husband bought everything from farm implements to cows and even the odd table at the Green Dragon farmers' market.

Much has changed since then, but a trip to Lancaster County is still a treat for me. There is an unpretentiousness about the people and the series of small towns interspersed with farmland that I find quite captivating. It reminds one of America's countryside as it used to be . . . or the way we hoped it was. You'll find an idyllic landscape, dotted with villages complete with community parks, country stores, and small family run businesses.

Whether you are looking for a safe haven, a perfect escape, or a shop 'til you drop experience, Lancaster County has it all.

WHY COME TO LANCASTER COUNTY?

With a little effort and time to explore, there are back roads to travel that hold the serendipity of a wooden toy shop, a farmland vista of Amish harvesting corn, or a spring stream rimmed with eager trout fisherman of all faiths.

Lancaster County is quite rural for the most part, but it has the advantage of being within range of New York City, Philadelphia, and Washington, DC. It offers fascinating glimpses of the Plain People. Their simpler way of life keeps alive the almost forgotten arts of painted furniture, quilting, and home grown food. The influences of the Pennsylvania Dutch *(Deutsch)* lifestyle of simplicity, frugality, hard work, and cleanliness are felt throughout the region.

Lancaster offers diverse pleasures. It makes a perfect destination for railroad buffs, antique hunters, quilt lovers, bicyclists, and families. It has a rich historical heritage with breathtaking country landscapes and many activities for the outdoor enthusiasts. Dining options vary from the sophisticated to the hearty and simple. Lodging is available both for visitors who come to be pampered or for those who want a campsite overlooking farm country. There is something for everyone, both plain and fancy.

I have tried to include the best of Lancaster County in this book, as well as some of the notable destinations outside its borders. I found, after logging thousands of miles, that the most interesting places are often not highly visible or well marketed. I hope you take the opportunity to discover your own favorite places to see and things to do.

I intend to update this book approximately every two years. Your thoughts, questions, criticisms, or suggestions are welcome and may be incorporated in the next version of *Lancaster County: The Best Fun, Food, Lodging, Shopping and Sights.* I can be reached at (215) 844-3850 and at the following address: *The Philadelphia Food Companion*, P.O. Box 27266, Philadelphia, PA 19118-0266. My email address is Philafoodi@AOL.com.

I look forward to hearing from you.

Helpful Information for Enjoying Your Visit to Lancaster County

The conundrum of tourism and the Amish is that people are drawn to the Lancaster area because of the Amish and their unique way of life, yet the Amish want to live quietly without people trying to snap their photos, gawking at them, or asking inconsiderate questions. When visiting the area, it is important to respect the privacy of the Amish and their wish not to be photographed or videotaped.

This may seem an obvious recommendation, but it is important not to trespass on an Amish farm or school. This is private property and unless you've been invited, you are probably not welcome.

Due to the presence of horse drawn buggies and farm equipment, it is important to be aware that traffic in the area may be slow going at times. There may also be congestion on the heavily traveled numbered routes. Allow plenty of time to commute and keep your traveling speed lower than usual, particularly on the small back roads where the Amish and Old Order Mennonites tend to live and work.

VISITORS' CENTERS

Besides the information centers particularly useful for learning about the Amish and Mennonites listed on page 39, the following places are also good sources for information:

DOWNTOWN VISITORS' CENTER
South Queen Street
Lancaster, PA 17603
(717) 397-3531
Mon-Fri 8:30-5, Sat 9-4, Sun 10-3

LEBANON VALLEY TOURIST AND VISITORS' BUREAU
Quality Inn
Lebanon, PA 17042
(717) 272-8555
Mon-Sat 9-12 and 1-5

READING AND BERKS COUNTY VISITORS' BUREAU
VF Factory Outlet Complex
Hill Avenue
Wyomissing, PA 19610
(717) 375-4085
Mon-Fri 9-5, Sat 10-2

STRASBURG VISITORS' INFORMATION CENTER
Route 896, Historic Strasburg Inn
Strasburg, PA 17579
(717) 687-7922; Open daily: 7-11

SUSQUEHANNA HERITAGE TOURIST INFORMATION CENTER
Linden Street
Columbia, PA 17512
(717) 684-5249
Mon-Fri 9-4:30, Sat 10-4, Sun 12-4

CALENDAR OF EVENTS

JANUARY

◆ Pork and Sauerkraut Dinner at the Leola Fire Company, Route 23, Leola. New Year's Day. (717) 656-9881.

◆ Pennsylvania Farm Show at the Harrisburg Farm Show Building, Harrisburg. Held during the second week. If you haven't been, you gotta go! (717) 787-5373.

◆ Rug Sale and Seminar, Ten Thousand Villages, 240 North Reading Road, (Route 272), Ephrata. End of the month, call to confirm dates. Over 1,000 handknotted Persian, Bokhara, Kilim, and Afghani tribal rugs made with fairly paid adult labor. (717) 721-8400.

MARCH

◆ Gordonville Fire Company Auction, Old Leacock Road between Route 30 and 340, Gordonville. Held the second Saturday. Quilts, farm machinery, livestock, furnishings, antiques, and crafts sale. (717) 768-3869.

APRIL

◆ Annual Quilters' Heritage Celebration at the Holiday Inn Lancaster Host Resort. Held on the first full weekend with hundreds of quilts on display. There are also classes, lectures, vendors, and contests. $12,000 in prizes awarded. Call the Quilters' Heritage Celebration for show information (217) 854-9323.

A sit in at an old-time quilting bee during the Lancaster County Quilt Festival

Photograph courtesy of the PA Dutch Convention and Visitors Bureau

Call the Holiday Inn for accommodations (717) 299-5500.

Photograph courtesy of Ron Bowman Visual Communications

Happy faces at the Rhubarb Festival.

◆ Pennsylvania Relief Sale, Quilt Auction, and Country Auction at the Harrisburg Farm Show Building. Held the first weekend. All proceeds are channeled through Mennonite Central Committee for support of international relief projects. Featuring arts, crafts, quilts, antiques, and all sorts of Pennsylvania Dutch foods. (717) 787-5373.

◆ Gourmet Fest at the ARTWORKS Expo Center, 100 North State Street, Ephrata. Meet cookbook authors and celebrity chefs and sample specialty foods. Call for dates. (717) 738-9500.

◆ Antiques Extravaganza at Stoudt's Antique Mall, Route 272, Adamstown. Held on the last Saturday and Sunday, featuring hundreds of additional dealers. (717) 484-4385.

MAY

◆ A Gathering of Local Art and Artists at the Kitchen Kettle Village, 3529 Old Philadelphia Pike, Intercourse. First Saturday. See original artwork of Lancaster County and the local art of quilting, tool making, leather working, tinsmithing, and bread making. (800) 732-3538.

◆ Old Fashioned Sunday at Wheatland, 1120 Marietta Avenue, Lancaster. Third weekend. Featuring tours of the mansion, storytelling, magic shows, a bird show, jazz band, and children's games. (717) 392-8721.

◆ Rhubarb Festival Kitchen Kettle Village, 3529 Old Philadelphia Pike, Intercourse. Held on the third Saturday. Pie baking contest, quilting bee, and a rhubarb derby. (800) 732-3538.

JUNE

- Outdoor Woodcarving Show at Kitchen Kettle Village in Intercourse. First Saturday. See 40 of the nation's finest woodcarvers. Whittling contests and food are offered throughout the day. (800) 732-3538.

- Children's Festival, Ten Thousand Villages, 240 North Reading Road, (Route 272), Ephrata. Held the first Saturday. Children gather in a tent outside for hands on experiences in rugmaking, eating with chopsticks, and puzzles. There are rickshaw rides as well. Call for dates. (717) 721-8400.

- Pennsylvania Dutch Food Fair on Route 340 in Bird-in-Hand. Held in a large tent on the third Friday and Saturday. Showcasing the food of eight of the County's favorite restaurants, live music, and demonstrations of horse drawn farming techniques. Benefits the Lancaster County Food Bank.

- Food, Farm, and Fun Fest at the ARTWORKS Expo Center, 100 North State Street, Ephrata. Foods from local restaurants and food purveyors are for sale and sample. Call for dates. (717) 738-9500.

- Summer Evening Tours at the Ephrata Cloister. On Saturdays and Sundays. Costumed guides conduct tours through 18th century medieval style buildings. (717) 733-6600.

- Antiques Extravaganza at Stoudt's Antique Mall, Route 272, Adamstown. Held on the last Saturday and Sunday, featuring hundreds of additional dealers. (717) 484-4385.

- Columbia Craft, Antique, and Art Show in Locust Street Park and downtown Columbia. Last Saturday. Juried show. (717) 684-5249.

- Kutztown "Pennsylvania German" Festival. Held at the Kutztown Fairgrounds and the adjacent Kutztown University campus. Begins the last weekend of June through Fourth of July. This new festival celebrates the colorful Pennsylvania Dutch culture and provides an authentic representation of the foods, arts, customs, and lifestyle of Pennsylvania's plain and fancy settlers. Featuring Pennsylvania German dance, music, food, folklife activities, quilting, and a country auction. (800) 963-8824.

JULY

- Kutztown "Pennsylvania German" Festival. See last entry in June.

- Outdoor Music Series at Nissley Vineyards, 140 Vintage Drive, Bainbridge. Saturday evenings through Labor Day. (717) 426-3514.

◆ Pennsylvania State Craft Show and Sale at Franklin and Marshall College, Lancaster. Begun in 1946. Features 275 juried members of the Pennsylvania Guild of Craftsman. Call for dates. (717) 291-3911.

◆ Warehouse Sale, Ten Thousand Villages, 240 North Reading Road, (Route 272), Ephrata. Usually the third weekend, call to confirm dates. Overstocked, discontinued, or slightly damaged items for sale. (717) 721-8400.

August

◆ Goschenhoppen Historians Annual Folk Festival at Goschenhoppen Park, Route 29, East Greenville (Montgomery County). Held on the second Friday and Saturday. Begun in 1966, effort is made to portray authentic homestead skills: crafts, cooking, farming, and other everyday family activities. (215) 234-8953.

◆ Pennsylvania Renaissance Faire at Mount Hope Estate and Winery, Route 72, Cornwall. Weekends in August and September. Features jousting, a working village of artisans, a spitted pig, and costumed entertainers. (717) 665-7021.

◆ Heritage Day at the Hans Herr House, 1849 Hans Herr Drive, Willow Street. First Saturday. Colonial period and rural life demonstrations such as hearth cooking, blacksmithing, gardening, broom making, and soap making. (717) 464-4438.

◆ Lebanon Bologna Festival at the Lebanon County Fairgrounds. Second weekend. (717) 272-8555.

◆ Circus Days at the Rail Road Museum of Pennsylvania, Route 741, Strasburg. Hundreds of miniature circus exhibits displayed throughout the Museum's main exhibit hall. Call for dates. (717) 687-8628.

September

◆ The Long's Park Art and Craft Festival at Long's Park, Lancaster: Features nearly 200 artists and crafts people from around the country. Held the first weekend. (717) 295-7054.

◆ Pennsylvania Renaissance Faire at Mount Hope Estate and Winery, Route 72, Cornwall. Weekends in August and September. Features jousting, a working village of artisans, a spitted pig, and costumed entertainers. (717) 665-7021.

◆ Pennsylvania Dutch Balloon and Craft Festival. Historic Strasburg Inn, Route 896, Strasburg. Over 20 hot air balloons, craftspeople, food and entertainment. Call for dates. (717) 687-7691.

◆ Southern Lancaster County Fair, Legion Park and Fairgrounds, Quarryville. One of the few remaining agricultural fairs with animal judging, sewing, cooking, crafts. Call for dates. (717) 786-4884.

◆ Seven Sweets and Sours Festival at Kitchen Kettle Village, 3529 Old Philadelphia Pike, Intercourse. Held the third Thursday through Saturday. Demonstrations on preserving fruits and vegetables for the winter. (800) 732-3538.

The Orangery at Longwood Gardens.

Photograph courtesy of L. Albee/Longwood Gardens

◆ German Oktoberfest at the Lancaster Liederkranz, 722 South Chiques Road, Lancaster. Third weekend. Features German bands, accordion players, German folk dancers, activities for children, German food, contests, and games. (717) 898-8451.

◆ Festival of Fountains at Longwood Gardens, Route 1, Kennett Square, (Chester County). A celebration of flowers, fountains, and music. Lovely gardens with alfresco concerts and musically illuminated fountain displays three evenings a week. Call for dates and times. (610) 388-1000.

◆ Quilt Auction at the Gordonville Fire Company, Old Leacock Road between Route 30 and 340, Gordonville. Fourth Saturday. Quilts, buggies, sleighs, wagons, and building materials. (717) 768-3869.

◆ Antiques Extravaganza at Stoudt's Antique Mall, Route 272, Adamstown. Held on the last Saturday and Sunday, featuring hundreds of additional dealers. (717) 484-4385.

◆ Ephrata Fair. Last week of the month. Ephrata, PA. (717) 733-8132.

OCTOBER

◆ Bridge Bust, Route 462 bridge between Columbia and Wrightsville. Held the first Saturday. Featuring 270 stands with foods and crafts. (717) 684-5249.

◆ 50's Auto Club of America at the Historic Strasburg Inn, Route 896, Strasburg. First weekend. Antique cars from the 50s on display. Flea market. (717) 687-7691 or (609) 927-4967.

◆ Snitz Fest at the Hans Herr House, 1849 Hans Herr Drive, Willow Street. First Saturday. Snitz Fest celebrates the importance of the apple harvest to early Pennsylvania German settlers in Lancaster County. Lots of activities pertaining to apples and the fall harvest. (717) 464-4438.

◆ Rug Sale and Seminar, Ten Thousand Villages, 240 North Reading Road, (Route 272), Ephrata. Usually the third Thursday, call for dates. Over 1,000 handknotted Persian, Bokhara, Kilim, and Afghani tribal rugs made with fairly paid adult labor. (717) 721-8400.

◆ Harvest Days Landis Valley Museum, Route 272, Lancaster. Columbus Day weekend. See old-fashioned, harvest time activities including apple butter making and lace and rug making. (717) 569-0401.

◆ Pumpkin Patch Weekend at the Landis Valley Museum, Route 272, Lancaster. Two weekends after Columbus Day weekend. Enjoy horse drawn wagon rides to the pumpkin patch and pumpkin decorating. Tour the historic buildings and watch various demonstrations. (717) 569-0401.

◆ Murder at the Mansion at Wheatland, 1120 Marietta Avenue, Lancaster. Murder mystery tour of the mansion. Guests become the detectives and help to find who was murdered, how, and why. Call for dates. (717) 392-8721.

◆ Halloween Lantern Tours and Halloween Phantom Train at the Strasburg Rail Road, Route 741, Strasburg. Take a train ride in the dark. Then go to the Pennsylvania Rail Road Museum which has been turned into a haunted house. Call for dates (717) 687-7522.

◆ Ghosts of Lancaster Past Walking Tour sponsored by the Historic Lancaster Walking Tour. Usually held the weekend before Halloween. Call to confirm place and time. (717) 392-1776.

NOVEMBER

◆ Donecker's Wine and Food Festival at the ARTWORKS Expo Center, 100 North State Street, Ephrata. Featuring Pennsylvania wineries and food. Call for dates. (717) 738-9500.

DECEMBER

◆ Christmas Candlelight House Tour in Marietta. Held on the first Sunday. House tour, antique show, Abe Lincoln and Civil War encampment, music, special displays, and Victorian tea. (717) 684-5249.

◆ Days of the Belsnickel at the Landis Valley Museum, Route 272, Lancaster. Thursday through Saturday on the first weekend. Hear the legend of the Belsnickel, a Christmas Eve visitor of bygone days during museum tours. (717) 569-0401.

◆ Christmas Candlelight Tours at the Hans Herr House, 1849 Hans Herr Drive, Willow Street. First Friday and Saturday evenings. Features activities at the 1719 home which is decorated for the season. Wagon rides, caroling, and refreshments are included. (717) 464-4438.

◆ Christmas Show at Living Waters Auditorium, Route 896, Strasburg. One of America's most elaborate water, light, and screen shows. See thousands of dazzling designs of exploding water from an 80' pool. Call for dates. (717) 687-7854 or 687-7800.

◆ "The Joys of Christmas" at Sight and Sound Entertainment Centre, Route 896, Strasburg. The nation's largest professional Christian theatre. Watch special effects, surround sound, live animals, and wrap around side stages in a state-of-the-art, 1,400 seat theatre. Call for dates. (717) 687-7800.

◆ Christmas Tours (Candlelight tours on weekends) of James Buchanan's Wheatland, 1120 Marietta Ave., Lancaster. First two weeks. See the mansion decorated as it would have been during James Buchanan's time. (717) 392-8721.

◆ "Annual Candlelight Carol"at the Historic Rock Ford, Lancaster. Second weekend. Candlelight tours of 18th century home of General Edward Hand, Washington's Adjutant General. Features holiday decorations and entertainment. (717) 392-7223.

◆ Santa Trains - The North Pole Express at the Strasburg Rail Road, Route 741, Strasburg. Santa Claus rides each train and gives children treats. Call for dates. (717) 687-7522.

◆ "Home for the Holidays" at the Rail Road Museum of Pennsylvania, Route 741 East, Strasburg. Experience 100 years of holiday rail travel and meet engineers, ticket agents, conductors, and passengers from the 1850s-1950s. Call for dates. (717) 687-8628.

◆ Christmas at Landis Valley, Landis Valley Museum, Route 272, Lancaster. Tuesday night, the week before Christmas. Free tours of several decorated buildings. Sing carols by a bonfire accompanied by the Lititz Moravian

Choir. Free refreshments. (717) 569-0401.

◆ Christmas at Longwood, Longwood Gardens, Route 1, Kennett Square, (Chester County). Open daily. Wonder at the thousands of poinsettias, 400,000 lights, Christmas trees, and daily concerts. (610) 388-1000.

◆ HERSHEYPARK Christmas Candylane, HERSHEYPARK, Hershey. Throughout the month. Half a million twinkling lights, rides, games, and seasonal entertainment. (717) 534-3900.

How This Book Works:

I've structured this book so it can be used by traveler and resident alike to find information on restaurants, lodging, historic sites, shopping, and recreation. I've provided tips on learning about the Plain People, discovering the bed and breakfast suited to your personality, and finding that special shop for your very own quilt or antique.

Before choosing a place to stay, I recommend referring to Chapter 6 on the towns of Lancaster County. This will help you determine what part of the County you would most like to explore. Then decide whether you enjoy bed and breakfast accommodations, prefer the amenities of a hotel, want to pamper yourself at an inn, or go camping.

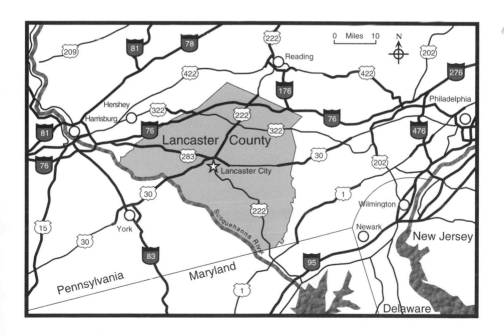

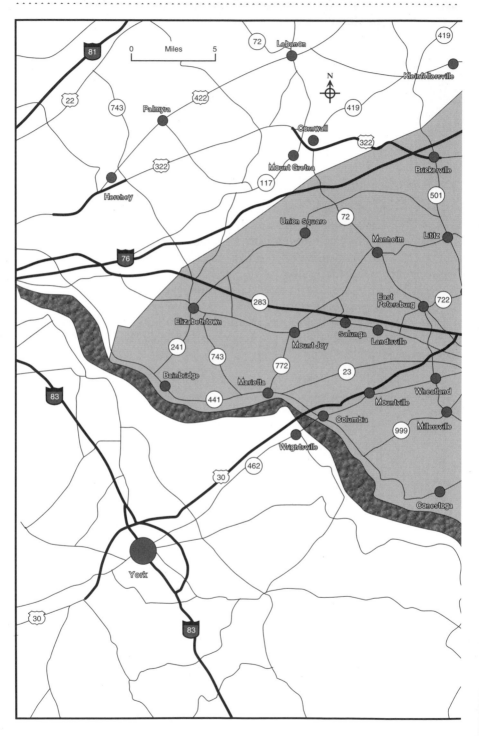

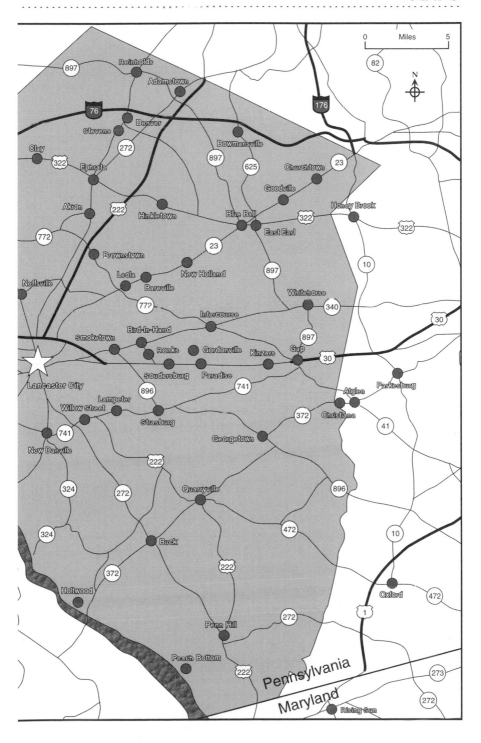

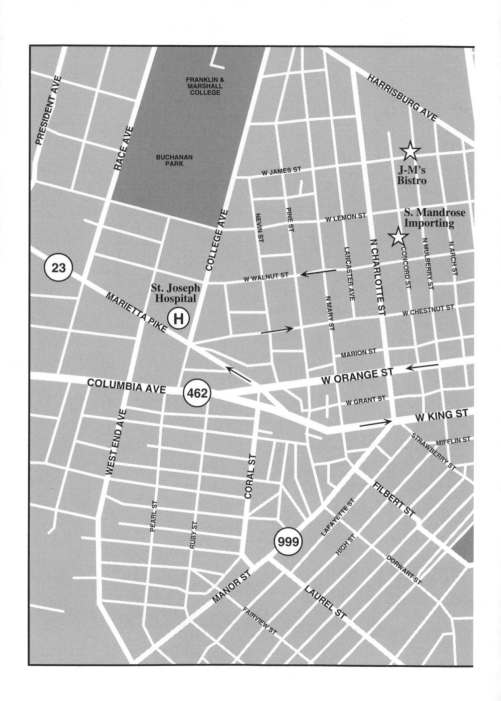

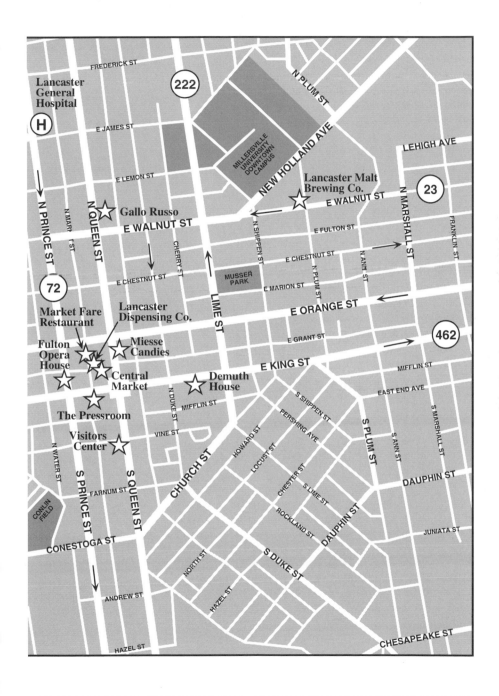

A BRIEF HISTORY

◆1◆

LANCASTER COUNTY: PAST AND PRESENT

Getting Settled 30
Today 31

WHO ARE THE PENNSYLVANIA DUTCH?

Who Are the Plain People? 32
Who Are the Anabaptists? 33
WhoAre the Mennonites? 33
Who Are the Amish? 34
Resources 39

CHAPTER ONE:
LANCASTER COUNTY:
A BRIEF HISTORY

THE STATE OF PENNSYLVANIA

In 1681 William Penn, a Quaker, was granted a charter by King Charles II of England for land along the east coast of America. The king named it "Pensilvania" and Penn began his "Holy Experiment," offering a government that insisted on religious freedom for all people. Pennsylvania has always been an important agricultural state, and even today, though it has become a major commercial and manufacturing state, agriculture remains the state's number one business. It also has more rural residents than any other state.

> ### THE "CIRCLE"
>
> **The church is the "circle," the gathering of people, no matter what kind of "house" they meet in. The ground we stand on is holy, not because we have erected a shrine, decorated it, . . . but because God meets us here.**
>
> **John L. Ruth,**
> *A Quiet and Peaceable Life*
>
> ◆◆◆

LANCASTER COUNTY

GETTING SETTLED

In 1709 a settlement of Swiss Mennonites with the surnames Herr, Mylin, and Kendig established the first European Lancaster County community. French Huguenots followed shortly thereafter to settle in Strasburg. Welsh, Scottish, and many other immigrants from Germany came as farmers, artisans, and skilled laborers.

Eighteenth century industry included iron making, glass making, grain milling, and the manufacturing of rifles, textiles, hardware, and the famous Conestoga wagons. Lancaster is also noted for its fine cabinetmakers, silversmiths, and pewterware. During the Revolutionary War, these contributions to the Continental Congress were in evidence. Lancaster even served as the United States capital for a day on September 27, 1777, as the Congress fled from the British invasion of Philadelphia.

TODAY

Lancaster County's strength is still its hard working, diverse population, and its ability to adapt to the economic realities of "progress." Forges that once smelt iron are quiet, and many candy, cigar, and textile factories are closed. Today, many countians make their living by farming, in the light manufacturing industry, or within the tourist industry.

Lancaster County is often called the "garden spot of the world" because it has some of the richest non-irrigated farmland in the United States. Some 65% of its land is still used for farming. A majority of these farms are family owned; almost half by the Amish and Mennonites. Today, 80% of the available farmland in the county is purchased by the Amish. This area, like many regions in the United States, has difficulty achieving a balance between housing and commercial development, on the one hand, and agriculture on the other. The County has set up an Agricultural Preserve Board dedicated to the preservation of farmland. The Lancaster Farmland Trust is a non-profit land trust that also works with residents to preserve historic buildings, farms, and park lands. Together, these two entities have preserved over 21,000 acres through the purchase of conservation easement rights to keep the land available for farming. If you would like to know more about farm preservation, call the Lancaster Farmland Trust at (717) 293-0707.

The County's population still leans heavily toward those who have German heritage; about 90% have one or both parents of German ancestry. Seventeen percent of the inhabitants claim some English, Scotch, or Irish blood. The newest arrivals are Latino (mainly Mexican and Puerto Rican), and their population has doubled in the last decade. They have settled primarily in the city of Lancaster.

THE PLAIN PEOPLE

If the Plain People of North America are to be understood in terms of their own concerns, we must consider sympathetically their own expressions, and the biblical cadences they echo. Having maintained, with the tolerance of their society, a simple life as the quiet in the land, these folk still prize such passé virtues as modesty, humility, and humble obedience to God's will, as interpreted by a disciplined community of faith. Their values, difficult to appreciate in a world bemused by progress, are seldom if ever articulated, except as curiosities, as our mass media.

John L. Ruth,
A Quiet and Peaceable Life

◆◆◆

WHO ARE THE PENNSYLVANIA DUTCH?

The Pennsylvania Dutch are natives of central Pennsylvania, particularly Lancaster County and several other nearby counties. They are of many different faiths with the common bond of a German heritage. The term Pennsylvania Dutch is actually a mispronunciation of *Deutsch*, or German. Technically, they are Pennsylvania Germans! Besides sharing a common ancestry, these people speak a dialect which is a combination of German, from the Pfalz area, and English. Pennsylvania Dutch is therefore a cultural, not a religious, term.

> ### SMALL-SCALE THINGS
>
> **From egos to organizational units, the Amish prefer small-scale things. They fear that bigness will lead to pride and the abuse of power. Smallness also encourages informal social relationships. The bureaucratic structures and formal procedures that proliferate in modern societies are completely missing in Amish life.**
>
> Donald B. Kraybill & Steven M. Nolt, *Amish Enterprise: From Plows to Profits*
>
> ◆◆◆

There a quite a few small religous groups who immigrated to Pennsylvania. The Huguenots came from France, the Moravians from Bohemia (in present-day Czechoslovakia), and the Dunkards (also known as German Baptists) and Schwenkfelders from Germany. They thrived on the rich farmland, religious freedom, and peace they found in Pennsylvania.

Some Amish and Mennonites, who are also Pennsylvania Dutch, immigrated through Pennsylvania, and many moved on to distinct settlements in Elkhart and Berne (Indiana), Harrrisonburg (Virginia), Holmes County (Ohio), Kitchener (Ontario), and parts of Maryland, West Virginia, Illinois, and Iowa.

WHO ARE THE PLAIN PEOPLE?

There are 650,000 people living in the greater Lancaster County region (which includes the population bordering Lancaster County with significant Amish settlements). Approximately 10% of that population is made up of 48 different plain sects, numbering some 65,000 people. These groups include the German Baptist Brethren, also known as Dunkers or Dunkards, and the River Brethren, who drive cars and dress plain as do the Old Order Mennonites. Add to this mix New Order Amish, who drive cars and have electricity, and

Clip clopping along country roads.

the so-called Team Mennonites, who drive buggies and eschew electricity.

The term plain in "Plain and Fancy" refers to the plain, simple, unadorned Amish and Mennonites. The Plain People account for only a small part of the Pennsylvania Dutch population. The Fancy or "Gay Dutch" enjoyed brightly colored fabrics, painted furniture, and hex signs. These Pennsylvania Germans often were Lutheran or of other Protestant religions.

WHO ARE THE ANABAPTISTS?

The Anabaptists (rebaptizers) believed that only adults who had confessed their faith should be baptized, and that they should remain separate from the larger society. Swiss Brethren, Hutterian Brethren, and the Dutch Mennonites all suffered repeated persecutions and migrated to America for religious freedom.

WHO ARE THE MENNONITES?

During the Reformation, Anabaptists were persecuted as heretics because they rejected the rituals and doctrine of both the Protestants and Catholics. Many fled to the mountains of Switzerland and southern Germany. In 1536 a young Catholic priest from Holland named Menno Simons joined the Anabaptist movement. His writings and leadership united many of the Anabaptist groups, who were subsequently often called Mennonites.

BIG BUSINESS

Big business is most dangerous because it so easily leads to pride, self-confidence, and a spirit of independence. When an owner begins to exhibit an attitude of arrogance, the church knows that the business has become too large.

Donald B. Kraybill & Steven M. Nolt, *Amish Enterprise: From Plows to Profits*

Engraving by Reinier Vinkeles.

Menno Simons.

Taking advantage of William Penn's safe haven, the first group of Mennonites settled in Germantown (now a part of Philadelphia) and established a religious meeting in 1683, which continues to this day. Mennonites primarily came from Switzerland, Holland, and Germany.

The Mennonite and Brethren in Christ (a closely related Anabaptist group) churches numbered close to 975,000 worldwide in 1994. More than half of this number are located in continents other than North America with membership growing fastest in Asia and Africa. Mennonites have a reputation for being hardworking, frugal, and pious. The Mennonite Central Committee and Mennonite Disaster Service are two agencies supported by churchwide membership contributions. They are the channel through which most non-Mennonites learn about these denominations, particularly if they do not live in proximity of a Mennonite or Brethren in Christ congregation. These agencies work throughout the world to "demonstrate God's love . . . among people suffering from poverty, conflict, oppression, and natural disaster."

Mennonites today can be of the Old Order sect, dress plain and drive buggies, or they can look like the average American, live in an urban setting, and play tennis.

WHO ARE THE AMISH?

Some 150 years after the start of the Anabaptist movement, a man named Jakob Ammann felt the Mennonite Church of the late

MENNONITE IMMIGRATION

Swiss and South German immigrants began coming to the United States and settled in eastern Pennsylvania, some eventually moving south and west to Ohio, Indiana, Illinios, Virginia, and Maryland. Some 60,000 Dutch-Prussian-Russian immigrants settled primarily in Manitoba, Minnesota, South Dakota, Nebraska, and Kansas. The total Mennonite immigration is estimated to be between 70,000 and 75,000.

17th century didn't exercise enough church discipline or maintain a strong enough spiritual life. He encouraged the practice, called shunning today, which separates church members from those who are disciplined and expelled from the church. The followers of Ammann were then called Amish.

There are more than 150,000 Amish in North America. Sixty-five percent live in Pennsylvania, Ohio, and Indiana. There are Amish settlements in 22 states and in Ontario, Canada. Ironically, no Amish remain in Switzerland or Germany, where the first migrations came from in the 1720s. The oldest group of Old Order Amish, about 16,000-18,000 people, live in Lancaster County, Pennsylvania. According to historian David Luthy, the Amish population nearly doubles every 20 years, and an average of seven new settlements are founded each year.

THE HOME AND FAMILY

The Old Order Amish farmstead is distinguished by its neatness. Often a windmill or water wheel posted nearby provides water pressure. Many farms have tobacco sheds and cows are contained by wooden fences. The family vehicle is a horse drawn, gray-topped buggy. Backyards are often festooned with wash-lines covered with family laundry. The Amish live without electricity, and their clothes are simple, modest, and often dark-colored.

This idyllic picture requires very hard work by all family members as soon and as long as they are able. An Amish woman is expected to care for house and garden, cook three meals a day, and sew her family's clothes. All this with appliances powered by bottled gas.

The Amish pay taxes, including those to support public schools which their children do not attend. They are exempt from paying social security because they have chosen not to collect it. Children are taught to respect authority and learn responsibility early on. They are given chores to do as soon as they are able. Amish children speak Pennsylvania Dutch at home and are taught English in school. They are only required to attend school until grade eight, often in small, one-room buildings within a reasonable bike ride from home. At age 16, teenagers join "supper gangs" which meet to sing and

THE ORDNUNG

The Ordnung, an oral communal understanding within the Amish community, forbids the filing of a lawsuit, divorce, and entering into military service. It contains guidance about men's hat styles, the style of buggies, and the order of the worship service. It is the means for cultivating order and group identity.

◆◆◆

play games. Dating begins, and the Amish elders are indulgent if the errant wild oat is sewn.

You may think of a rural town in the19th century when you meet the Amish. Plainness and simplicity are not a matter of ignorance or archaism. The Amish do accept change, but only after they determine that the object or activity in question will not interfere with their desire to lead a simple life.

AT WORK

During the persecution of the Amish and Mennonites in Switzerland and Germany, many found that the best way to live was as farmers. This lifestyle allowed families to live and work closely together. Parents could provide instruction on serving God while avoiding much of the distraction from outside influences. They emphasized humility, family, community, and separation from the world.

The Amish continue to uphold these basic principles. There is an appreciation for the land and a deep sense of stewardship of the resources God has entrusted to them. They care for it lovingly, seeking the most up-to-date agricultural information. Through hard work and careful planning, they harvest a wide variety of crops: alfalfa, corn, tobacco, and other grains. The average Amish farm in Lancaster County is 55 acres. Old Order farmers use horse drawn equipment and rely on Amish craftsman to build and repair their outdated equipment.

Due to development pressure and an ever increasing population, farmland is at a premium in Lancaster County. Land prices are high, and the ability of an Amish father to give his sons a start in farming is a luxury more and more cannot afford. A few

Some of the many roadside invitations to buy goods and services.

families have moved to Maryland, Ohio, or Kentucky where start-up costs are more reasonable. Most young Amish men, however, do choose to stay in the County. Some 50% work at non-farm jobs such as carpentry, furniture making, welding, blacksmith, silo building, and making products for tourists. Many of these small businesses are Amish-owned, and many have become quite successful. The tourist industry, while putting pressure on the Amish way of life, has also benefited many Plain People because of the demand for quilts, handmade toys, furniture, fresh produce, and baked goods.

The Amish commitment to community life is illustrated in their legendary barn raisings. Much more invisible to the "English" (what many Amish call anyone who is not Amish) are Amish efforts in helping out not only family members, but also other members of their church community. A successful businessman, for example, may help another Amish person start up a business, rather than growing his own business and becoming much wealthier than his neighbors. Becoming so wealthy that you cause envy is considered something to be avoided by most Amish.

At Worship

Amish family life revolves around the church community. Church districts are organized with 20-30 households geographically near each other. Sunday services are held in homes, every other Sunday. The Amish use a High German Bible, and that is the language of the sermon as well. The alternate Sunday is often spent visiting family and friends.

There is no formal hierarchy to oversee the Old Order churches. Each district makes decisions about what is acceptable based on the Bible and the *Ordnung*, a set of teachings, often unwritten, that guide Amish life and help create a sense of order and identity.

Meekness

Meekness is the fairest virtue

In the Christian treasure-store

For she ornaments the youthful,

And the aged even more.

Do not those whom Fortune raises

Also seek to sound her praises?

She is more than gold in worth,

Or what glitters on the earth.

Demuth ist die Schoenste Tugend,
a Mennonite hymn

BASIC MENNONITE AND AMISH TENETS

The Amish and Mennonites both adhere to the following beliefs:

Christianity: They believe they are sinners, saved only through the confession of their sins through Jesus Christ. They also believe that the Bible is the final word on how to live one's life.

Adult baptism: They believe persons should be old enough to make this choice for themselves. Also called believers' baptism.

Community: They emphasize what many call brotherhood, helping each other out in practical ways.

Non-resistance: They refuse to fight in wars.

Non-conformity: They believe that to maintain the beliefs and values of the church, it is necessary to live separately from the world.

Underpinning these tenets is an attitude of humility which often also means avoiding competition within the community.

RESOURCES

If you are interested in learning more about Lancaster County's Plain People, the bibliography at the back of this book may be of use. The following resources are also good places to start.

INFORMATION CENTERS:

AMISH MENNONITE INFORMATION CENTER

Route 23 (R.D. 1, Box 120)
Morgantown, PA 19543
(610) 286-9870; Mon-Sat 9:30-4
Easter through Thanksgiving

MENNONITE INFORMATION CENTER

Millstream Road,
Lancaster, 17602
(717) 299-0954; Mon-Sat 8-5

PENNSYLVANIA DUTCH CONVENTION AND VISITORS' BUREAU

Greenfield Road,
Lancaster, 17601
(717) 299-8901; Mon-Sat 8-6,
Sun 8-5

THE RIVER INN TEA BREAD

3 cups all-purpose flour
1 1/2 teaspoons salt
1 1/2 teaspoons baking powder
2 tablespoons poppy seeds
2 1/4 cups sugar
3 eggs
1 1/2 cups milk
1 1/8 cups oil
1 1/2 teaspoons vanilla extract
1 1/2 teaspoons almond extract
1 1/2 teaspoons butter extract

1/4 cup orange juice
3/4 cup sugar
1/2 teaspoon vanilla extract
1/2 teaspoon almond extract
1/2 teaspoon melted butter

In a large bowl mix the first 11 ingredients. Pour into 2 greased 9 by 5-inch loaf pans, filling the pans two-thirds full. Bake in a 350°F oven for 40 to 60 minutes. Cool for 5 minutes. In a small bowl combine the orange juice, sugar, vanilla, almond extract, almond extract, and melted butter. Glaze the warm bread. Makes 2 loaves.

—Recipe from Joyce Heiserman, *The River Inn*

TOURS:

MENNONITE INFORMATION CENTER

Millstream Road, Lancaster, 17602

(717) 299-0954;

see page 155 for more information.

RED ROSE EXCURSIONS

Butler Avenue, Lancaster, 17601

(717) 397-3175;

Reservations required, best 3-4 days in advance.

No Sunday tours.

SCALLOPED SAFFRON POTATOES

Give a new twist to an old favorite, scalloped pototoes. The saffron sauce adds a rich flavor.

3 tablespoons butter or margarine
1 teaspoons salt
1/4 teaspoon pepper
1/8 teaspoon crushed saffron threads (about 40 to 50 threads)
3 tablespoon flour
3 cups milk
2 pounds potatoes (about 6 medium potatoes or 5 cups sliced)

Wash and peel potatoes. Crush the saffron carefully on a sheet of paper. Melt the butter or margarine in a saucepan over low heat. Add salt, pepper, saffron and flour and blend well. Cook and stir mixture over low heat until it is smooth and bubbly. Remove from heat, add milk, stir constantly over medium heat until mixture comes to a boil. Remove from heat and set aside. Cut potatoes into thin slices. Place the sliced potatoes in four layers in a greased two-quart casserole or baking dish (8 by 8 by 2-inches). Top each layer with about a quarter of the saffron sauce. Bake in a preheated 350°F oven for about 1-1 1/2 hours. Allow to cool 5 to 10 minutes before serving.

— Recipe from
R. Martin Keen and Family,
M & J Greider Farms, Inc.

LODGING

2

Bed and Breakfasts 44
Inns 61
Farms and Guest Houses 69
Camping 74
Resorts, Hotels, Motels, and Travel Lodges 78
Lodging Outside Lancaster County 82

CHAPTER TWO: LODGING

There is a wide variety of lodging available in the Lancaster area. The bed and breakfast industry has blossomed in the last ten years, and these business owners do a remarkable job in keeping their guests happy. One of the keys to having an enjoyable visit is to take some time in choosing the right accommodation for you. Do you have children? Do you want to be in the thick of things or out in the country? Are you sociable in the morning? Does an inn or hotel work better for you? What amenities must you have, and what can you live without? Do you have allergies? I have tried to answer these questions for the following recommendations.

> **Hospitality consists in a little fire, a little food, and an immense quiet.**
>
> Ralph Waldo Emerson,
> *Journal, 1856*
>
> ◆◆◆

Unless otherwise specified in the lodging reviews, English is the only language spoken, pets are not welcome, children of all ages are accommodated, smoking is not permitted indoors, and the rates stated are for two people per room per night.

Check-in typically starts at 3:00 to 4:00 p.m., and check-out varies from 10:00 to 11:30 a.m. Some hosts are more flexible than others, and it is important to discuss the timing of both the beginning and the end of your visit so there aren't surprises for either party. If you plan to arrive later than expected, please stop to call ahead, giving an updated schedule. I have found bed and breakfast owners, in particular, to be quite gracious in this regard.

Each lodging business has its own requirements regarding deposits, cancellation policies, and length of stay. Please make sure you know what these are before you make reservations.

If you are looking for a quiet spot, western and northern Lancaster County are worth considering. I am particularly fond of Lititz, the Ephrata/Akron area, and Marietta, a river town on the western edge of the County. For those who like hustle and bustle and want to be close to shopping, the mid-eastern part of the County is more appropriate. For this the town of Strasburg is particularly lovely.

I have taken particular pains to research the bed and breakfast establishments in the area because staying at these places offers the advantage of having hosts who know their way around. Many come from families who have lived here for generations. I also enjoy visiting with fellow travelers from around the world over breakfast. What is also fun about bed and breakfasts is that each one is unique, a reflection of the owner's personality and interests.

ABOUT BED AND BREAKFASTS

Lancaster County offers a wide range of bed and breakfasts, from a get-away complete with Jacuzzis and afternoon tea to a farm home perfect for families with children. If you would like assistance in locating the perfect bed and breakfast vacation beyond my reviews, you can contact the Authentic Bed & Breakfasts of Lancaster County (800) 552-2632 or Farm Vacations (717) 665-4231.

Your need for privacy is a major factor in deciding what lodging would be most suitable. Even bed and breakfasts differ in how much sociability is expected. Some breakfasts are served with all guests seated around a common table. Others serve each party individually at separate tables and even times.

Amenities can include anything from fresh flowers and mints for the pillow to afternoon refreshments and dinner reservations with a nearby Amish family. Most bed and breakfasts do not have telephones or televisions in the guest rooms but have them available for use in a central location.

There are three main types of breakfasts offered: full, continental, and continental plus. A full breakfast usually includes a hot entree, fruit, breakfast meat, and beverages. The continental meal offers beverages and some sort of bread. Cereal and/or fruit are added for continental plus breakfasts. If you have your heart set on a full country breakfast, make sure this is one of your research questions when choosing a place to stay. As an added treat, many bed and breakfasts have kitchen gardens from which they gather fresh produce to serve as part of the breakfast repast.

Restrictions on alcohol are not uncommon at bed and breakfasts. Many Amish and Mennonite hosts are non-drinkers and do not feel comfortable with guests drinking alcohol in their homes.

OTHER TYPES OF LODGING

There are a number of lovely old historic inns in the area, and they make a good alternative to the bed and breakfast. These offer especially good accommodations if you would like more privacy and don't have small children with you.

A tourist home has guest rooms in the family home, baths can be private or shared and breakfast is not usually served.

TOP HONEYMOON HIDEAWAYS

Inn at Twin Linden,
The Palladian Suite

The King's Cottage,
The Carriage House

Gardens of Eden,
The Beecher Cottage

BED AND BREAKFASTS

ADAMSTOWN INN - A BED & BREAKFAST
West Main Street
Adamstown, PA 19501
(800) 594-4808

Centrally located for shoppers of all kinds, the Adamstown Inn with its Victorian architecture and relaxed small town setting can become that necessary oasis between bargain hunting jaunts. Adamstown is billed as the Antiques Capital of the World and Reading, not much more than ten minutes away, is called the Outlet Capital of the World. This bed and breakfast is guilded with leaded glass windows and doors, chestnut woodwork, oriental rugs, and family heirlooms. There are four rooms with features such as king-sized beds and two-person Jacuzzis; all have private baths. Breakfast is continental plus with the added bonus of coffee, tea, or hot chocolate at your door in the morning. Children over 12 are welcome, and smoking is permitted in certain areas. Room rates range from $65 to $95 per night. Tom and Wanda Berman, the owners of this bed and breakfast, have garnered three diamonds from AAA for their hospitality.

ALDEN HOUSE BED & BREAKFAST, THE
East Main Street, (Route 772)
Lititz, PA 17543
(800) 584-4808

The Alden House graces the main street of my favorite Lancaster County town, Lititz. Within walking distance is a great coffee shop, the first pretzel bakery in America, a chocolate factory, and a map museum. An excellent place from which to sally forth, this 1850 brick, Victorian house has six tastefully appointed rooms, three of which are two room suites. All rooms have a private bath, a queen-sized bed, and a television. A full breakfast is served in the dining room or on one of the porches, weather permitting. Room rates range from $85 to $125. Children over six are welcome.

THE APPLE BIN INN
2835 Willow Street Pike
Willow Street, PA 17584
(800) 338-4296

Located in the small town of Willow Street, this bed and breakfast provides a convenient place to stay either for business or pleasure. Originally (over 100 years ago) a country store, this colonial home offers a comfortable place to relax. Each of the attractively furnished, country style rooms have air conditioning, a telephone in each room, and a fax machine. Debbie Hershey is an attentive host and serves up a tasty, full breakfast in the morning. She will advise you on your itinerary, and make dinner reservations upon request. With advance notice, she will even prepare a picnic lunch. There are four rooms; some have private baths and some have shared baths. Bed sizes are either double or queen-sized. Rates range from $60 to $95. Children over twelve are welcome.

THE BELLA VISTA BED & BREAKFAST
1216 East Main Street
Akron, PA 17501
(717) 859-4227

Built in 1911, this large Georgian style house is situated in the small town of Akron across from a lovely park, complete with a pond and fountains, playground equipment, and a bike trail. There are six attractive and comfortably furnished rooms with high ceilings and early American furniture. Several of the rooms share a bath and several have their own private baths. There are a variety of bed sizes. Along with offering a full breakfast, your hosts, Don and Mary Ella Wallace, are good resources for planning your itinerary. The rooms range from $85 for the largest room with a queen-sized bed and private bath to $65 for the smaller rooms with shared baths. Don't forget to visit Martin's Pretzels down the block and watch the Mennonite women hand twist pretzels. Children 12 and over are welcome.

BOXWOOD INN BED & BREAKFAST
Corner of Tobacco Road & Diamond Street
Akron, PA 17501
(800) 238-3466
PA turnpike exit 21. Rte. 222 S. to Brownstown - Rothsville exit. R. to Route 272, 2 miles, R. onto Main St. 1/2 mi. R. onto Diamond.

The beautiful sun porch at Boxwood Inn.

Photograph by Tom Bagley

Situated in the small town of Akron, the Boxwood Inn was built by Mennonite settlers in 1768. The two-story stone house overlooks neighboring farms but offers contemporary comforts. The inn has five elegantly furnished guest rooms; all have private baths. The Hunt

Room is an extra-large room with a queen-sized bed and bath with a Jacuzzi. The largest accommodation is the Carriage House which is several steps away from the main house. It has a king bed, fireplace, Jacuzzi, refrigerator, and private balcony. In addition to a full country breakfast, afternoon tea is served in the garden. Room rates are $75 to $135 a night. Children are welcome, and there is an additional $10 per night charge for each child.

THE CANDLELIGHT INN

2574 Lincoln Highway East, (Route 30)

Ronks, PA 17572

(800) 772-2635

1/4 mile East of the intersection of Route 896 and Route 30.

This large country home has been lovingly restored by Heidi and Tim Soberick, two professional classical musicians. Regular events such as chamber music recitals are held on weekends throughout the season. Located along the busy Route 30, the Inn is elegantly furnished with Victorian antiques. The handsome guest rooms have queen- and king-sized antique beds, robes, and extravagant linens. Guests can lounge in the parlor, complete with fireplace and oriental rugs, or sit on the porch and enjoy the gardens. Amenities include late afternoon refreshments and a full, candlelit breakfast. Room rates range from $65 for rooms that share a bath to $105 for a large suite. Children over eight are welcome.

CEDAR HILL FARM BED & BREAKFAST

305 Longenecker Road

Mount Joy, PA 17552

(717) 653-4655

Built in 1817, the limestone barn and farmhouse of Cedar Hill Farm overlook the Little Chickies Creek. Russel Swarr is the third generation to make a living at farming here, and his wife, Gladys, oversees the bed and breakfast. Both make guests feel at home in their attractive, but unpretentious, home. There are five guest rooms; all have private baths. Rooms feature one or more of the following: whirlpool, private balcony, or claw-foot bathtub. A rollaway bed and crib are available. Breakfast is continental plus, served beside the old, walk-in fireplace. Typical offerings are fruit, cheese, cereal, and delicious homemade breads. Room rates are $65 and $75 per night.

◆◆

CLEARVIEW FARM BED & BREAKFAST

355 Clearview Road

Ephrata, PA 17522

(717) 733-6333

From Ephrata on Route 322, turn right onto Clearview Road and look for the first farm on your right.

Home for Glenn and Mildred Wissler is a beautiful limestone farmhouse built in 1814 on 200 acres of farmland. They have lovingly restored their 11-room homestead to create a peaceful home away from home for their guests. The living room overlooks the pond on which glides a pair of swans. There are five guest rooms furnished with antiques, Victorian collectibles, handmade Amish quilts, cozy armchairs, and private baths. The two rooms on the third floor are a cozy retreat tucked under exposed, hand-pegged beams. One of the rooms has a double bed, and the others have queen-sized beds. Seven days a week, a big country breakfast is served on antique china in the formal dining room. The Wisslers both grew up in Lancaster County and know how to find the most interesting corners of the countryside for those who like exploring. Room rates range from $95 to $115. Children ten and over are welcome. Clearview Farm Bed and Breakfast has the distinction of being the only bed and breakfast in Pennsylvania with AAA's Four Diamond Award, and they've been awarded that honor for three years running.

A peaceful spot: Clearview Farm Bed and Breakfast.

Drawing courtesy of Clearview Farm Bed and Breakfast

THE COLUMBIAN BED & BREAKFAST

360 Chestnut Street

Columbia, PA 17512

(800) 422-5869

Route 30 West to the Route 441 Columbia exit. South on 441 to Chestnut.

Left and go one block.

This turn-of-the-century mansion, built in Colonial Revival style, has a wrap-around porch, stained glass windows, and a grand sweeping staircase. The bed and breakfast was restored in 1988, and the current owners, Chris

◆◆

and Becky Will, are gracious hosts. Their five guest rooms are decorated either in high Victorian style or filled with country antiques. Each has a private bath, queen-sized beds, flowers, and a television. One of the two-room suites has its own balcony. Breakfast is a hearty country affair. Room rates range from $70 to $85 per night. Because the Wills have a small child of their own, children are welcome. Columbia is a small river town located in western Lancaster County along the Susquehanna River. Traveling to Hershey takes approximately 40 minutes, and traveling to central Lancaster County takes approximately 30 minutes.

COUNTRY GARDENS FARM BED & BREAKFAST
686 Rock Point Road
Mount Joy, PA 17552
(717) 426-3316

Andy and Dotty Hess welcome their guests with open arms. Andy has lived on this farm since he was six years old. Along with one of his sons, he farms 170 acres. Together they care for goats, cows, hogs, chickens, and sheep. Dotty is a vivacious hostess who thoroughly enjoys her guests. She is also an accomplished gardener, and her flowers grace the lawn and house. Mornings bring a large and delicious breakfast, featuring locally grown ingredients. Breakfast includes seasonal fresh fruit, vegetables from her garden, and breakfast meats.

Their large Georgian farmhouse is tastefully decorated with country furnishings. A local Amish woman makes quilts and quilted wall hangings that are displayed throughout the house and are available for sale. There are four guest rooms; two have private baths with showers and two share a bath. The rooms are cheerfully decorated with flowers, lace curtains, and old prints or paintings of the local countryside. My favorite room has a balcony furnished with chairs for fair weather lounging. Room rates are reasonably priced from $55 to $70 for two people.

This is an excellent place for families with small children. After breakfast Dotty rounds up the kids and goes to gather eggs, feed the goats, or watch the baby lambs (during April and May) play in the meadow. The Hesses had seven children of their own, and they take obvious pleasure in their small guests.

COUNTRY PINES FARM
1101 Auction Road
Manheim, PA 17545
(717) 665-5478
PA turnpike exit 20 and go South on Route 72 for 7.6 miles. Turn right onto Auction Road.
Go 2.2 miles and turn left into lane.

Country Pines Farm is located in quiet, western Lancaster County in a valley full of farms. The comfortable 18-room brick house was built in 1817 and is the center of a 100-acre working farm. Children are welcome, and there are many animals to feed and play with. There are two guest rooms in the main house that share a bath; one has two double beds and one has a double bed and a single bed. The rates for these rooms are $40 for two. There is a cottage that sleeps six and has a full bath and air conditioning. Additional adults are $10 per night and children three and above are $5 per night. Breakfast, at $2.50 for each adult, is a hot farmer's meal. Children under 14 eat for free.

Creekside Inn Bed & Breakfast

44 Leacock Road

Paradise, PA 17562

(717) 687-0333

Go North on Leacock from Route 30 and their entrance is on Singer Avenue.

Cathy and Dennis Zimmerman are exceptional hosts at their handsome, 1781 Georgian homestead. Tucked inside a curve of the Pequea Creek and centrally located, this house has five guest rooms; two have fireplaces and all have private baths. The Zimmerman's Amish neighbors made the quilts that grace the beds. The house is furnished with antiques and collectibles gathered by Cathy and Dennis over the years. Creekside dreaming can be done on Amish-made chairs or on a swing on the banks of the Pequea, named for a local Indian tribe. A full breakfast is served and dinner with their Amish neighbors is arranged upon request. Room rates range from $80 to $100 for two in season. Children over 12 are welcome.

Cricket Hollow Bed & Breakfast

240 Evans Road

Lititz, PA 17543

(717) 626-4083

Take Newport Road 2 miles North of Route 501, make a right onto Evans Road, go 1 mile and, they are on the right.

To reach this lovely cottage in the woods, you travel a country lane that winds itself around a pond where geese and ducks summer. Dressed with flowers and a burbling brook, this bed and breakfast offers three pretty rooms; all have private baths and king-sized beds (one room also has a single bed). The room downstairs has a whirlpool and opens onto the patio. Bernice Wagner is a relaxed and gracious hostess and presides over a full country breakfast come morning. The room rates are $75 each. Check-in and check-out times are flexible but are stated as 3:00 p.m. for check-in and 11:00 a.m. for check-out. Children are welcome.

FLOWERS & THYME BED & BREAKFAST

238 Strasburg Pike
Lancaster, PA 17602
(717) 393-1460
PA turnpike exit 21 to
Route 222 S. Take
Route 30 E and exit at
Route 462 (Lincoln
Highway). Right onto
462. Make a left at the
first traffic light onto
Strasburg Pike. Go
slighty more than 1 mile.

The hospitality is warm at Flowers and Thyme Bed and Breakfast.

Staying with Don and Ruth Harnish is a treat. The hospitality is warm, the rooms are handsome and comfortable, and the breakfasts are delicious. This bed and breakfast is in a country setting but only about four miles from the historic villages of Strasburg or Bird-in-Hand. The Harnish home was built in 1941 by an Amish man for a Mennonite family. In 1992 the house underwent extensive remodeling, and a large gathering room with cathedral ceiling was added where a full breakfast is served. The house is surrounded by flower and herb beds with plenty of chairs for enjoying the view. There are three guest rooms: the Garden Room overlooking the gardens with a queen-sized bed, sitting area, and private bath; the Country Room with a double bed and private bath in the hall; and the Thyme Room furnished with reproduction Shaker furniture, a queen-sized, pencil post bed, and a private bath with a shower and Jacuzzi. Room rates range from $65 to $95 per night. Children over 12 are welcome.

FROGTOWN ACRES BED & BREAKFAST

44 Frogtown Road
Paradise, PA 17562
(717) 768-7684
From Route 30 take Belmont Road North to Queen Road,
and then make a right onto Frogtown Road.

Nestled in the Amish countryside, this bed and breakfast has four rooms located in an 1810 stone carriage house. There are two bedrooms on the first floor and two on the second; all have private baths, queen-sized beds, and unique features. The forge room has a bathtub and what remains of a once-working forge. One room has a balcony and another a fireplace. All are beautifully furnished with early American and country furniture. Hosts Phyllis and Patrick Reed offer a full country breakfast to get you started in the morning. Room rates range from $65 to $75.

◆◆

GARDENS OF EDEN BED & BREAKFAST

1894 Eden Road
Lancaster, PA 17601
(717) 393-5179
From Route 30 take Route 23 E 0.8 of a mile. Make a right onto Eden Road 0.4 of a mile and make a right just before the bridge.

Gardens of Eden is home to a remarkable variety of wild flowers (nearly 100), birds, small animals, and your hosts, Marilyn and Bill Ebel. Their beautiful Victorian house was built in 1867 by an iron master and overlooks the Conestoga River. Marilyn's terraced gardens and surrounding grounds have trails for hiking and wildlife spying. There are three guest rooms in the main house, lovingly furnished with family antiques and quilts. All have private baths with bed sizes ranging from a full-sized bed to king-sized bed. The Beecher Cottage is a restored summer kitchen and has a full-sized platform bed upstairs, private bath, living room area with a large working fireplace, and an efficiency kitchen.

There is canoeing, rowboating, and fishing on the river. Two County bike routes pass by the house, and summer brings garden tours. A full breakfast is served in the main house. During warm weather, breakfast is served on the screened porch. Room rates range from $85 to $130 for the cottage. Gardens of Eden has a two-night minimum on weekends and a three-night minimum on holidays. Cash or travelers checks are requested for payment. Children over 12 are welcome in the main house, and children of any age are welcome in the cottage.

Photograph courtesy of Gardens of Eden B and B and Tom Bagley

Gracious comfort at Gardens of Eden Bed and Breakfast.

THE INN AT MT. HOPE

2232 East Mount Hope Road
Manheim, PA 17545
(717) 664-4708
Take Route 72 North of Manheim. Turn right onto Mountain Road and left onto East Mount
Hope Road.

Built in 1800, The Inn at Mt. Hope has been restored to its original charm. It is situated in a quiet, wooded setting, and there are full-length porches from which to watch the birds. There are five well-appointed guest rooms; some have private baths, some have queen-sized beds, and all are elegantly furnished. The suite has a fireplace, separate dressing room, and an alcove with a child's bed. Mary's Room has a charming view of the grounds with a private bath and claw foot tub for soaking away life's troubles. The hearty breakfast buffet, served up daily, consists of granola, fruit and cereals, and a hot entree such as pancakes or French toast. Room rates vary from $60 to $110 per night for two people. Well-behaved and supervised children are welcome at an additional charge of $15 per child for the same room.

THE KING'S COTTAGE

1049 East King Street
Lancaster, PA 17602
(717) 397-1017

A beautifully restored Spanish style mansion, The King's Cottage is listed on the National Register of Historic Places, as well as having been named to the American Historic Inns Top 10 List. This bed and breakfast is situated just east of downtown Lancaster in a residential area.

Along with eight rooms in the main house, there is a newly renovated

Carriage House that pampers guests with privacy, antique furnishings, a fireplace, Jacuzzi, a king-sized canopy bed, and an intimate breakfast for two. The rooms in the main house are all charming and comfortable, furnished with antiques, 18th century reproductions, and terry cloth

The King's Cottage is a special place to stay that is centrally located.

◆◆

robes for lounging. All rooms have private baths. Amenities range from claw foot bathtubs, private porches, queen- and king-sized beds, and a private balcony.

Karen and Jim Owens are gracious hosts, and their full gourmet breakfast is something special. In season rates range from $90 to $160 for the Carriage House. Children over 12 are welcome. The Carriage House is handicapped accessible. Weekends require a two-night stay and holidays or special events a three-night stay.

MANHEIM MANOR BED & BREAKFAST

140 South Charlotte Street
Manheim, PA 17545
(717) 664-4168

Located on a quiet street one block off Manheim's Market Square is a Victorian splendor called the Manheim Manor. There are seven rooms, each with a private bath, television, air conditioner, and refrigerator. One room has a double Jacuzzi and another offers a private balcony. The house has a large living room and dining room, each resplendent with fine woodwork. The owners live in New York City, and the house is run locally. They are open year round, children are welcome, and no smoking is allowed. Prices vary from $85 to $140, depending on features. The room with the Jacuzzi is high end, and most rooms are around $120.

MILL CREEK HOMESTEAD BED & BREAKFAST

2578 Old Philadelphia Pike, (Route 340)
Bird-in-Hand, PA 17505
(717) 291-6419

This 18th century fieldstone farmhouse is one of the oldest homes in Bird-in-Hand. Mill Creek Homestead Bed & Breakfast has much old world charm while offering modern comforts. There are three guest rooms furnished with colonial and Victorian era furnishing; all have private baths and queen-sized beds. A hearty breakfast is served in the formal dining room, and there are a number of common rooms for lounging. Room rates range from $72 to $99 per night. Well-behaved children over ten are welcome. There is an outdoor swimming pool available for guest use. Centrally located along busy Route 340, you are within walking distance of the Bird-in-Hand Farmers' Market and other shops.

MOUNT GRETNA INN
16 West Kauffman Avenue
Mount Gretna, PA 17064
(800) 277-6602

Located in the small historic town of Mt. Gretna in northwestern Lancaster County, this inn is a peaceful place from which to explore. There are game lands nearby and your hosts will design mountain bike tours, by special arrangement, for an easy family ride or a more challenging expedition for expert riders. The 1921 arts and crafts style inn has a spacious living room with a fireplace, a large inviting dining room for full morning breakfasts, and eight uniquely furnished guest rooms. All bedrooms have a private bath. There is one suite, and some rooms have private porches. The antique beds are either queen- or king-sized. Furnishings include Stickley arts and crafts pieces. Room rates are $85 to $115.

NOBLE HOUSE BED & BREAKFAST
113 West Market Street
Marietta, PA 17547
(717) 426-4389

Elissa and Paul Noble are your friendly hosts at this delightful bed and breakfast. A restored, Federal style, brick house, their home was built in 1810 and has 12-foot ceilings. The Nobles have decorated it with family heirlooms, collectibles, art, and fresh flowers to give a happy, welcoming feel. There are two second-floor guest rooms with queen- or king-sized beds (which can also be changed to two twin beds) . They have private baths, and one has a gas fireplace. Candlelight breakfast is served in an elegant dining room. There is a living room with a fireplace for watching television, reading, or visiting. Room rates range from $75 to $95. There are three cats and a dog on the premises, but they are kept in the Noble's own living space. Children are accommodated only by special arrangement.

O'FLAHERTY'S DINGELDEIN HOUSE B & B
1105 East King Street, (Route 462)
Lancaster, PA 17602
(717) 779-7765
On Route 462 which becomes Route 30 traveling East.

Jack and Sue Flatley have created a warm home away from home for their guests. The house is surrounded by lovely flower beds and patios for lounging. A colonial era house, it is traditionally, but very comfortably, furnished. Several common rooms serve as welcome rooms for relaxing. There are four guest rooms; two have private baths and the other two share a bath. Room rates range from $80 to $100 per night for two. Come morning, much effort goes into a full country breakfast.

This bed and breakfast is centrally located (just a mile from Lancaster City's Central Market) and the Flatleys are excellent guides to nearby attractions, including dinner with Amish neighbors.

SAUSAGE BISCUIT PINWHEELS

4 cups all-purpose flour
1 1/4 teaspoon powder
1/2 teaspoon soda
1/4 teaspoon salt
1 cup shortening
1 1/2 cups buttermilk
1 pound sausage

Sift 3 1/2 cups flour into a large bowl. Make well in center, add baking powder, soda, and salt. Cut in shortening, add buttermilk, mix well. Add last 1/2 cup flour. Blend completely. Wrap in waxed paper and chill one hour.

Divide dough in half. On floured surface roll each half to an 18 by 8-inch rectangle and 1/4-inch thick. Spread half the sausage on each dough. Leave 1/2 inch of dough uncovered on one long side. Starting at one long side, roll up jelly roll fashion, ending with uncovered edge of dough. Seal the dough. Rolls can be refrigerated overnight or chilled 30 minutes. Use bread knife to cut, 1/2 inch slices. Place on cookie sheet or broiler pan. Bake 450°F for 15 minutes or until sausage is cooked and dough is golden. Makes 40 to 60 rolls.

—Recipe from Jack & Sue Flatley,
O'Flaherty's Dingeldein House

THE OLDE SQUARE INN

127 East Main Street
Mount Joy, PA 17552
(800) 742-3533

Built as a neoclassic home in 1917 by a local builder, this bed and breakfast is situated on Mount Joy's historic square. Attractive public rooms boast leaded glass windows, a fireplace, and comfortable chairs for lounging. The four guest rooms all have a private bath, a television, and a VCR. Room rates range from $75 to $95 per night.

Your hostess, Fran Hand, loves to cook, and breakfast is one the highlights of the visit. Homemade croissants, muffins, and sweet rolls are served alongside fresh fruit and a hot entree. Hand also runs a food concession at the nearby Historic Columbia Market. On the weekends, children must be at least 12 years old.

OSCEOLA MILL HOUSE

313 Osceola Mill Road
Gordonville, PA 17529
(717) 768-3758
From Route 340, take Route 772 East 1.6 miles
and turn right onto Osceola Mill Road and go 1/2 mile.

Beautifully situated on the Pequea Creek in Amish country, this breathtakingly restored 1776 house offers a glimpse of traditional colonial living. There are four working fireplaces and an 18th century herb garden. The four guest rooms all have private baths (though three cannot be accessed directly from the bedrooms), queen-sized beds, and other modern comforts. A full breakfast is served in the elegant dining room. Children ages 12 and over are welcome, and there is a Newfoundland dog in residence. Room rates range from $105 to $135 per night.

GERMAN APPLE PANCAKE

Peel, core, and slice 2 firm, tart apples (e.g., Granny Smith) and saute over medium heat in 3 tablespoons butter in a 12-inch cast-iron skillet until they begin to soften. Remove from heat and sprinkle with a mixture of 1/2 cup sugar and 1 tablespoon cinnamon.

Make a batter of 1/3 cup flour, 1 tablespoon sugar, pinch of salt, and 1/3 cup half-and-half. In a separate bowl, lightly beat 3 large eggs and 1 egg yolk. Add batter to eggs and beat briefly to mix. Pour over apples and bake in a preheated 400°F oven for approximately 13 minutes until puffed and lightly browned. Sprinkle with vanilla sugar and serve immediately.

Vanilla Sugar: Slice a vanilla bean lengthwise and cut into 1/2-inch pieces. Add to one box of confectioner's sugar and let stand one week before using.

—Recipe from Robin Schoen, *Osceola Mill House*

RAIL ROAD HOUSE BED & BREAKFAST

West Front & South Perry Streets
Marietta, PA 17547
(717) 426-4141

The Rail Road House has had an exciting life. Built between 1820 and 1823 to accommodate the nearby river and canal traffic, it has braved brawls by rivermen, the Depression, the housing of a psychedelic coffee house, and the flood of 1972. Rick and Donna Chambers have rescued this historic inn, added fine food to the menu, planted flower, vegetable and herb gardens, and decorated 12 guest rooms with Victorian flair. All rooms have private baths. One room, called the Summer Kitchen and Breakfast Room, has a separate entrance off the patio with its own kitchenette, loft, and sitting area. A full breakfast is served to get your day off to a good start. Room rates range from $69 to $99.

THE RIVER INN BED & BREAKFAST

258 West Front Street

Marietta, PA 17547

(717) 426-2290

West on Route 30, exit at Columbia, N on Route 441. Left at first traffic light onto Market and left to Front St.

The handsome historic River Inn in Marietta.

The River Inn is a restored house built in 1790 and located in the national historic district of Marietta. Furnished with antiques and reproduction furniture, this inn makes an excellent starting point from which to explore this historic town on foot. There are three guest rooms; all have private baths and queen-sized beds. One room also has a single bed and yet another, a working fireplace. Joyce and Bob Heiserman are gracious hosts. Bob loves to fish and, with advance notice, is happy to take guests out on his boat for a fishing expedition on the nearby Susquehanna River. Joyce oversees a delicious full breakfast that is served on the porch, weather permitting.

The Heisermans have lived in the area most of their lives and are full of information about present-day Marietta, as well as its interesting history. Room rates run from $60 to $75 for two with a $10 charge for each additional person. Children over ten are welcome.

SPRINGHOUSE INN BED & BREAKFAST

806 New Street

Akron, PA 17501

(717) 859-4202

PA Turnpike exit 21. Take Route 222 South to Brownstown exit. Turn right onto New Street.

Located in a quiet, small town setting, this lovely stone farmhouse has pine floors, bubble glass, and an 18th century ambiance. A comfortable parlor is an inviting place to read or visit. Three comfortable guest rooms are available with either private baths or a shared bath, queen beds or twin beds.

Room rates range from $59 to $79.

Breakfast is a full one served at small tables for added privacy. Visit the nearby Ephrata Cloister, outlet shopping in Reading, or antique shopping in Adamstown.

Photograph courtesy of Swiss Woods Bed and Breakfast

The idyllic Swiss Woods Bed and Breakfast.

SWISS WOODS BED & BREAKFAST

500 Blantz Road
Lititz, PA 17543
(800) 594-8018

Built in 1986, Werner and Deborah Mosiman patterned their bed and breakfast after the chalets that dot the hillsides of Werner's Swiss home-land. Set in the north-ern Lancaster County countryside by a pond and landscaped with flowers, this retreat is a winner. Inside there is lots of light, natural oak and pine, and a massive fireplace in the common room. The seven guest rooms each have their own bath. All have either a balcony or patio, where one may lounge and contemplate life, and are furnished with contemporary comfort. A suite, with a private deck, is ideally suited for families. Two rooms have a Jacuzzi.

A full breakfast is served on the patio in the summer or next to the fire in the winter. Swiss breads and pastries, freshly baked quiche, casseroles, soufflés with muffins, and scones will get you off on the right foot. Deborah grew up in this area and is a good source of information. The nearby Speedwell Forge Lake is a perfect place for hiking and fishing. German and Swiss German are spoken here. Rates range from $75 to $125 per night. Certain holiday weekends require a minimum three-night stay, and weekends during the season require a minimum two-night stay.

VOGT FARM BED & BREAKFAST

1225 Colebrook Road
Marietta, PA 17547
(800) 854-0399

This 26-acre working farm is home to the Vogt family, assorted sheep, beef cattle, and lovable cats. The farmhouse, built 1868, has three porches and homey, common areas for relaxing. Accommodations include two guest rooms with shared baths that are $60 per night. A suite which includes king-sized bed (which can be changed to twin beds), a private bath, and a single bed in a separate cozy room goes for $99 per night. A full breakfast is generally served at 8:30 during the week and 8:00 on Sunday. Additional features of interest for the business traveler are private phones, desks, a copier on the premises, and flexible breakfast hours. The country setting is centrally located between Hershey, Lancaster, Harrisburg, and York.

WALNUT HILL FARM BED & BREAKFAST

801 Walnut Hill Road
Millersville, PA 17551
(717) 872-2283

For families who want to be out in the country, Walnut Hill Farm is a good place to stay. The Shertzers are farmers and have three bedrooms in their 11-room farmhouse, as well as a guest house with two bedrooms, a living room, kitchen, and bath. One of the rooms has a private bath; all are comfortably furnished and have air conditioning. The guest house is rented to one party at a time, whether or not they need both bedrooms. A full country breakfast is served for guests staying in the main farmhouse. There are fun farm things for the children to do: gather eggs, feed calves and lambs, and play with the kittens. The rooms are $50 to $65 per night for two people. There is an additional charge of $10 per night for each adult and $5 per night for each child 12 and under. The guest house is $65 per night with additional fees as described above.

WATERFORD HOUSE BED & BREAKFAST

18 East Front Street
Marietta, PA 17547
(717) 426-3056

The Ritchey's historic home on Front Street is adorned with old dolls, quilts, and antiques. Two guest rooms are comfortably furnished; both have double beds and share a bath. A full breakfast is served in a handsome dining room. Children are welcome, and smoking is permitted in specific areas of the house. Guests are welcome to use a sitting room with a television and VCR.

WEST RIDGE GUEST HOUSE

1285 West Ridge Road
Elizabethtown, PA 17022
(717) 367-7783

Take Route 230 West into Elizabethtown. At 3rd light, left. 1 mile, left onto Rutt Road. Right onto W. Ridge.

This large country house, overlooking a 23-acre farm, and its guest house offer a pampered holiday in the country setting of western Lancaster County. There are five rooms in the guest house that variously offer a fireplace, whirlpool tub, or a deck. The main house has an additional four rooms; two are suites with fireplaces and whirlpool tubs. All rooms are comfortably furnished in traditional style with private baths and have access to a refrigerator with drinks, a television, and a telephone. Amenities also include an exercise room, a hot tub, and two fishing ponds for recreation. A full country breakfast is served in the guest house. Rates range from $60 to $100. If there are more than two persons to a room, an additional charge of $15 per person is added. Children under ten are $10 per night, and there is a $5 fee for setting up a crib. The location of this bed and breakfast makes traveling to Harrisburg and Hershey a reasonably short ride away.

OTHER BED AND BREAKFASTS TO TRY:

BED & BREAKFAST - THE MANOR
830 Village Road
Lampeter, PA 17537
(717) 464-9564

THE DECOY BED & BREAKFAST
958 Eisenberger Road
Strasburg, PA 17579
(800) 726-2287

GREYSTONE MANOR
2658 Old Philadelphia Pike, (Route 340)
Bird-in-Hand, PA 17505
(717) 393-4233

HERSHEY BED & BREAKFAST RESERVATION SERVICE
P.O. Box 208
Hershey, PA 17033
Monday-Friday 10-4. (717) 533-2928

THE GEORGE ZAHN HOUSE
6070 Main Street
East Petersburg, PA 17520
(717) 569-6026

LINCOLN HAUS INN
1687 Lincoln Highway East, (Route 30)
Lancaster, PA 17602
(717) 392-9412

NEW LIFE HOMESTEAD
1400 East King Street (Route 462)
Lancaster, PA 17602
(717) 396-8928

ROSE MANOR ENGLISH
124 South Linden Street
Manheim, PA 17545
(717) 664-4932

THE WALKABOUT INN
837 Village Road
Lampeter, PA 17537
(717) 464-0707

INNS

CAMERON ESTATE INN
1895 Donegal Springs Road
Mount Joy, PA 17552
(717) 653-1773

Owned by David and Becky Vogt and tucked away on 15 secluded acres, this grand manor makes for a quiet getaway. The grounds include beautifully landscaped lawns and a trout stream meandering through the meadow. The 1804 Federal house was built by President McKinley's great-grandfather and has a grand foyer and formal public rooms for visiting. The second floor bedrooms are large and furnished as appropriate for the period with a federal and Victorian look. The rooms under the eaves on the third floor are much cozier.

Get away from it all at the Cameron Estate Inn.

Photograph courtesy of the Cameron Estate Inn

Cameron Estate Inn has a total of 17 rooms; all have private baths and seven have fireplaces. The rooms with fireplaces and the single suite run $125 per night. The rest of the rooms are $100 per night. Dinner is served in the inn's restaurant, which specializes in continental cuisine with daily specials to capitalize on seasonal produce, game and fish. Dinner is not included in the lodging fee. Overnight guests are offered a complimentary, continental plus breakfast on the porch. Muffins, ham and cheese, and fruit are typically offered. Afternoon brings tea and cookies in the library. Children over 12 are welcome though pets are not.

CHURCHTOWN INN
Route 23
Churchtown, PA 17555
(717) 445-7794
In the center of Churchtown.

Jim Kent, Hermine and Stuart Smith are your convivial hosts in their 18th century fieldstone inn. The innkeepers go out of their way to bring their guests together. Special events include an annual Victorian ball, a murder mystery weekend, and musical weekends. Stuart Smith is a choir director and evenings find him at the grand piano.

Eight guest rooms in full Victorian splendor offer private baths (with two exceptions), queen-sized beds, and antique furnishings. The first floor suite also has a large sitting area. Room rates begin at $55 for two per night and go to $135 for the suite. A big, five-course breakfast with fresh squeezed orange juice and homemade breads is served in a glass enclosed garden room. Dinner with Amish or Mennonite families can be arranged with prior notice.

COUNTRY LIVING INN
2406 Old Philadelphia Pike, (Route 340)
Lancaster, PA 17602
(717) 295-7295

This centrally located inn, owned and managed by Judy and Bill Harnish, has been pleasing travelers since 1989. It is located in East Lampeter Township but has a Lancaster address. The 34 rooms and two suites (one with a Jacuzzi) are tastefully furnished with an elegant country look. Master craftsmen used the old German art of wallprinting for a lovely effect. The extra long beds are quilt covered, and even the most inexpensive rooms are generously proportioned and include a telephone, cable television, bath and shower, and a table and chairs for catching up on your reading. Most of the rooms have two double beds, but there are rooms with queen-sized beds. Be sure to be specific about your requirements.

The staff is very helpful and pleasant. Complimentary coffee, tea, and hot chocolate are served from 8-10 a.m. On weekends between May and October, pastries are also served on the porch. This inn has the usual amenities, including wake-up calls, air conditioning, ice and soda machines, and guest rooms for smokers. Children are welcome and complimentary cribs are available. Children under five stay free. There is an additional person charge of $8.00, but cots are free. If you require wheelchair accessibility, you must request a first floor room. Room rates range from $70 to $125 in season.

DONECKERS: THE 1777 HOUSE
301 West Main Street
Ephrata, PA 17522
(717) 738-9502
Exit 21 from the PA turnpike and take Route 322 West which is also Main Street.

In the town of Ephrata, there are four inns owned by H. William Donecker with a total of 40 rooms and suites, all within a short distance of the rest of the Doneckers' community: Doneckers Fashion Stores, The Restaurant at Doneckers and The Artworks at Doneckers. The 1777 House is located on Main Street and just six blocks from Doneckers Fashion Stores.

◆◆

Built by one of the members of the Ephrata Cloister, the clockmaker Jacob Gorgas, this stately home now offers ten guest rooms and two carriage house suites. Tile flooring, stone masonry, hand-hooked rugs, and hand-cut stenciling add to the beauty of this handsome house. The rooms are named for members of the Ephrata Cloister. They all have private baths and various bed sizes. Rooms feature a variety of amenities, including Jacuzzis, fireplaces, refrigerators, and private entrances. Room rates range from $89 to $175 for the suites. A continental plus breakfast is served.

THE GUESTHOUSE AT DONECKERS

318-324 North State Street

Ephrata, PA 17522

(717) 738-9502

Exit 21 from the PA turnpike and take Route 322 West. Make a right onto N. State Street for two blocks.

This inn has 20 attractive and comfortably furnished rooms with many original features such as inlaid wood floors and stained glass windows. Antiques, hand-stenciled walls, and designer linens add to a feeling of country

elegance. All rooms have private baths; some also have fireplaces, Jacuzzis, private entrances, or balconies. Room rates range from $59 to $149 for the Fulton Suite. See the 1777 House at Doneckers entry for more information. A continental plus breakfast is served.

Photograph courtesy of Doneckers

Country elegance at The Guesthouse at Doneckers.

THE INNS AT DONECKERS-THE HOMESTEAD

251 North State Street

Ephrata, PA 17522

(717) 738-9502

Exit 21 from the PA turnpike and take Route 322 West. Make a right onto N. State Street for two blocks.

This is the original site of the first Donecker family business. Today it offers four suites and rooms, each with a Jacuzzi and /or a fireplace. The inn is decorated with local handcrafts, and each room has a television and mini-refrigerator. Room rates range from $125 to $165. See the 1777 House at Doneckers entry for more information. A continental plus breakfast is served.

THE INNS AT DONECKERS-THE GERHART HOUSE

287 Duke Street

Ephrata, PA 17522

(717) 738-9502

Exit 21 from the PA turnpike & take Route 322 W. Make a R onto N. State Street for 3 blocks & left onto Duke St.

Built in 1926 by the local builder Alexander L. Gerhart, this lovingly restored home features five guest rooms. There are original pine floors, leaded and stained glass windows, and chestnut doors and trim. All rooms have private baths; some have a canopied queen-sized bed, private balcony, and private entrance. Room rates range from $69 to $89 for two. See the 1777 House at Doneckers entry for more information.

FULTON STEAMBOAT INN

Routes 30 & 896

Strasburg, PA 17579

(717) 299-9999

Children especially will enjoy sleeping in a steamboat firmly anchored on land. This inn was built in the shape of a boat and has three levels: the Promenade Deck (first floor), the Observation Deck (second floor), and the Sun Deck (third floor). The room rates and amenities increase the higher up you stay. All rooms have a refrigerator, microwave, cable television, telephones, and queen-sized beds. The rooms on the top floor are generously sized and have whirlpool bathtubs and access to a balcony. All units are comfortably furnished with Early American, country, or traditional furniture. There is a gift shop, a cafe, and a dining room with reasonably priced food. Other amenities include an indoor pool and Jacuzzi, universal fitness room, video game room, laundry facilities, and conference and banquet facilities. Room rates range from $47 to $124 depending on the floor, time of year, and amenities. There are various discount packages available.

Drawing courtesy of the General Sutter Inn

Enjoy the historic town of Lititz with a stay at the General Sutter Inn.

General Sutter Inn
14 East Main Street
Lititz, PA 17543
(717) 626-2115
On the square at the corner of Route 772 and 501.

The General Sutter Inn was established in 1764 by Moravians under the name Zum Anker (the sign of the anchor). It was renamed during the 19th century in honor of General John Sutter who was a Lititz resident and a famous California gold digger. The inn also has the distinction of being one of the oldest continuously operating inns in the Pennsylvania Dutch area. Boasting 12 Victorian rooms and decorated with period antiques and quilts, this inn is a comfortable place to be waylaid. All rooms have private baths, televisions, and telephones.

There is a coffee shop where breakfast and lunch are served and a more formal dining room for lunch and dinner. The Victorian lobby is graced by finches and lovebirds in their wire cages. Pets are permitted, but must not be left in the room unattended. Small, quiet, well-behaved dogs that understand they must stay off the furniture are preferred. Lititz is a charming and historic town, and the inn is within walking distance of America's first commercial pretzel factory, an idyllic park, The Wilbur Chocolate Factory, and the Lititz Museum.

The Historic Strasburg Inn
Route 896
Strasburg, PA 17579
(800) 872-0201

This modern, colonial style inn offers 104 guest rooms. On-site amenities include a game room, an outdoor swimming pool, a volleyball court, bicycle rental, and valet service. Dogs are welcome with an additional fee of $10 per night. Room rates begin at $119 on the weekend during the season. A restaurant on the premises serves breakfast, lunch, and dinner.

THE INN AT TWIN LINDEN
2092 Main Street, (Route 23)
Churchtown, PA 17555
(717) 445-7619
Exit 22 from the PA turnpike. Route 10 S to West 23. Travel 4 miles. The Inn is in the center of town on the left.

Donna and Bob Leahy got their appetite for innkeeping while running a summer getaway in Maine. They enjoyed it so much they decided to look for an inn they could run full-time within a reasonable commute of Bob's Philadelphia-area job. Since 1987 the Leahys have pampered guests with delicious, elegant food, sumptuous guest rooms, and bucolic views.

The seven rooms (including one suite) have private baths, antique furnishings, stenciled walls, and cable television. The Palladian Suite is the ultimate retreat: private entrance, fireplace and stove, two-person Jacuzzi, tiled wet bar, and a farmland view. With one exception, all the other rooms have a queen-sized bed and a special feature such as a fireplace, canopy bed, or a two-person Jacuzzi. Room rates range from $100 per night to $210 per night for the suite.

Breakfast is an affair to remember. Donna, as chef and author of *Morning Glories* (Rizzoli), a breakfast cookbook, prepares extraordinary eye openers. Smoked salmon and brie frittata or pesto eggs with leeks and asparagus are possible entrees. Sweets such as blueberry-peach cobbler or croissant cinnamon raisin buns are worth twice the calories.

Candlelight dinners are served on Friday and Saturday nights with reservations only. Preference is given to the inn's guests. Donna is chef again and her creativity and attention to ingredients come to the fore. Appetizers such as wild mushroom ravioli with chèvre and plum tomato precede entrees such as veal chop with pear, ginger, and pecans or Maine lobster fricas-

Pamper yourself with a stay at The Inn at Twin Linden.

see with chanterelles and dill cream. Appetizers start at $8.25 and entrees range from $18.95 to $23.95.

The handsome Limestone Inn
is in the charming town of Strasburg.

LIMESTONE INN

33 East Main Street
Strasburg, PA 17579
(717) 687-8392

Slightly East of the intersection of Route 896 and 741.

A Georgian stone house built in 1786 for the first chief burgess of Strasburg, this inn is a lovely spot to hang your hat. It is located in Strasburg's historical district and is listed on the National Register of Historic Places. The rooms are tastefully decorated with a large living room on the first floor and a cozy library on the second floor. There are five guest rooms; all have private baths and a variety of bed and room sizes to choose from. A full breakfast is served in the formal dining room in the morning. An evening meal with an Amish family may be arranged in advance, and there is room to store bicycles. Room rates range from $75 to $95 per night. Holidays and weekends require a minimum two-night stay. Children over 12 are welcome. You are within a short distance of both the Rail Road Museum and the Strasburg Rail Road. Your hosts, Jan and Dick Kennell, also speak some French and German.

THE SMITHTON INN

900 West Main Street
Ephrata, PA 17522
(717) 733-6094

Highway 222 to Ephrata exit. Turn West on Route 322 for 2.5 miles to the Inn.

This site has a long history of comforting weary travelers. Built by Henry and Susanna Miller, who were a part of the Ephrata Cloister, this stone inn began hosting lodgers in 1763. Dorothy Graybill, the current owner, has lovingly restored the inn and has operated it since 1982. It has seven guest rooms and one three-room suite; all have working fireplaces, private baths, a sitting area, and a writing desk. Most beds have canopies, goose down pillows, and handmade quilts. Added touches include private refrigerators, night shirts, and flowers in every room. There is a great room for chatting and a library for reading. A full breakfast is served in the morning. Room rates range from $65 to $170 for the suite. Saturday and holiday reservations require a two-night minimum stay. Mannerly children and pets are welcome.

THE VILLAGE INN OF BIRD-IN-HAND
Old Philadelphia Pike, (Route 340)
Bird-in-Hand, PA 17505
(800) 914-BIRD
7 miles East of Lancaster on Route 340.

The Smucker family runs The Village Inn, built in 1734. It is a Victorian eleven-room inn which has the distinction of being listed on the National Register of Historic Places. There are four suites (two with whirlpools); all have private baths, cable television, and king- or queen-sized beds. A complimentary continental plus breakfast is served on the Sun Porch. Room rates range from $74 for the rooms to $170 for the suites. This makes a good place to stay if you want to be centrally located. Children are welcome, and it has the coziness of a bed and breakfast and the privacy of an inn. Guests have free use of both an indoor and outdoor pool and tennis courts.

OTHER INNS TO CONSIDER:

CONTINENTAL INN
2285 Lincoln Highway East, (Route 30)
Lancaster, PA 17602
(717) 299-0421

MCINTOSH INN
2307 Lincoln Highway
East, (Route 30)
Lancaster, PA 19602
(800) 444-2775

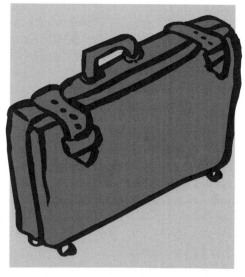

FARMS AND GUEST HOUSES

CLEARWOOD FARM

494 Compass Road
Gap, PA 17527
(717) 442-8229

Route 340 E., right onto Compass Road at the light where Route 10 and Compass intersect.

Jonathan and Lydia Lantz are your hosts at this guest home on a working Amish dairy farm. Located on a quiet road in the far eastern corner of Lancaster County, Clearwood Farm is a good place to relax. There are four simply, but comfortably, furnished guest rooms that share a bath. Children are welcome as long as they are supervised. (A trip to the cow stable during morning or evening milking is a good way to entertain them.) Breakfast is

continental plus with juice, cereal, and some homemade bread to get you on your way in the morning. The rooms are all $20 per night for one person and $30 for two. Baby cribs are available. Smoking and alcoholic beverages are not permitted.

Children have lots to do to keep themselves busy and happy in Lancaster County.

GREEN ACRES

1382 Pinkerton Road
Mount Joy, PA 17552
(717) 653-4028

This lovely country spot is an excellent place for families to stay. The farmhouse is a beautiful large brick affair surrounded by a big yard complete with a life-sized playhouse. There is a whole menagerie of animals to play with: pygmy goats, sheep, and kittens. Pony cart and hay wagon rides are offered to the small guests.

The seven guest rooms each have a private bath with extra beds to accommodate families. Room rates are $75 for two to four people with an additional $5 per extra person. Breakfast is a big country event, and your hosts, Wayne and Yvonne Miller, are willing to help plan your itinerary. They also book dinners with a local Amish family.

◆◆

GROFF FARM HOME
766 Brackbill Road
Kinzer, PA 17535
(717) 442-8223
Just South of Route 30.

Surrounded by Amish farmland, Harold and Mary Ellen Groff are gracious hosts on their working farm. The farmhouse was built in 1857 and offers very comfortable rooms at a very reasonable price. Baths are shared, and there are various bed and room sizes; some large enough to sleep a family with several children. A living room and porch are available for relaxing, and there are animals to visit. The farm has calves, sheep, cows, a goat, and a donkey. Room rates are $25 for two adults and $40 for a family with two children. Breakfast is not served.

LANDIS FARM GUEST HOME
2048 Gochlan Road
Manheim, PA 17545
(717) 898-7028
Take Route 30 to Route 283 W to the Landisville exit. Take Route 722 North. Make a left onto S. Colebrook and a left onto Gochlan Road.

Landis Farm Guest Home makes a charming family getaway.

Photograph courtesy of Landis Farm

The Landis family operates a dairy farm, and they are genial hosts. Available for guests is a cottage with a full kitchen, an original walk-in fireplace, and polished plank floors in the living room. The two bedrooms with two double beds in each, and a full bath are perfect for families. There are swings for the children, and they are invited to help milk a cow or feed the calves. The Landis family home has one guest room with a bathroom next door. Breakfast is served for guests who stay in the home. Room rates for the guest house are $70 for two and $5 for each additional child. The home's guest room is $45 per night.

◆◆

MAPLE LANE FARM GUEST HOUSE

505 Paradise Lane
Paradise, PA 17562
(717) 687-7479

Perched atop a hill on the south side of Paradise, this home is located in a modern brick house on a working farm. The Rohrer family has four guest rooms. Two rooms share a bath; all beds are

Those who never sink into this peace of nature lose a tremendous well of strength, for there is something healing and life-giving in the mere atmosphere surrounding a country house.

Eleanor Roosevelt

doubles in these well-appointed rooms. Both Edwin and Marion grew up nearby, and they know the County well. For a relaxing treat, sit on the front porch and watch the horses graze in the meadow below. Breakfast is continental plus. The rooms are all $55 per night and children of all ages are welcome.

MORNING MEADOWS FARM

103 Fuhrman Road
Marietta, PA 17547
(717) 426-1425
Route 30 West to Columbia. 441 N. to 4th light. Right onto 743 N. Go 1 block, make right onto Fuhrman Rd.

An 1840 brick plantation farmhouse is the centerpiece of a 240-acre working farm. Unusually fancy for the country, the house has a large veranda, a balcony with a view of the surrounding countryside, and rooms with French country furnishings. There are four rooms with private baths, a fireplace, and a television. Barbara and Harold Frey are warm hosts, and morning brings a hearty farm breakfast. It is an excellent place to bring children because there are donkey rides, eggs to gather, cows to milk, and sheep, goats, kittens, calves, and a pig to feed. Room rates are $55 to $65 per night.

NEFFDALE FARM OF PARADISE

610 Strasburg Road, (Route 741)
Paradise, PA 17562
(717) 687-9367
Between Black Horse Road and Belmont Roads on Route 741.

Ellen Neff and her husband Roy live in a contemporary brick home on the family farm. Three generously sized guest rooms have air conditioning and televisions. Choose from private or semi-private baths. Room rates are $40 per night for rooms with one double bed and $42 per night for rooms with two double beds. Amenities include animals for children to discover and a screened patio for lounging. Breakfast is not served.

OLDE COUNTRY LOG HOUSE FARM

1175 Flory Road
Mount Joy, PA 17552
(717) 653-4477

The original part of this handsome farmhouse is made of logs, hence the name. This is a working farm which has been in the family over 50 years, and the Brubakers go out of their way to give their guests a full farm experience. There are goats, sheep, laying chickens, and a hayride to the next farm where they raise pigs. There are five guest rooms; one has a private bath. Another of the five has a queen-sized bed; the rest have full-sized beds. Breakfast is continental plus, and room rates range from $60 and $80.

OLDE FOGIE FARM

106 Stackstown Road
Marietta, PA 17547
(717) 426-3992

Self-described leftover hippies, Tom and Biz Fogie run an organic farm which is home to a few of almost every sort of farm animal. On this relaxed family centered farm, children can enjoy activities like pony rides or helping with the evening chores: milking the goats, gathering eggs, or feeding calves. Accommodations include two small guest rooms (double beds); one has a private bath and one shares a bath with the Fogie family. There are also two suites in a separate house with bathrooms, televisions, kitchens, queen or double beds, and a trundle bed or cribs for small children. Breakfast is served only to those who stay in the main house's guest rooms. The guest rooms start at $55 with an additional $10 for each child per night. The suites start at $65 with an additional $10 for each child. There is a two-night minimum stay.

ROCKY ACRE FARM

1020 Pinkerton Road
Mount Joy, PA 17552
(717) 653-4449

The Benner family has lived on this land for more than 75 years and has been hosting guests on their working farm for over 30 years. The original part of the house (it has been added onto three times) was built in the 1700s, and it features an Indian door and a walk-in fireplace. Legend has it the house was once part of the Underground Rail Road. Guests of Rocky Acre Farm can wade and fish in nearby Little Chickies Creek.

The eight guest rooms are furnished with Victorian and country antiques; all have private baths. There are a variety of bed sizes and number of beds to a room. A two-bedroom apartment is also available complete with kitchen and sitting room. A full country breakfast is served in the morning. Activities for children include a playhouse, watching the cows being milked, or playing with the many cats outside. The apartment rents for $120 and all the other rooms are $60 per night.

OTHER FARMS AND GUEST HOUSES TO VISIT:

BEN-MAR GUEST HOME
5721 Old Philadelphia Pike, (Route 340)
Gap, PA 17527
(717) 768-3309

FARM VIEW GUEST HOUSE
280 White Horse Road
Gap, PA 17527
(717) 442-9055

SMOKETOWN VILLAGE GUEST HOUSE
2495 Old Philadelphia Pike, (Route 340)
Smoketown, PA 17576
(717) 393-5975

STONE HAUS FARM BED & BREAKFAST
360 South Esbenshade Road
Manheim, PA 17545
(717) 653-5819

> If God gave me the choice of the whole planet or my little farm, I should certainly take my farm.
>
> Ralph Waldo Emerson
>
>

CAMPGROUNDS AND CABINS

COUNTRY HAVEN CAMPGROUND
354 Springville Road
New Holland, PA 17557
Open all year. (717) 354-7926
East of Lancaster along Route 897 between Route 322 & 340. 4.5 miles South of Route 322.

This 55-site campground is perched on a hill with delightful views. It is open all year and has all the modern hookups.

FLORY'S CAMPING & COTTAGES
North Ronks Road
Ronks, PA 17572
Open all year. (717) 687-6670
Between Routes 30 & 340.

Enjoy a centrally located, but quiet, country setting in your choice of accommodations: a cottage, guest room with private bath, mobile home, or your very own campsite. There are 71 campsites with the latest hookups and cable television. Facilities include a laundry, pavilion, and a game room.

OAK CREEK CAMPGROUND
Maple Grove Road
Bowmansville, PA 17507
Open all year. (717) 445-6161
1 1/2 miles East of Bowmansville.

This large campground has 311 sites, 136 with sewer hookups. There are cabin rentals, a pool, laundry facilities, a recreation hall, fishing, and miniature golf.

OLD MILL STREAM CAMPING MANOR
2249 Route 30 East
Lancaster, PA 17602
(717) 299-2314
Located just of East of the Dutch Wonderland Entertainment Complex.

Though it is sandwiched between the heavily trafficked Route 30 and a corn field, this campground manages to be a pleasant spot. There are 150 campsites with either 30- or 50-amp hookups, but sewer is not available. Amenities include two dumping stations, game room, pavilion, sundeck, playground, two air conditioned bathhouses, and cable television.

RED RUN CAMPGROUND

877 Martin Church Road
New Holland, PA 17557
Open April-November. (717) 445-4526
From PA turnpike exit 21, take Route 272 south to Church Street. Left and go 1.6 miles and left
on Red Run

Lancaster County countryside.

Set in the lovely Lancaster County countryside, these 115 sites each have a table, fireplace, electricity, and water (18 have sewer hookups). There is a four-acre lake for swimming and boating. No motorboats are permitted, but canoes are available for rental. Other amenities include on-site dumping, ice, propane, campstore, playground, planned activities, and a recreation hall. AAA approved.

ROAMER'S RETREAT CAMPGROUND

5005 Lincoln Highway, (Route 30)
Kinzer, PA 17535
(717) 442-4287
7 1/2 miles East of Route 896, 1/1/2 miles West of Routes 41 and 30.

Nestled in the Amish countryside but centrally located, this campground with its 100 sites is a good place from which to explore Lancaster County. Each site includes a picnic table and electric and sewer hookups. You have a choice of an open grassy site or a shaded one. Amenities include a log campstore and game room, weekend activities, a small grocery store, a laundry, playground, and convenient non-denominational church services. Roamer's Retreat is AAA rated and open all year, though there are limited facilities from November 1 through March 31.

◆◆

SILL'S FAMILY CAMPGROUND

Bowmansville Road

Adamstown, PA 19501

Open April 1 - Oct 31 (800) 325-3002

PA turnpike exit 21, 222 North, 3 1/2 miles to 272 South, 1/4 mile to Bowmansville Road E, 1/4 mi.

This family campground has 125 sites (100 with sewer), a swimming pool, and a game room. Pets are welcome.

SPRING GULCH RESORT CAMPGROUND

475 Lynch Road

New Holland, PA 17557

Open March 8-Nov 1 (800) 255-5744

3.4 miles south of Route 322 on 897. Make a left onto Lynch Road.

This AAA rated campground offers everything one could possibly want and more. It has 450 campsites situated on 115 acres of forest and farmland, and a variety of other lodging options. There are air conditioned lodges that sleep six, country "farmhouses" that sleep up to eight people, and A-frames with two bedrooms that sleep eight. Amenities include the latest in hookups, a lake with a beach, two heated pools with an adult spa, a pond stocked with trout, a game room, miniature golf, laundry, athletic equipment and facilities (tennis, basketball, volleyball, and shuffleboard courts), and regular weekend activities. There is a security gate at the ground's entrance. Pets are allowed at campsites if attended but are not permitted in the indoor lodging.

STARLITE CAMPING RESORT

1500 Furnace Hill Road

Stevens, PA 17578

Open May 1 -Nov 1 (800) 521-3599

This family run campground boasts a large pool, a kiddie pool, tennis court, volleyball court, half court basketball, an air conditioned recreational hall, an outdoor pavilion, an air-conditioned teen room, three bathhouses, two laundries, a playground, and an 18-hole miniature golf course. 130 sites are available for campers; 60 have sewer hookups. Campsites are situated in wooded or open areas. The campground is located on farmland in northern Lancaster County.

◆◆

CRANBERRY POACHED APPLES

6 small apples
(about the size of a peach)
3 cups cranberry juice
1/2 cup sugar
1 small lemon, puréed
3/4 cup finely chopped figs or dates
2 tablespoons brown sugar
1/4 cup finely chopped walnuts
2 tablespoons lemon juice

Peel the apples and core 3/4 of the way to the base. Put the cranberry juice, sugar, and puréed lemon into a saucepan large enough to hold the apples in one layer. Bring to a boil, stir, and add the apples to the pan. Add enough water so the liquid comes halfway up the sides of the apples. Cover the pan and bring to a simmer. Uncover and spoon poaching liquid over the apples every few minutes, turning them gently in the liquid so they are coated often. Depending on the size of the apples, they should simmer 10 to 20 minutes to become fork tender. Be careful not to over cook them or they will fall apart. When the apples are fork tender, remove the pan from heat and let apples cool in the poaching liquid.

In a small bowl, mix the figs, brown sugar, walnuts, and lemon juice. When the apples are cool, stuff the cavities with the fig mixture. Refrigerate stuffed apples overnight and reheat in the morning just before serving. Serves 6.

—Recipe from Karen Owens,
Innkeeper of The King's Cottage

SUN VALLEY CAMPGROUND
Maple Grove Road
Bowmansville, PA 17507
Open all year. (800) 700-3370
PA turnpike exit 22, Route 10,
4 miles Northwest on Maple
Grove Road, 4 miles.

Sun Valley Campground has 265 sites; 200 have sewer hookups. Amenities include cable television, a pool, a game room, and a laundry room.

OTHER CAMPGROUNDS TO VISIT:

PINCH POND FAMILY CAMPGROUND
3075 Pinch Road
Manheim, PA 17545
Open all year. (800) 659-7640

WHITE OAK CAMPGROUND
White Oak Road
Strasburg, PA 17566
Open all year. (717) 687-6207

RESORTS, HOTELS, MOTELS, AND TRAVEL LODGES

BIRD-IN-HAND FAMILY INN
Route 340
Bird-in-Hand, PA 17505
(800) 768-8271

On the site of the Smucker Homestead in the heart of Pennsylvania Dutch country, the Smucker family operates a family focused inn and restaurant. In addition to attractive, modern rooms, there are indoor and outdoor pools, lighted tennis courts, a hot tub, playground, and a game room. Within walking distance are the Bird-in-Hand Farmers' Market, quilt and craft shops, and a general store. The inn has 100 rooms and two suites, all with television, telephone, and in-room coffee. Room rates range from $85 to $90 and children 16 and under stay free.

HERSHEY FARM MOTOR INN
Route 896
Strasburg, PA 17579
(717) 687-8635
1.5 miles south of Route 30.

Hershey Farm Motor Inn makes a good family destination. Amenities include an outdoor pool, a central location, and the nearby Hershey's Family Restaurant. Room rates range from $74 to $89. There are 59 rooms. Children 15 and under stay free.

RED CABOOSE LODGE
Route 741 East
Strasburg, PA 17579
(717) 687-7522

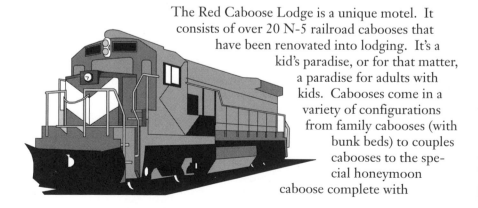

The Red Caboose Lodge is a unique motel. It consists of over 20 N-5 railroad cabooses that have been renovated into lodging. It's a kid's paradise, or for that matter, a paradise for adults with kids. Cabooses come in a variety of configurations from family cabooses (with bunk beds) to couples cabooses to the special honeymoon caboose complete with

Photograph courtesy of Ron Bowman Visual Communications

Children enjoy sleeping at the Red Caboose Lodge.

whirlpool bath and a private deck. The Red Caboose also has a restaurant housed in two 80-ton P-70 dining cars renovated in Victorian splendor. Yes, the rooms are inevitably a bit cramped, but that is a part of the charm.

The best thing about the Lodge, other than the cabooses, is probably the location. It is next door to the National Toy Train Museum (see page 154) and is only a short walk from the Strasburg Rail Road (see page 152) and the Rail Road Museum of Pennsylvania (see page 154). The tracks of the Strasburg Rail Road pass right by the Red Caboose so, as a visitor, you'll be hearing and seeing the old number 90 as it steams past. Prices vary by season. Reservations four to six weeks in advance are recommended due to demand.

WILLOW VALLEY FAMILY RESORT

2416 Willow Street Pike
Lancaster, PA 17602
(800) 444-1714
Three miles south of Lancaster on Route 222.

This large family resort features lodging, a restaurant known for its family dining, and recreational facilities. Room amenities can include king-sized beds, Jacuzzis, and pullout sofas for extra sleeping space. Room rates range from $102 to $142 for two people during the busy summer season. Additional adults are $10 each per night and children six to eleven are $5 each per night. Children under five stay free. All weekends require a two-night minimum and all holidays a three-night minimum. Other amenities include two game rooms, three pools, tennis courts, a nine-hole golf course, and a fitness room with saunas, whirlpools, and Jacuzzis.

OTHER RESORTS, HOTELS, MOTELS, AND TRAVEL LODGES TO CONSIDER:

BEST WESTERN EDEN RESORT INN
Eden Road, Rts. 30 & 272
Lancaster, PA 17601
(800) 528-1234
Room rates range from $139 to $195 per night for weekends.

BEST WESTERN INTERCOURSE VILLAGE MOTOR INN
Routes 340 & 772
Intercourse, PA 17534
(800) 528-1234
Room rates begin at $119 for two people.

BEST WESTERN REVERE MOTOR INN
3063 Lincoln Highway, (Route 30)
Paradise, PA 17562
(717) 687-7683
Room rates begin at $64 per night for two people.

THE BLACK HORSE LODGE & SUITES
2180 North Reading Road, (Route 272)
Denver, PA 17517
(717) 336-7563
Take Exit 21 of PA Turnpike
Room rates begin at $69 per night for two people and include a continental breakfast.

COMFORT INN
624 West Street
New Holland, PA 17557
(800) 228-5150
Room rates begin at $72 per night for two people.

COMFORT INN
500 Centerville Road
Lancaster, PA 17601
(800) 228-5150
Room rates begin at $98 per night for two people.

DAYS INN OF LANCASTER
30 Keller Avenue
Lancaster , PA 17601
(717) 299-5700
Room rates range from $86 to $101 per night for two people.

HAMPTON INN
Route 30 at Greenfield Road
Lancaster, PA 17601
(800) 426-7866
Room rates begin at $74 per night for two people.

HOLIDAY INN
Lititz Pike, (Route 501)
Lancaster, PA 17601
(800) 465-4329
Room rates begin at $95 per night for two people.

HOLIDAY INN LANCASTER HOST
Lincoln Highway East, (Route 30)
Lancaster, PA 17602
(800) 233-0121
Room rates begin $149 per night for two people.

HOTEL BRUNSWICK
Queen & Chestnut Streets
Lancaster, PA 17603
(800) 233-0182
Room rates begin at $70 per night for two people.

HOWARD JOHNSON
2100 Lincoln Highway East, (Route 30)
Lancaster, PA 17602
(800) 446-4656
Room rates begin at $79 per night for two people.

LANCASTER HILTON GARDEN INN
101 Granite Run Drive
Lancaster, PA 17601
(800) 445-8667
Room rates begin at $99 per night for two people.

LANCASTER TRAVELODGE
2101 Columbia Avenue
Lancaster, PA 17603
(800) 255-3050
Room rates start at $66 per night for two people.

MILL STREAM MOTOR LODGE
170 Eastbrook Road
Smoketown, PA 17576
(800) 444-1714
Room rates range from $79 to $99 per night.

RAMADA INN
2250 Lincoln Highway East, (Route 30)
Lancaster, PA 17602
(800) 272-6232
Room rates start at $79 per night.

SOUDERSBURG MOTEL
Route 30
Soudersburg, PA 17577
(717) 687-7607
Room rates are $66 per night.

THE TRAVELERS REST MOTEL
3701 Old Philadelphia Pike, (Route 340)
Intercourse, PA 17534
(800) 626-2021
Room rates are $76 per night.

HARVEST DRIVE MOTEL
3370 Harvest Drive
Intercourse, PA 17534
(717) 768-7186
Room rates are $66 per night.

LODGING OUTSIDE LANCASTER COUNTY

HERSHEY

THE HERSHEY LODGE
University Drive
Hershey, PA 17033
(800) 533-3131
Off Route 322.

Billed as "the ideal family vacation resort," The Hershey Lodge offers indoor and outdoor pools, an exercise facility, game room, tennis, movie theatre, miniature golf, and regulation golf. Room rates begin at $142 for two adults per night for the room only. Prices vary depending on additional children, the inclusion of tickets to various Hershey attractions, or the inclusion of meals.

THE HOTEL HERSHEY
Hotel Road
Hershey, PA 17033
(800) 533-3131
Off HERSHEYPARK Drive.

The Hotel Hershey is the place to stay if you need pampering. Styled after hotels on the Mediterranean, there are formal gardens, attentive service providers, and 241 guest rooms. Amenities include an indoor pool, exercise room, sauna, whirlpool, and 24-hour room service. There are also two restaurants; one casual and the other special enough for a celebratory dinner. Room rates begin at $220 per night for two people for the

GRANDMOTHER MOYER'S BROWN SUGAR BREAKFAST CAKE

2 cups brown sugar
2 cups flour
1/2 cup margarine
pinch of salt

Combine these four ingredients until crumbly. Set aside 2/3 cup of this mixture for crumbs. Add to the remaining ingredients:

1 cup milk
1 egg
1 teaspoon baking powder
1 teaspoon baking soda
1 teaspoon vanilla

Beat together and pour into a well greased and floured pan. Sprinkle crumbs on top. Bake at 350°F for 30 to 35 minutes.

room only. There are many different package options from which to choose, including breakfast, golf, HERSHEYPARK admission, or dinner.

PINEHURST INN HERSHEY

50 Northeast Drive

Hershey, PA 17033

(800) 743-9140

Built by Milton Hershey, this large brick home originally provided lodging for the orphaned boys who attended the Milton Hershey School. The living room is ringed with windows, and there are large porches with rocking chairs. There are 15 guest rooms, simply furnished as a reminder of this building's past use. They feature a range of bed sizes, and three rooms have their own baths. Morning brings a full breakfast. For those with allergies, please be aware there is a cat in residence. Room rates start at $65 for two people, each additional person is $5 per night. Children are welcome.

READING

THE HOUSE ON THE CANAL BED

4020 River Road

Reading, PA 19605

(610) 921-3015

The House on the Canal Bed is a lovely, large farmhouse that was built by a wealthy farmer in the late 1700s. The decor leans toward Victorian with antique dolls as accents. An acre of grounds runs down to the Susquehanna Canal with fishing, bike paths, and walking trails for recreation. There is a very nice back porch and patio for the more relaxed guests. Three guest rooms are generously proportioned; all have private baths, televisions, VCRs, and phones. The $80 room has a large whirlpool tub and a queen-sized bed; the $85 room has a separate sitting room and a view of the canal with a double bed, and the $95 room is a suite with a kitchen and a queen-sized bed. Morning brings a large, tasty country breakfast. Children and pets are welcome and the owners have two dogs themselves. Smoking is permitted in restricted areas but not in the bedrooms.

THE INN AT READING

1040 Park Road

Wyomissing, PA 19610

(800) 383-9713

This colonial style inn has friendly staff, a restaurant and sports bar, and an outdoor pool. It is handicapped accessible and has non-smoking rooms. Special group and business rates are offered. Room rates begin at $119 for two people per night.

◆◆◆

FOOD

◆3◆

INTRODUCTION 86

RESTAURANTS 89
American and Continental 89
Breakfast 95
Ethnic 96
Family and Pennsylvania Dutch 102
Fine Dining 108
Lunch 113
Pub Grub 114
Restaurants Outside Lancaster County 118

PURVEYORS 121
Bakeries 121
Butchers 124
Candy 126
Coffee and Tea 127
Country Stores 128
Farm Stands 129
Farmers' Markets 133
Flour 136
Herbs 136
Honey 136
Ice Cream 137
Imported Foods 138
Jams and Jellies 139
Natural Food Stores 140
Pretzels 141
Trout 143
Wine and Beer 144

◆ ◆ ◆ ◆ ◆ ◆ ◆ ◆ ◆ ◆ ◆ ◆

CHAPTER THREE: FOOD

Food is one of the more universal means for creating a sense of community and strengthening cultural bonds. This is true of the Pennsylvania Germans of many different faiths who came to America from Germany, Switzerland, and Alsace in the 18th and 19th centuries. William Woys Weaver, in his book *Pennsylvania Dutch Country Cooking*, contends that Pennsylvania Dutch cooking is most like the food of the Alsace, though highly influenced by North American cookery.

Pennsylvania Dutch food is unpretentious, hearty food, best suited to the family table. Recipes, with an eye to the kitchen garden and the seasons, are handed from mother to daughter for generations. They are often one-pot meals such as chicken potpie, pork and sauerkraut, or chicken corn soup. These popular dishes stick to the ribs and are economical, both in time and money.

In contrast to Pennsylvania Dutch cooking before the Civil War, today's cooking uses herbs sparingly. When an herb is in evidence, it is usually parsley. Thanks to the efforts of a well-known cook, Clara Landis, M.D. with the Philadelphia Electro-Hygienic Institute and author of *The Improved Hygienic Cookbook*, Pennsylvania Dutch cooks were persuaded to eschew herbs and spices. Dr. Landis believed that highly seasoned food had the effect of "drying up the secretions, causing false appetites." The hygienic movement went so far as to declare simple foods evidence of moral and religious superiority.

Many of the foods served at a Pennsylvania Dutch table are quite familiar to the average American. German food has been incorporated into our daily lives: hamburgers, hot dogs, potato salad, sauerkraut, sausages, pickles, and pot roast.

FAVORITE FOODS

Savory foods associated with Lancaster County today include pretzels, potato chips, corn fritters, Lebanon bologna, chow chow (pickled vegetables), red beet eggs, corn fritters, horseradish as a condiment, root

Photograph courtesy of Ron Bowman Visual Communications

These are a few of the favorite foods of Lancaster.

beer, pork and sauerkraut, chicken potpie, and chicken corn soup.

Pennsylvania Dutch women are also known for their baking prowess. For those with a sweet tooth, there are shoofly pies, whoopie pies, sticky buns, snickerdoodles, and many wondrous fruit desserts. In fact, there are pies for practically every time of the day. At breakfast the sweet, gooey, shoofly pie gets you started. Chicken potpie makes a perfect lunch or dinner. For evening desserts and snacking, there are all sorts of fruit and custard pies.

As with the rest of the country, baking for a festive occasion is a serious and mouthwatering business for Pennsylvania Dutch cooks. Christmas brings cookie baking, and local favorites include gingerbread cookies, walnut kisses, *pfeffernusse*, almond cookies, sandtarts, and *springerle* (molded cookies with aniseed). Shrove Tuesday, the day before Ash Wednesday, would not be complete without "fastnachts" or raised doughnuts.

Cool cellars hold apples throughout the winter, and this readily available ingredient shows up in many guises. Apples appear as apple butter (which has nothing to do with butter, but is a combination of apples, cider, and spices boiled to a thick consistency), cider, dumplings, fritters, sauce, pancakes, pie, and dried apples. They are transformed into *Schnitz un Gnepp* or apples and dumplings.

The dried stigmas of the fall-blooming crocus, *Crocus sativus*, saffron has a long history in Lancaster County. It became an everyday ingredient in the mid 19th century and was valued as a medicinal herb and sometimes used as a dye. It is now primarily used for flavoring and coloring food. In Pennsylvania Dutch cooking, saffron shows up in the comforting chicken corn soup, noodles, stuffed pig's stomach, and holiday breads. Marty and Carol Keen, who grow saffron under the name M & J Greider Farm, are one of the few families in the area who still produce saffron. Their half-acre saffron patch is carefully hand-picked during the three-week blooming season. The stigmas are then dried. The intensive labor required to harvest saffron makes it the most expensive herb or spice on the market. Look for M & J Greider Farm saffron at the Landis Valley Museum, the Ephrata Cloister, and other locations throughout the area.

RESTAURANTS

Lancaster County dining runs the gamut from family dining to brew pubs with good food and from American food served in old taverns to fine dining and ethnic choices. The ethnic restaurants in the area are a relatively new and welcome addition to the culinary scene. In general the food and restaurants are unpretentious, the service is unusually pleasant, portions are huge, and prices are very reasonable.

One of the ways I judge restaurants is by the bread they serve. The handcrafted, European style breads have not made their appearance in the area yet. Nor is most of the bread served at restaurants in the area reminiscent of the bread baked in the wood-fired ovens of earlier days. These ovens, found on most Pennsylvania Dutch homesteads, yielded a crusty, chewy, and flavorful addition to the meal. When the bread renaissance finally hits Lancaster County, it will add much pleasure to the Pennsylvania Dutch table.

Restaurants serving Pennsylvania Dutch food are usually organized so the food is served either family style or smorgasbord. For family style service, waitresses bring serving bowls filled with food which are passed around the table. Most often, several families or parties of diners are seated together at one table. Smorgasbords on the other hand are more commonly known as buffet style dining. Each party typically has its own table, and diners can choose from a wide array of foods.

PURVEYORS

Butchers and bakers make up a preponderance of the following purveyors. For the Pennsylvania Dutch, November traditionally was butchering month, and the lowly pig most often provided lots of necessary protein. Today, old-fashioned butchers continue to butcher, smoke their own hams, and manufacture a wide variety of pork products.

Pennsylvania Dutch cooks are known for their ability to turn out a myr-

iad of delicious cakes, pie, and cookies. When they run out of time, there are bakeries that still rely on traditional recipes and help to satisfy the area's unabashed sweet tooth.

FARM STANDS

Because of the large number of farmers, Lancaster County has always been blessed with impeccable fresh produce. Farm stands spring up spontaneously along country roads as the bountiful gardens and kitchens produce more than families can eat. If you want to hit a lot of farm stands in a short distance, I recommend Route 23 between Churchtown and Route 897 or Route 625 from Route 23 north to Bowmansville.

RESTAURANTS

AMERICAN AND CONTINENTAL

ALEX AUSTIN STEAKHOUSE

2481 Old Philadelphia Pike, (Route 340)
Lancaster, PA 17602
Daily 11-9. (717) 394-2539

This casual eatery offers up tasty steaks, chicken, and seafood options, served by pleasant waiters. New York strip au poivre is a good choice, and prime rib is served on Fridays and Saturdays. Entrees range from $5 for a burger to $22.95 for a 10-ounce steak stuffed with crabmeat. Liquor is not served, but you can BYOB.

THE DINING CAR
AT THE STRASBURG RAIL ROAD

Route 741 East
Strasburg, PA 17579
Lunch served daily from March to December. Call for days and time.
Reservations suggested for lunch and required for dinner. (717) 687-6486

Eat aboard the Lee E. Brenner Dining Car at the historic Strasburg Rail Road. Enjoy lunch or dinner on a beautifully restored, wooden coach while traveling through scenic Amish farms. The Lee E. Brenner is a wooden railroad car with a woodburning stove, mahogany paneling, and brass lamps. Lunch is casual American food. Dinner lasts approximately two hours and selections are of the American variety: prime ribs, chicken, or flounder stuffed with crab meat. Cost for the four-course meal is $27.95 and includes the train ride, tax, and entertainment. Or stop here at the Dining Car Restaurant (a stationary restaurant near the train station) or the Sweet and Treat shop and buy a picnic lunch to take along on the Strasburg Rail Road. You can be let off at Groff's Picnic Grove, have lunch at the picnic tables, and hop the next train back to the station.

Photograph courtesy of the Strasburg Rail Road

Dine while trundling through Amish countryside on the Lee E. Brenner Dining Car.

DOC HOLLIDAYS

College Square
931 Harrisburg Pike
Lancaster, PA 17603
Dining Room: Mon-Sun 11-11. Saloon: Sun-Thurs 11-1, Fri & Sat 11-2.
(717) 397-3811

This popular new restaurant is the sort of place that keeps both the local Franklin and Marshall College students happy, as well as their parents. The large contemporary dining room, outfitted with high ceilings, brass, and wood tables, makes a good setting for digging into a Doc's famous prime rib. There are ribs, burgers, seafood, rotisserie roasted chicken, and very good steaks. This is down home cooking at good prices: entrees range from $5.25 for a burger to $19.95 for surf and turf.

J-M'S BISTRO & PUB

300 West James Street
Lancaster, PA 17603
Mon-Sat 11-11. Sun 4-9. (717) 392-5656

I love bistro food. Who doesn't have a craving for roast chicken or meatloaf with mashed potatoes at least once a week? J-M's, new to the Lancaster restaurant scene, is overseen by chef and owner Jean-Maurice Jugé. Other than the aforementioned bistro staples, the dinner menu variously offers up Parisian chicken with caramelized shallots and mushrooms in a thyme scented sauce, grilled duck breast with orange sauce, or filet mignon done as you like it with a béarnaise sauce or encrusted with peppercorns with a brandy dijon cream sauce. Starters can include Louisiana oyster beignets, garden ravioli, or a wild mushroom spring roll. Appetizers run from $5.95 to $6.95 and entrees from $8.95 for meatloaf to $23 for rack of lamb. This is

also a good place for lunch or lighter evening fare such as ribs, burgers, pastas, or pizzas.

Comfort food is the specialty of J-M's Bistro.

KEGEL'S SEAFOOD RESTAURANT

551 West King Street
Lancaster, PA 17603
Tues-Fri 11-9. Sat 2-9:30. Sun 12-7. (717) 397-2832

Kegel's Seafood is a family owned restaurant that has been serving up seafood since 1941. All the standard favorites are offered: sautéed frog legs, lobster thermidor, and sautéed softshell crabs along with shad roe, and a fried oyster platter. When in season clam and oysters are given the full treatment. Dining is casual in this neighborhood spot, and special requests to the kitchen are accommodated when possible. Parking is available at 619 Marietta Avenue and 516 West Grant Street. Entrees run from $8.50 to $23 for a large, broiled seafood platter.

MARKET FARE RESTAURANT

50 West Grant Street
Lancaster, PA 17603
Lunch: Mon-Sat 11-2:30. Dinner: Sun & Mon 5-9, Tues-Sat 5-10. Sunday Brunch 11-2.
(717) 299-7090
Entrance at the corner of Grant and Market Streets.

A favorite Lancaster eatery, Market Fare Restaurant can be counted on for good food from 9:00 a.m. (in the cafe) until they close at night. The intimate dining rooms have a genteel British club feel with 19th century paintings, upholstered armchairs, and well-spaced tables. Come here for a romantic dinner, a festive brunch, or a light bite at the Market Fare Cafe, open from 9:00 to 3:00. Featuring imaginative American cuisine, typical menu choices include Victorian chicken, a chargrilled chicken breast with oven-roasted vegetables and a sauce of white balsamic vinegar, tarragon, and dijon vinaigrette. Rack of lamb with dijon crumb topping or lemon peppered crab sauté over jumbo chicken ravioli are other representative menu items. Dinner entrees range from $13.95 to $25.95 for the rack of lamb, and dinners run around $32 per person with a glass of wine. Reservations are suggested.

PEPPERS

1280 Plaza Boulevard
Lancaster, PA 17601
Mon-Sat 4-11. Bar open until 12:00. (717) 299-1900

Hungry for a burger? You'll have a difficult time settling for just one with the 40 different choices at this casual eatery. Are you in an extravagant mood? The Dom Pérignon burger features a bottle of Dom Perignon and two burgers made just the way you like them for $99.95. If you're feeling a little less flush, maybe the Australian burger with bacon, cheddar, and one egg over easy will be just the thing. Or maybe the gyro burger topped with onions, tomatoes, olives, and sour cream on pita will fit the bill. The burgers are good, but this restaurant also has an extensive selection of pastas, stir frys, and entrees from the grill. Entrees run from $4.95 for an all-American cheeseburger to $17.95 for a steak. The service is congenial. There is a good beer selection, and this is a great late night place to nosh.

RAIL ROAD HOUSE BED & BREAKFAST

West Front & South Perry Streets
Marietta, PA 17547
Tues-Sat 11-2, Tues-Thurs 5-9, Fri-Sat 5-10, Sun: Brunch 11-2,
Lunch 11-4, Dinner 11-9 (717) 426-4141

Once an old hotel, this historic building is home to a bed and breakfast inn as well as a restaurant. Serving up American standards, this comfortable spot has several attractive dining spaces. A tavern room with a copper bar for light fare and three other dining rooms variously featuring oriental rugs, wood floors, and a fireplace. In good weather, the outdoor courtyard with wrought iron furniture is the place to be.

Drawing courtesy of the Rail Road House B & B

The dinner menu offers old favorites like Steak Diane, Caesar salad, and Veal Normandy. There is a variety of seafood, chicken, and pasta. Entrees run from $13.95 to $19.95. The lunch and light fare menu has a good selection of soups, sandwiches, and salads.

Rail Road House Bed and Breakfast
serves up American standards.

REFLECTIONS FINE FOOD & SPIRITS

1390 Oregon Road, (Route 722)
Leola, PA 17540
Daily 11-12. Reservations suggested. (717) 656-3717

Located in an old stone house in the small village of Oregon, Reflections is named for a 200-hundred-year-old, 38-foot, hand dug well that surfaces in one of the dining rooms. Lit and covered with glass, it is possible to eat and make wishes at the same time! If you want a good alternative to the ubiquitous family style restaurants, your first wish has come true. Reflections serves up good American fare with a creative use of fresh ingredients. The service is pleasant, and the dining room is decorated with tiffany lamps and many plants. The convivial bar is surrounded by stained glass partitions. The porch, which is particularly inviting during the day, is a handsome room surrounded with cheerful windows.

The lunch menu offers soups, salads, and hot or cold sandwiches ranging from $4.95 to $7.95. Dinner brings a varied menu of seafood, veal, steak, and chicken options. An appetizer of smoked trout and salmon with capers and red onions would be a good start. The prime rib with Yorkshire pudding (Friday and Saturday only) is my choice as an entree. All main course dishes are prepared to order and range from $13.95 to $21.95. Sunday brunch offers up all sorts of omelets and specialties like smoked salmon on a bagel or steak and eggs.

THE STOCKYARD INN
1147 Lititz Pike
Lancaster, PA 17601
Mon 4-9. Tues-Fri 11:30-9. Sat 4-9:30. (717) 394-7975
1/2 mile South of Route 30 on Route 501.

The Stockyard Inn is an old Lancaster County standby serving up American and Continental food in a gracious setting. A building with many stories, it was constructed around 1750 and owned by President James Buchanan from 1856 to 1864. It has been used as an inn since 1900. Prime rib, steaks, and seafood are the specialty of the house. Dinner entrees run from $14 to $25.50.

TOBIAS S. FROGG
1766 Columbia Avenue
Lancaster, PA 17603
Mon-Tues 11-12. Wed-Sat 11-2. Sun 12-12. (717) 394-8366

Burgers are a favorite at this casual neighborhood restaurant which is a good place for noshing on interesting sandwiches such as the salmon burger, prime rib, or crabcake. Dinner options include honey glazed pork chops, smothered blackened chicken, and ribs. There is a children's menu, and several heart healthy entrees to choose from. Entree prices run from $4.95 up to $16.95 for the 10-ounce filet mignon.

OTHER AMERICAN AND CONTINENTAL RESTAURANTS YOU MIGHT LIKE TO TRY:

THE BLACK HORSE RESTAURANT

2180 North Reading Road, (Route 272)
Denver, PA 17517
Lunch: Mon-Thurs 11:30-2. Fri-Sun 11:30-5.
Dinner: Mon-Sat 5-10, Sun 5-9. (717) 336-6555

D & S BRASSERIE

1679 Lincoln Highway East, Route 462
Lancaster, PA 17602
Lunch: Mon-Fri 11:30-2.
Dinner: Sun-Thurs 5-10. Fri & Sat 5-11. (717) 299-1694

ED STOUDT'S BLACK ANGUS

Route 272
Adamstown, PA 19501
Mon-Sat 5-11. Sunday 12-9.
(717) 484-4385

HISTORIC REVERE TAVERN

3063 Lincoln Highway East, (Route 30)
Paradise, PA 17562
Mon-Sat 5-10. Sun 4-9. (717) 687-8602

HORSE INN

539 East Chestnut Street
Lancaster, PA 17603
Tues-Sat 5-10. Sun 5-9. (717) 392-5528

THE OLDE LINCOLN HOUSE

1398 West Main Street, (Route 322)
Ephrata, PA 17522
Open Tues-Sat for lunch and dinner from 11-9:30. (717) 733-3490

OVEN FRENCH TOAST

1 cup light brown sugar
1/4 to 1/2 cup light margarine
2 tablespoons corn syrup

Cook until syrupy and pour into greased 9 by 13-inch baking dish.

8 eggs or egg substitute
2 cups skim milk
1 1/2 teaspoons vanilla
1 loaf French bread sliced 3/4 to 1 inch thick

Place bread and eggs over syrup. Bake uncovered at 350°F for 35 minutes. Serve with bacon and sausage. This can be made the night before. Serves 8.

—Recipe from
Bella Vista Bed and Breakfast

WASHINGTON HOUSE RESTAURANT

At the Historic Strasburg Inn
Route 896 & Historic Drive
Strasburg, PA 17579
Lunch: Mon-Sat 11:30-2. Sunday Brunch 11-2. Dinner begins at 5:00 daily and ends at 8:30 Sun-Thurs and at 9:30 Fri and Sat. (717) 687-9211

BREAKFAST

BUBBIE'S BAGELS

Cloister Shopping Center
Route 272
Ephrata, PA 17522
Tues-Fri 6-3. Sat 7-3. Sun 7-2:30. Closed Mon. (717) 733-3955

Bubbie's Bagels is a good place to satisfy your craving for a good old-fashioned New York style bagel with all the trimmings. The bagels are made the proper way: boiled than baked daily. Classic flavors like plain, cinnamon, onion, and salt share the billing with blueberry, chocolate chip, and cheddar cheese rivals. There are various cream cheese spreads from the traditional lox to the nouveau raspberry swirl. Sandwiches on a bagel include an excellent whitefish salad, chopped herring or liver, and tuna, egg, or chicken salads. All cold cuts are the Boarshead brand. Bubbie's also has a soup of the day and cookies or cake for an appropriately sweet ending.

BUBBIE'S BAGELS

2046 Fruitville Pike
Lancaster, PA 17602
Mon-Fri 6:30-3. Sat and Sun 7:30-3:00. (717) 560-3988

The various Bubbie's locations have different owners but carry the same excellent bagels with all the trimmings.

Take a walk down memory lane at Glassmyer's Restaurant.

GLASSMYER'S RESTAURANT

23 North Broad Street
Lititz, PA 17543
Breakfast 6:30-11:30. Lunch 11-3. (717) 626-2345

This old-fashioned luncheonette offers comfort foods and friendly service. The old soda fountain still produces phosphates (fruit-flavored sodas), egg creams, malts, and milkshakes. The country cooking is tasty, satisfying, and cheap. If it's available, order baked oatmeal. It's great!

HINKLE'S RESTAURANT
Corner of Locust and Route 441
Columbia, PA 17512
Mon-Fri 7-9. Sat 7-7:30. Sun 11:30-3. Please note that only cold sandwiches are available one hour before closing. (717) 684-2888

Opened in 1893 as a family owned drug store, seating at Hinkle's is in 1970s style booths. The soda fountain is still one of Hinkle's main attractions. The food is solidly American at this Columbia institution which serves the purpose of town hall and golf course. One old-timer in the know contends that much local business gets done here.

JENNIE'S DINER
Lincoln Highway East, (Route 30)
Ronks, PA 17572
Open 24 hours a day. Seven days a week. (717) 397-2507

Jennie's will make diner lovers feel right at home. This stainless steel specimen is a watering hole for locals, truck drivers, and travelers alike. Breakfast brings two eggs, toast, and a mound of home fries large enough to feed a family of four for a mere $1.95. Along with the usual diner fare, Jennie's serves Pennsylvania Dutch favorites such as braised beef over noodles, scrapple, and pork and sauerkraut.

ETHNIC

CAJUN

PRUDHOMME'S LOST CAJUN KITCHEN
Rising Sun Hotel
519 Cherry Street
Columbia, PA 17512
Mon-Sat 11:30-2:30, 4:30-10. (717) 684-1706

David and Sharon Prudhomme are the proprietors of a restaurant that is one of my favorite new casual dinner spots in Lancaster County. Despite its reputation, Cajun food is not knock your socks off spicy though David will gladly add more heat if you are a hot pepper fan. He is the nephew of Paul Prudhomme of K-Paul's in Louisiana. When in season, start with the crayfish sampler which is finger-lickin' fun. Oyster po-boys, David's Cajun country burger, or Sharon's chicken joes make a tasty middle-of-the-day treat. Choose between crawfish etouffée, blackened (or fried) catfish platter, blackened pork chops, or fried alligator platter for dinner. There is live Cajun music on Friday and Saturday evenings from 7-10. This restaurant has a liquor license.

CHINESE

PEKING PALACE

1025 Dillerville Road
Lancaster, PA 17603
Mon-Thurs 11:30-10. Fri & Sat 11:30-11. Sun 11:30-10. (717) 291-1614/5

The Peking Palace has been offering a respite from fried chicken and shoofly pies since 1986. This attractive dining room with its crisp, white linens and pleasant, efficient wait staff offers a pleasant dining experience. Choices include a large selection of beef, chicken, seafood, pork, and vegetable dishes. Seasonal specials take advantage of available fresh produce, and menu items are well flavored and spicy when indicated. One of my favorites is Hunan Chicken with its black beans and just the right amount of glow. Inexpensive lunch specials are offered daily. They have a liquor license.

TONY WANG'S CHINESE RESTAURANT

2217 Lincoln Highway East, (Route 30)
Lancaster, PA 17602
Mon-Thurs 11-10. Fri-Sat 11:30-11. Sun 12-10. (717) 399-1915
Across from Tanger Outlets.

Billed as Lancaster County's favorite Chinese restaurant, the dining room is hosted by a gregarious Mrs. Wang while the kitchen is overseen by her husband Tony. Tony Wang worked at various area restaurants before he and his wife opened their own place in 1991. The menu covers all the favorite Chinese dishes and has a low calorie section with steamed meats for those watching calories. Ingredients are fresh and well prepared. An unusual feature of this restaurant is the glass enclosed kitchen where you can watch the chefs at work. Free delivery to nearby hotels on Fridays and Saturdays ($15 minimum) from 5:00 to 9:00.

GERMAN

EAST OF EDEN PUB

680 Millcross Road

Lancaster, PA 17601

Mon-Thurs 11-10. Fri 11-11. Sat 4-11. Sun 4-9. (717) 299-0159

This friendly neighborhood restaurant is a good place to satisfy those cravings for spätzle and wurst. The Austrian and German specialties, particularly the ham, pork, and wursts, are quite good. The spätzle is excellent. East of Eden features a large selection of imported beers and, weather permitting, a beer garden, along the Conestoga River, for relaxing with a drink. Entrees run from $10.95 to $16.95.

INDIAN

THE TAJ MAHAL

Hechinger Plaza

2080 Bennett Avenue

Lancaster, PA 17603

Lunch: Mon-Sat 11:30-2:30. Sun 12-3. Dinner: Sun-Thurs 5-10. Fri & Sat 5-10:30.

(717) 295-1434

Just south of the intersection of Routes 30 & 741.

Indian food at its best is a sophisticated amalgam of many spices. The term curry is confusing because it means a blend of spices and varies widely depending on the region of India and the food being flavored. It can also mean a dish in which these spices are used. The Taj Mahal brings authentic northern Indian cuisine to Lancaster County. The pleasant dining room is gaily decorated with various Indian instruments and other cultural items, many of which are explained on accompanying plaques.

Good starters are the vegetable samosa, a turnover with potatoes and green peas, or the papadum, a thin crispy wafer with specs of black pepper. The tandoori choices are always a favorite, with or without curry. The menu is arranged so that your entree includes choice of seven different sauces with chicken, lamb, or shrimp. (The meat selection is topped with the sauce.) Sauces include a spicy vindaloo, a milder tikka masala (my favorite), or saag, a delicious blend of spinach, fresh onions, ginger, and spices. There are great vegetarian choices, and the home-made breads should not be missed. Appetizers are $1.25 to $5.95 and entrees run $9.95 to $14.95. Servers are attentive and helpful in explaining the various dishes.

ITALIAN

LORETO'S RISTORANTE

173 South Fourth Street
Columbia, PA 17512
Lunch: Tues-Fri 11-2. Dinner: Tues-Thurs 4-9. Fri and Sat 4-10. Sun 4-8. (717) 684-4326
Route 462 to Union Street. Turn left and go 2 blocks.

With eleven members of the Loreto family involved in this restaurant, you could say it's a family affair. Mary Loreto is the matriarch and one of the chefs. It is her special sauces and homemade pastas that get the raves. The executive chef, Bob

Leon, learned his trade at the Philadelphia Restaurant School, Le Cordon Bleu, and La Varrene in Paris. The menu offers primarily northern Italian with an emphasis on impeccably fresh ingredients. Steaks and veal are handcut, and there is also a variety of chicken and seafood. Dinner entrees run from $8.50 to $20.95. The casual dining rooms are dressed with white linens and fresh flowers.

PORTOFINO

254 East Frederick Street
Lancaster, PA 17604
Open daily from 11-10. Dinner served all day Sunday with brunch buffet from 11-3.
(717) 394-1635

Portofino is situated in a residential neighborhood in the city of Lancaster. Low lighting provides an atmosphere that is both gracious and casual. You can tuck yourself into a booth and have an intimate dinner. The food is a combination of old favorites and new Italian cuisine. Start with

> **The only real stumbling block is fear of failure. In cooking you've got to have a what-the-hell attitude.**
>
> Julia Child
>
> ◆◆◆

stuffed cherry peppers, fried calamari, or smoked salmon and trout. Pastas can be ordered in half or full portion and run the gamut from fettucine alfredo to smoked chicken capellini with rosemary and wild mushrooms in a Madeira wine demi-glaze. The veal, chicken, beef, and seafood choices offer the comfort of tradition along with a nouveau twist. Appetizers range from $4.95 to $7.50 and entrees from $13.95 to $21.95. Portofino offers a large selection of varietal wines.

Also see Gallo Rosso in Fine Dining page 109.

THAI

LEMON GRASS THAI RESTAURANT
2481 Lincoln Highway East, (Route 30)
Lancaster , PA 17602
Sun-Thurs 11:30-9. Fri & Sat 11:30-10. (717) 295-1621
Across from Rockvale Square Outlets.

Thai cooking is similar to Chinese food in its reliance on rice as a foundation with fresh vegetables and various condiments for flavoring. Thai dishes are unique for their use of lemon grass, a long slender root with a distinct lemony flavor. In addition they feature fish sauce (a very aromatic salty liquid), lime juice, various curry pastes, and tamarind juice. The owners of this restaurant also own an eatery with the same name in Philadelphia that I've enjoyed. Though the food is tasty at the Lancaster location, I miss the intense flavors of its urban kin.

Appetizer choices include crab sausage, crispy rolls, or a flavorful satay (chicken or beef marinated in Thai spices and grilled). Entrees include the favorite Pad Thai, stir fried rice noodles with shrimp, tofu, bean sprouts, scallions, and ground peanuts, as well as basil salmon, a char-grilled fresh fillet of salmon with red curry sauce and basil. The food is not hot enough for my taste, and I have a fairly low threshold for pain. There is a wide variety of vegetarian appetizers, soups, and entrees. Appetizers run $3.50 to $7.95 and entrees are $9.95 to $15.95.

VARIOUS

NAV JIWAN INTERNATIONAL TEA ROOM

Ten Thousand Villages
240 North Reading Road, (Route 272)
Ephrata, PA 17522
Mon-Sat 10-3. Fri 10-8. (717) 738-1101
1/4 mile North of the intersection of Route 272 and 322.

The Nav Jiwan International Tea Room, inside the largest Ten Thousand Villages store, offers an introduction to a wide variety of international flavors at an excellent lunch destination. (Dinner is served on Fridays only.) Despite the challenge of ever changing menus, I've always found the food to be remarkably tasty and satisfying. Entrees are $4.50 to $7.00, and all gratuities support disadvantaged school children in Calcutta, India. Don't miss the adjacent crafts store, supporting the work of artisans from over 30 countries.

OTHER ETHNIC RESTAURANTS YOU MIGHT LIKE TO TRY:

CARLOS & CHARLIE'S
2309 Columbia Pike
Lancaster, PA 17603
Sun-Thurs 11-11. Fri and Sat 11-12. (717) 399-1912

CARLOS & CHARLIE'S
915 Plum Street
Lancaster, PA 17602
Sun-Thurs 11-12 (kitchen closes at 11). Fri & Sat 11-12. (717) 293-8704

CARLOS & CHARLIE'S
62 West Main Street
Mount Joy, PA 17552
Sun-Thurs 11-12 (kitchen closes at 11). Fri & Sat 11-12. (717) 653-1220

LOMBARDO'S ITALIAN AMERICAN RESTAURANT
216 Harrisburg Avenue
Lancaster, PA 17603
Mon-Thurs 11-9 (until 10 at the bar). Fri & Sat 11-10 (until 11 in the bar). (717) 394-3749

HONG KONG GARDEN
1807 Columbia Avenue
Lancaster, PA 17603
Lunch: Tues-Thurs 11:30-9. Fri & Sat 11:30-10. Sun 11:30-8:30. (717) 394-4336

YANG'S RESTAURANT
1232 Lititz Pike
Lancaster, PA 17601
Mon-Thurs 11-10. Fri & Sat & 11-11. Sun 11-10. (717) 397-8600

FAMILY AND PENNSYLVANIA DUTCH FOOD

AKRON RESTAURANT
Route 272 - 333 South 7th Street
Akron, PA 17501
Open Mon-Sat 6-8. Sunday 11-7. Summer hours Fri & Sat until 9. (717) 859-1181

Akron Restaurant is a favorite of locals and travelers alike. The service is friendly and efficient; the food is simple, tasty, country cooking; and the bill is easy on the wallet. Of particular interest to me are the slightly smaller portions for those of us who are light eaters. This allows room for the delicious, homemade desserts. I recommend the raisin pie, a local specialty sometimes called funeral pie because it is often served at Amish funerals. Also in the dessert lineup are peach, cherry, and strawberry pies, as well as such prosaic selections as graham cracker pudding.

THE COUNTRY TABLE RESTAURANT
740 East Main Street
Mount Joy, PA 17522
Mon-Thurs 6-8. Fri-Sat 6-9. (717) 653-4745

Serving up country food the way it should be, this restaurant is run by a Mennonite family. The homestyle cooking is inexpensive, but generously proportioned, and very good. Specials can include pork and sauerkraut, chicken potpie, barbecued meatloaf, turkey croquettes, or a fantail shrimp feast. Standard menu items include a good selection of grilled, charbroiled, broiled, or fried seafood, poultry, and meats. Particularly helpful is the For the Smaller Appetite section. (You don't have to be under five or over 65 to order from it.) Homemade soups are excellent, but the highlight of any meal at Country Table are the outstanding pies, cakes, homemade ice cream, and apple dumplings. They have a retail bakery on the premises so you can even bring these tasty treats home. They don't accept credit cards or reservations. Weekend evenings often require a wait for a table.

DIENNER'S COUNTRY BAR-B-Q
The Village of Dutch Delights
2855 Lincoln Highway East (Route 30)
Ronks, PA 17572
Breakfast: 7-11 daily except Sunday. Lunch & dinner: Mon-Thurs & Sat 11-6. Fri 11-8.
(717) 687-9571

This Amish-Mennonite family owned restaurant features excellent country cooking. The locals swear by the baked oatmeal. (Even if you don't like oatmeal, you should try Dienner's as it's like eating a big oatmeal cookie.) There is a breakfast buffet 7-10:30 (Thurs-Sat during the winter) and a lunch buffet from 11-3 (until 2 on Sat). Dinner buffet from 3:30-6 (Sat 2-6). Wednesday is pork and sauerkraut day and Thursday is chicken potpie.

GOOD 'N PLENTY FAMILY STYLE EATING

Route 896
Smoketown, PA 17576
Mon-Sat 11:30-8. Closed mid-December through January. (717) 394-7111

Good 'n Plenty is a large family style restaurant and the staff can keep up to 600 patrons happy at one time. Housed in a Pennsylvania Dutch farmhouse and true to its name, it serves up large quantities of good old-fashioned country cooking. Dining is family style which means there are no private dining arrangements available. Open since 1969, Good 'n Plenty has friendly service and homemade cooking down to a T. A typical dinner may include pork and sauerkraut, mashed potatoes, baked country sausage, baked country ham, roast beef, crispy fried chicken, noodles, homemade bread, homemade apple butter, shoofly pie, and more. There is a fun gift shop for browsing, and a retail bake shop so you may come away with even more goodies. Dinners are $14.50 for adults and $6.50 for children from four to ten.

GROFF'S FARM RESTAURANT

650 Pinkerton Road
Mount Joy, PA 17552
Lunch: Tues-Sat 11:30-1:30.
Dinner: Tues-Fri 5-7:30. Sat
5-8 (seatings at 5 and 8). Sun
Brunch 10:30-2.
Appointments required for
dinner. (717) 653-2048

This Lancaster County favorite gets my vote for very good country food. Betty Groff, the wife of a farmer, started out cooking for friends and family. She received such an enthusiastic response that she moved her family out of their sprawling stone farmhouse and started this restaurant. Her work came to the attention of some well-known

HAM AND CHEESE STRATA

8 slices white bread
1 1/2 cups diced ham
1 1/2 cups shredded cheddar cheese
4 eggs beaten
2 cups milk
Buttered crumbs

Line bottom of square Pyrex dish with 4 slices of bread. Add 1/2 of the ham and cheese. Repeat layers of bread, ham, and cheese. Beat eggs, add milk, and stir. Pour egg and milk mixture over ingredients in dish. Cover and refrigerate overnight or several hours. Put buttered crumbs on top and bake at 325°F for 45 minutes to 1 hour.

—Recipe from Andy and Dotty Hess, *Country Gardens Farm Bed & Breakfast*

food authorities in New York, and Groff now has quite a few cookbooks to her name, Chicken Stoltzfus (a delicious dish with a hint of saffron), prime rib, hickory smoked ham, and fresh seafood are menu standards. You may choose to eat family style or from the a la carte menu. Her son, Charlie, has taken over day-to-day management of the kitchen. He is a Culinary Institute of America graduate and continues his mother's tradition of serving delicious, hearty, Pennsylvania Dutch fare.

INTERCOURSE VILLAGE RESTAURANT
Routes 340 & 772
Intercourse, PA 17534
Mon-Sat 6 a.m.-8 p.m. (717) 768-3636
9 miles East of Lancaster on Route 340. Near the Best Western.

Serving as a local gathering place, this restaurant's regulars belly up to the counter and exchange gossip over traditional Amish and Mennonite diner fare. The small dining room is served by longtime Amish waitresses. The strong suit here is meat and potatoes; particularly the roast turkey and filling.

KREIDER DAIRY FARMS FAMILY RESTAURANTS
1461 Lancaster Road
Manheim, PA 17545
Mon-Sat 6 a.m.-11 p.m. (717) 665-5039

Centerville Road & Columbia Avenue
Lancaster, PA 17603
Mon-Sat 6 a.m.-11 p.m. (717) 393-3410

Briarcrest Square
Hershey, PA 17033
Mon-Sat 6 a.m.-11 p.m. (717) 533-8067

Tasty, plentiful country food and good service keep 'em coming back for more. Best of all, this family restaurant makes its own excellent ice cream. Dessert should definitely include one of the great ice cream sundaes. My favorite is the smores sundae with graham cracker crumbs, vanilla ice cream, and chocolate sauce, of course.

LAPP'S FAMILY RESTAURANT

1525 Manheim Pike, (Route 72)

Lancaster, PA 17601

Mon-Sat 6 a.m.-8 p.m. Sun 11-2. (717) 560-9302

2270 Lincoln Highway East, (Route 30)

Lancaster, PA 17602

Tues-Thurs 7 a.m.-8 p.m. Fri & Sat 7 a.m.-9 p.m. Sun 7 a.m.-8 p.m. During the summer they are open until 9 p.m. during the week. (717) 394-1606

Lapp's offers solid, country cooking and efficient, pleasant service. With few exceptions, their baked goods are made on the premises. My choice for dessert is an addictive lemon sponge pie. This is a favorite breakfast destination.

> **Them that works hard, eats hearty.**
> Pennsylvania Dutch saying
>

LEOLA FAMILY RESTAURANT

Route 23

Leola, PA 17540

Mon-Sat 6 a.m.-8 p.m. Sun 10:30-2. (717) 656-2311

The food and service are what I have come to expect from these family restaurants: simple, tasty food and pleasant, efficient service. A good choice either for lunch or dinner is chicken potpie, a large bowl of homemade noodles in a flavorful chicken broth topped with tender white chicken meat. All baked goods are made on the premises and include a good assortment of pies, cakes, and muffins (at breakfast).

PEOPLES RESTAURANT

140 West Main Street (Route 23)

New Holland, PA 17557

Mon-Fri 7-8. Sun 10:30-7 (dinner only). Closed Sat. (717) 354-2276

The Peoples Restaurant has been serving up satisfying home cooked meals since 1907. It offers a fairly standard American menu with the usual meat, seafood, and sandwich items, but the daily specials are of more interest to me. A typical special is roast capon with homemade filling and choice of two vegetables which makes a great lunch for only $6.30. Ingredients are fresh, and desserts are made by the restaurant. Seasonal fruit pies or the lemon sponge pie are a good way to top off your meal.

PLAIN & FANCY FARM RESTAURANT

Route 340
Bird-in-Hand, PA 17505
Summer hours: Mon-Sat 11:30-8. Sun 12-7. Winter hours: Mon-Sat 12-8. Sun 12-7.
(717) 768-4400
1 mile east of Bird-in-Hand

Located in a renovated barn, this is Lancaster County's original family style restaurant. The all-you-can-eat menu includes Lancaster County sausage, chicken potpie, roast beef, four vegetables, five desserts, and homemade breads and relishes. Seating is at large tables with fellow diners.

SHADY MAPLE SMORGASBORD

1352 Main Street, (Route 23)
East Earl, PA 17519
Mon-Sat 5 a.m.-8 p.m. Closed Sunday. (717) 354-8222
One mile East of Blue Ball.

This very popular restaurant has been satisfying big appetites for over a decade. The staff has refined the task of feeding large numbers of people three meals a day in a cavernous dining room to a science. At the height of a meal hour, you may encounter fairly long lines. The country and Pennsylvania Dutch food is plentiful and reasonably priced. Lunch is $7.49 and dinner on weeknights is $9.99. Lunch and dinner buffet choices include 46 salad items, 3 soups, 8 homemade breads, 8 meats, 14 vegetables, and over 20 kinds of dessert and soft ice cream with an assortment of toppings. This is a good place to bring the kids for a fast, family meal. A large gift shop downstairs features baked goods, handcrafts, gifts, collectibles, and unique clocks.

ALONNA'S FAVORITES

Potato chips: Bickles, made in Manheim, and Goods tie for first place

Hard pretzels: Martins of Akron

Shoofly pie: Glen Brook Bake Shop (dry bottom)
Bird-in-Hand Bakery (wet bottom)

Ice cream: Lapp Valley Farm

Whoopie pies: Bird-in-Hand Bake Shop on Gibbons Road

Coffee joint: Spill the Beans in Lititz

Rhubarb pie: Country Table Restaurant

Pork and sauerkraut: Dienner's Country Bar-B-Q (Wednesdays only) and Shady Maple Smorgasbord

Smoked meat products: Stoltzfus Meats and S. Clyde Weaver

STOLTZFUS FARM RESTAURANT

Route 772 East

Intercourse, PA 17534

Open daily except Sunday 11:30-8. Closed Nov. 1-May 1. (717) 768-8156

One block East of Intercourse.

Featuring family style meals on a more family style scale, this restaurant has its admirers. Chicken, pork, and beef sausage, as well as the requisite sweets and sours, add up to a big value. Those in the know make sure they don't miss the shoofly pie. The family owns a butcher shop across the street where they sell excellent meats, smoked and otherwise.

WILLOW VALLEY FAMILY RESTAURANT

2416 Willow Street Pike

Lancaster, PA 17602

Breakfast from the menu: Mon-Sat 6 a.m.-10:30 p.m. Dinner from the menu: 11 a.m.-9 p.m. Mon-Fri & Sun Smorgasbord 8-10:30, 11-2:30, 5-8. Sat breakfast smorgasbord from 8-10:30 & dinner smorgasbord 12-8. (717) 464-2711

Three miles south of Lancaster on Route 222.

Willow Valley makes a good mealtime destination for the whole family. Dining options include menu dining, a smorgasbord for several hours at breakfast, lunch, and dinner, and an all day breakfast menu. The dining rooms are pleasant as is the staff. The food is solid country cooking and plenty of it. I prefer choosing from the smorgasbord rather than ordering from the menu. Visit the bakery downstairs where they sell fresh baked cakes, pies, and other Lancaster County specialties. This restaurant is part of a resort that includes lodging and other amenities. See page 79 for more information.

OTHER FAMILY AND PENNSYLVANIA DUTCH RESTAURANTS YOU MIGHT LIKE TO TRY:

BIRD-IN-HAND FAMILY RESTAURANT

2760 Old Philadelphia Pike, (Route 340)

Bird-in-Hand, PA 17505

Mon-Sat 6 a.m.-8 p.m. Closed Sunday.

(717) 768-8266

FAMILY TIME RESTAURANTS

Route 322

Ephrata, PA 17522

Daily 11-8. (717) 738-4231

HERSHEY FARM RESTAURANT

Route 896

Strasburg, PA 17579

Summer hours: Sun-Fri 7-8. Fri & Sat 7-9.

Call for winter hours. (717) 687-8635

1.5 miles south of Route 30

ZINN'S DINER

Route 272

Denver, PA 17517

Open daily: 6 a.m.-11 p.m. (717) 336-2210

North at Exit 21 of the PA Turnpike

FINE DINING

ACCOMAC INN

South River Drive
Wrightsville, PA 17368
Dinner daily 5:30-9:30. Sunday brunch 11-2:30. Sunday dinner 4-8:30. (717) 252-1521
Exit off Route 30 at Wrightsville, turn North, and follow signs for 1 1/2 miles.

Located in eastern York County, this restaurant is definitely worth the pretty drive. It is one of my top choices for romantic dinners, celebrations, or a place to just plain pamper myself. The Queen Anne Dining Room is properly 18th century with oil paintings on the walls, a fireplace, and white-clothed tables graced with tall white tapers and fresh flowers.

Chef Bonnie Kurtz's heart lies with the more traditional French influences while her co-chef, Angelo Mango, introduces ingredients from around the world. Together, they create dishes that are pleasing to the eye as well as to the palate. Appetizers include oriental barbecued shrimp over cellophane noodles or terrine of goose and venison with apricot chutney. Entrees run from old favorites like New Zealand rack of lamb to tuna steak dredged in macadamia nut flour and served with pineapple-chipotle salsa. Special emphasis is given to the vegetables accompanying the entrees, as well as a vegetarian offering for those not eating meat. The kitchen will make substitutions to meet diners' dietary restrictions.

Service is attentive but unobtrusive. Entrees run from $16.95 to $28.95. An excellent place for Sunday brunch, particularly during warm weather, because a seat on the screened-in porch gives a smashing view of the Susquehanna River.

Photograph courtesy of Accomac Inn

Accomac Inn

GALLO ROSSO

337 N. Queen Street
Lancaster, PA 17603
Lunch: Mon-Fri 11:30-2. Dinner: Mon-Thurs 5:30-10. Fri-Sat 5:30-11. (717) 392-5616

Gallo Rosso offers very good northern Italian food served in a contemporary setting with lots of glass and marble. Tables are well spaced and the lighting is perfect for intimate dinners, though the noise level is a bit higher than I prefer. The food, delivered by an attentive wait staff, is the star of this show. Appetizers can include an excellent calamari fritti (fried calamari with tomato salsa), grilled portabello mushrooms, carpaccio, or sliced gravlax. Among the salad selections is a grilled duck breast salad with a spicy vinaigrette. Individual pizzas are topped with grilled chicken or smoked salmon with goat cheese.

> **Let food be your medicine and medicine your food.**
> Hippocrates
>

The pastas are excellent, especially the pappardelle verde (broad spinach noodles with lamb, fried eggplant, and goat cheese in a rich veal demi-glaze). Chicken al forno, a half chicken roasted with vegetables, and grilled swordfish are good choices from the meat side of the menu. Appetizers range in price from $4.95 to $7.25. Pastas from $8.95 to $16.95 for spaghetti con pesce, and meat and seafood entrees are $17.95 to $25.00 for the porterhouse steak. The lunch menu, served Tuesday through Friday, features sandwiches, pizzas, pastas, and salads.

HAYDN ZUG'S

1987 State Street, (Route 72)
East Petersburg, PA 17520
Lunch: Tues-Fri 11:30-2. Dinner: Mon-Sat 5-9. (717) 569-5746

This original, 18th century roadhouse serves up classic American fare with a flair. Dine in a handsome country setting with colonial furnishings and Armetal dinner service. Starters such as grilled lamb tenderloin or chicken fingers scampi are good choices. Entrees vary from Lancaster County smoked pork chops to medallions of veal Vienna (veal in a roquefort and marsala sauce with mushrooms). What I love about the menu are the half portions of entrees (commensurately priced) for those people with smaller appetites. Entrees run in the mid teens to high twenties.

JOSEPHINE'S

324 West Market Street

Marietta , PA 17547

Lunch: Tues-Thurs 11:30-2. Dinner: Tues-Sat 5:30-9 (To be seated). (717) 426-2003

Drawing courtesy of Josephine's Restaurant

Stepping into Josephine's is like dropping into a restaurant in small town France. Opened in 1995 in a 200-year-old log house, Josephine's is watched over by chef and proprietor Jean Luc Sandillon. His family owned a hotel and cafe in France, and he went through years of apprenticeship and training, studying with Roger Croechet at the Hotel de France. He combines a passion for excellent seasonal ingredients with a solid training in French cooking techniques. The result is noteworthy French cuisine.

The simple, but elegant, front dining room has a large fireplace, rustic wooden beams, hardwood floors, and fresh flowers. Furthering the sense of being in another place, nightly specials are presented on a chalkboard for each table. Snails, French onion soup, or lump crabmeat with salmon mousse baked in a casserole can be ordered for starters. Entrees include a seafood gratin, flounder stuffed with lump crabmeat, a sliced duck breast served with pear poached in honey and saffron, and lobster tail with beef tenderloin. Dessert time offers up such delicious standards as creme caramel, chocolate mousse, or a homemade apple tart. From cocktails and wine to homemade salad dressings to the delectable desserts, the food at Josephine's is excellent. Appetizers range from $3.25 to $8.25 for the baked brie. Entrees are $15.95 for pasta to $22.95 for the rack of lamb. Reservations are recommended, and off-street parking is available.

OLDE GREENFIELD INN

595 Greenfield Road

Lancaster, PA 17601

Dinner: Mon-Sat 5-10. Lunch: Tues-Sat 11-2. Sat & Sun Breakfast 8-11. Sunday brunch 11-2. (717) 393-0668

Housed in a farmhouse built in 1790, this relaxed country restaurant offers a romantic place to dine, whether in the wine cellar or by the fire at the first hint of chill. The traditional American choices include baby back ribs dijonnaise, baked pork tenderloin, seafood and pasta specials, or steaks cut to order. Weekend breakfasts and Sunday brunch are served outside on a trellis-covered patio during the season. A children's menu is available.

THE LOG CABIN RESTAURANT

11 Lehoy Forest Drive
Leola, PA 17540
Mon-Sat 5-10. Sun 4-9. (717) 626-1181
Take Route 272 (Oregon Pike) N from Route 30. Make a left onto Rosehill Road. Make a left onto Lehoy Forest Drive.

Locals come here for fine dining occasions or a variety of celebratory events. Consistent good food and attentive service make for a very civilized and memorable evening. The setting is country elegance with 18th and 19th century oil paintings on the walls, exposed log beams, and a fireplace. The menu starts with calamari fritti, shrimp cocktail, or alderwood smoked brook trout. There is an entree to please everyone: grilled Norwegian salmon, scampi, prime sirloin, lamb chops double cut, or chicken rosemary. Appetizers range from $4.75 to $8.00, and entrees from $16.50 to $35.50 for surf and turf. Cheesecake and after dinner drinks are a favorite finale.

THE RESTAURANT AT DONECKERS

333 North State Street
Ephrata, PA 17522
Daily 11-10 except Wed & Sun. (717) 738-9501
Exit 21 from the PA turnpike and take Route 322 West. Make a right onto N. State Street for three blocks.

This elegant restaurant is a Lancaster County favorite for its contemporary French cuisine. Located near the Fashion Store at Doneckers, lunching here is a good way to unwind after a morning of shopping. Dinner is a special occasion, offering up elegant food with impeccably fresh ingredients prepared without

Photograph courtesy of Doneckers

The Restaurant at Doneckers is an excellent place for fine dining.

heavy sauces. The chef uses flavor-infused oils, herbs, and marinades to add taste in a healthy way. A menu for light and casual dining features New American food. Table service is professional. Heart healthy options are available on all menus, along with a nice selection of wines by the glass. Doneckers hosts special events such as wine tastings and fashion show brunches. Banquets, business meetings, and receptions are accommodated.

ANOTHER FINE DINING RESTAURANT YOU MIGHT LIKE TO TRY:

THE LOFT RESTAURANT
201 West Orange
Lancaster, PA 17603
Lunch: Mon-Fri 11:30-2. Dinner: Mon-Sat 5:30-9. (717) 299-0661

ROASTED PIG'S STOMACH, DUTCH GOOSE
(Adapted from Mother Millie's pinch and toss recipe)

1 cleaned pig stomach (frozen and thawed, or fresh)
1 1/2 pounds ground sausage
1 quart diced potatoes
1 large onion
1 teaspoon salt
1 teaspoon pepper
2 cups breadcrumbs

Cover potatoes with water and bring to a rolling boil. Remove from heat and cool. Add to the other ingredients and mix. Fill the stomach and sew shut with needle and thread. Bake at 300°F for 3 1/2 to 4 hours in oven roaster bag until brown. Slice to serve.

—Recipe from Marilyn Ebel,
The Gardens of Eden Bed & Breakfast

LUNCH

A TOUCH OF TASTE

The Lancaster Shopping Center
Lititz & Oregon Pikes
Lancaster, PA 17601
Mon-Fri 10-7. Sat 10-5. (717) 291-5833

A Touch of Taste is a kitchen wares store *and* great casual lunch spot which also offers cooking classes. The cafe has a wide selection of very good homemade soups, sandwiches, salads, and desserts. Catering and a gift basket service are also available.

Grow you own saffron in flowerpots outside. Bulbs are available through mail order from:

**White Flower Farm
(800) 503-9624
and
Park Seed Company
(800) 845-3369.**

ISAAC'S RESTAURANT AND DELI

Cloister Shopping Center
Ephrata, PA 17522
Mon-Thurs 10-9. Fri & Sat 10-10. Sun 11-9. (717) 733-7777

44 North Queen Street
Lancaster, PA 17603
Hours same as above. (717) 394-5544

Route 741 East
Strasburg, PA 17579
Hours same as above. (717) 687-7699

1559 Manheim Pike, (Route 72)
East Petersburg, PA 17601
Hours same as above. (717) 560-7774

If you're looking for a lunch that will leave you alert but satisfied, this restaurant just might fit the bill. There is a list of sandwiches, all named after a different bird with an amazing number of variations. Diners looking for heart healthy choices have much to choose from, and the prices are right.

OTHER RESTAURANTS
YOU MIGHT LIKE TO TRY FOR LUNCH:

BRUNCH SUGGESTIONS

American: Reflections Fine Food
and Olde Greenfield Inn

**Downtown
Lancaster:** Market Fare Restaurant

Ethnic: Prudhomme's Lost
Cajun Kitchen
and The Taj Mahal

Family: Akron Restaurant

Fancy: The Restaurant
at Doneckers

Pub: Lancaster Malt Brewing Co.

**Outside
Lancaster:** Accomac Inn

THE MARION COURT ROOM
7 Marion Court
Lancaster, PA 17603
Mon 11-12. Tues-Sat 11-2 (light menu
from 10-12). Sun 5 pm-2 am (light
menu from 10-12). (717) 399-1970
Between Orange and Chestnut Streets.
Behind City Hall.

SMOKIN JAKE'S
1021 Dillerville Road
Lancaster, PA 17603
Mon-Thurs & Sat 11-12. Fri 11-2. Sun
11-12. (717) 291-6461

PUB GRUB

BUBE'S BREWERY, THE CATACOMBS & ALOIS'S
102 N. Market Street
Mount Joy, PA 17552
Alois's: Tues-Sun 5:30-9. Catacombs: Dinner nightly from 5:30-9. Bottling Works: Mon-Fri
11-2 and 5:30-9. (717) 653-2056

Built by a German immigrant, Alois
Bube, Bube's Brewery began making beer in
the 1800s. Though beer is no longer
made here there are three different
dining experiences to choose from.
For gourmet dining in a Victorian
setting, try Alois's in the brewery's
original hotel and tavern. The fare
is international in scope, and prices
run from moderate to expensive.
Reservations are recommended.
Forty feet underground in stone-
lined lagering cellars, more casual
fare is served in the Catacombs. Moderately priced and nicely varied, most
entrees are offered up in full or light portions. The Bottling Works has casual
cafe dining in the bottling works or the beirgarten, weather permitting.

LANCASTER DISPENSING COMPANY

33-35 North Market Street
Lancaster, PA 17603
Mon-Thurs 11-12. Fri-Sat 11-1. Sun 1-10. (717) 299-4602
On the corner of Market and Grant Streets.

This place reeks atmosphere you just can't buy. Located on the site of the Grape Tavern of 1893, this Victorian pub oozes with secrets. The focus of the dining room is a large, elaborately carved bar inset with stained glass windows and set off by 15-foot ceilings. The food is very good: chili, salads, sandwiches, vegetarian offerings, and Mexican food. As one might expect, the beer selection is large and includes the best local brews as well as imports from around the world. This is also a popular night spot with musicians performing folk music and rhythm and blues Wednesday through Saturday evenings. A great spot for lunch as well as a late night bite.

LANCASTER MALT BREWING COMPANY

Plum & Walnut Streets
Lancaster, PA 17602
Sun-Thurs 11:30-10 (Bar open until 11). Fri-Sat 11:30-11 (Bar open until 12). Tours daily 10-5. (717) 391-MALT

Housed in an old tobacco warehouse, Lancaster Malt Brewing Company is a fun place with its polished copper tables overlooking stainless steel brewing tanks, steel reinforced floors, and high ceilings. This restaurant and micro-brewery is one of my favorite places for lunch or a casual dinner, and I'm not much of a beer drinker. The menu is varied and includes certified heart healthy choices, a raw bar, and a beer tasting.

Starters are homemade potato chips with Cajun spices or Old Bay seasoning, beer cheese fondue, or hummus. The choices for entrees run from burgers (including a buffalo and a vegetarian option) to smoked pork chops to jambalaya. A sandwich I heartily recommend is the crabcake with tabasco tarter sauce. If you're into salads, they have a number of meal sized options that look intriguing: baked goat cheese with walnuts and roasted red peppers or the Jackson salad with grilled chicken, avocado, and toasted almonds. Match your food with one (or two) of the house beers including Golden Lager, Red Rose Amber Ale, or Plum Street Porter. There are always several seasonal beers available, and the beer tasting tray with four different beers is fun to sample. Tours of the brewery are available. Call for times.

MOLLY'S PUB

253 East Chestnut Street
Lancaster, PA 17603
Lunch: Mon-Sat 11:30-2:30. Dinner: Mon-Thurs 5-10. Fri & Sat 5-11. (717) 396-0225

This casual neighborhood eatery is a popular place for lunch and a late (relatively speaking) night bite.

THE PRESSROOM

26-28 West King Street
Lancaster, PA 17603
Lunch: Mon-Sat 11:30-3. Dinner: Tues-Thurs 5-9:30. Fri-Sat 5-10:30. (717) 399-5400

The Pressroom, a combination bistro and pub, is housed in an old hardware store built in 1886. Casual, yet sophisticated, it is a good first date destination as well as a family night out. The menu has favorites like burgers, pasta, specialty pizza, unique sandwiches, and a wide variety of entrees. Crab cakes, wild forest chicken, and Santa Fe cowboy steak are just a few, served with two side dishes. There is a good selection of wine and beer from the full bar. Entrees range from $4.25 for burgers to $19.95 for steak. The Pressroom works hard to give diners what they want. Special dietary requests are honored, pastas can be ordered in half portions, and there is a children's menu. Warm weather brings the added bonus of dining al fresco in Steinman Park with its large waterfall and fountain.

GRATUITOUS INFORMATION

The Pennsylvania Dutch delicacy scrapple is made from pork, pork liver, pork shoulder, pork heart, pork skin, cornmeal, and buckwheat.

QUIPS PUB

457 New Holland Avenue
Lancaster, PA 17602
Dinner: Mon-Wed 5-10 & Thurs-Sat 5-11. Bar: Mon 4-12. Tues-Sat 4-2. (717) 397-3903

Catherine Roland and her now ex-husband, who is British, opened Quips Pub in 1984. This British pub is located in the first building to house The Stockyard Inn, which continues its service as a Lancaster institution several blocks away along the Lititz Pike. While the old stockyards across New Holland Avenue were in operation, the men who came to buy and sell livestock would fortify themselves at this original Stockyard Inn and even secure a bed in the rooms upstairs.

Traveler and neighbor alike find this pub a friendly place to end the day with a pint of beer and light fare such as burgers, nachos, or Buffalo wings.

More ambitious entrees include Lucy Atherfield's shrimp (shrimp sautéed with capers, tomatoes, garlic, and black olives). Traditional British fare rounds out the menu with fish and chips, bangers and mash, British meat pies, and, my favorite, Cotswold chicken. The bread and salad dressing are home-made, and I was particularly impressed by the care given to the vegetables served with entrees. Desserts are appropriately homey and sweet. This is a happening place for a late night bite. On tap at the bar are great English beers like New Castle and John Courage.

SHANK'S TAVERN

36 Waterford Avenue
Marietta, PA 17547
Open Mon-Fri 12 p.m.-2 a.m. Kitchen hours: 12 p.m.-12 a.m. (717) 426-1205

Built in 1814, Shank's Tavern was originally called the Compass and Square and was operated by a retired riverboat captain, James Stackhouse. John and Kathryn Shank bought the tavern in 1930, and today the third generation of Shanks continues the tradition of a friendly neighborhood bar. A local micro-brew is on tap. Features include soft shell tacos on Wednesday nights and California sushi roll on Friday nights.

ANOTHER PUB TO TRY:

O'HALLORAN'S IRISH PUB & EATERY

High Street & Fairview Avenues
Lancaster, PA 17603
Mon-Thurs 7 a.m.-11 p.m. (Bar closes at 2). Fri & Sat 11-12 (Bar closes at 2). Sun 11-9 (Bar closes at 12). (717) 393-3051

RESTAURANTS OPEN FOR SUNDAY DINNER

American: Reflections Fine Food and Doc Hollidays

Family: Akron Restaurant or Willow Valley Family Restaurant

Fancy: The Log Cabin Restaurant

Casual: J-M's Bistro & Pub

Pub: Lancaster Dispensing Co.

Ethnic: Peking Palace and The Taj Mahal

Outside Lancaster: Accomac Inn

RESTAURANTS OUTSIDE LANCASTER COUNTY

HERSHEY AREA

HERSHEY PANTRY

801 East Chocolate Avenue
Hershey, PA 17033
Mon-Thurs 7-9. Fri & Sat 7-10. (717) 533-7505

If you crave very good sandwiches, salads, and soups, this is a good place for lunch. Dinner is casual American fare: broiled seafood, pasta favorites, and beef and pork entrees that run from $8.25 to $16.95 for filet mignon topped with lump crabmeat.

See also Kreider Dairy Farms Family Restaurants on page 104.

READING AREA

ANTIQUE AIRPLANE RESTAURANT

Dutch Country Inn
4635 Perkiomen Avenue, Reading, PA 19606
Breakfast: Daily from 7-11:30. Lunch: Mon-Sat 11:30-3. Dinner: Mon-Sat 5-9:30.
(610) 779-2345

Children and aviation fanatics will enjoy this restaurant whose focus is a 1927 Monocoupe suspended from the dining room ceiling. Other aviation collectibles such as Jake Arner's famous 1917 Curtiss OX-5 90-horsepower engine are also on display. The food and atmosphere are friendly and casual.

GREEN HILLS INN

2444 Morgantown Road
Reading, PA 19602
Mon-Sat 5 p.m.-9 p.m. (610) 777-9611

Formerly the Sorrel Horse Tavern, this site has been feeding the hungry traveler since 1805. The current elegant country inn is wowing diners with its country French food. Starters can include such mouthwaterers as quenelles de brochet-sauce Americaine (soufflé of pike with fresh lobster sauce) for $7.50 or paté maison for $4.95. Entrees range from bistro foie de vea aux poireaux confits (calf's liver with leeks and sage) for $19.95 to fine dining choices like le magret de canard aux figues (grilled moulard duck breast with merlot and fig purée) for $22.50 to variations of old favorites such as grilled filet of beef or rack of lamb with natural juices for $23.50. The wine list has some very good choices at reasonable prices, and the wait staff is attentive.

JOE'S BISTRO 614

614 Penn Avenue

West Reading, PA 19602

Lunch: Tues-Sat 11:30-2:30. Dinner: Tues-Sat 5-9. (610) 371-9966

Opened by Jack and Heidi Czarnecki of Joe's Restaurant fame, this attractive eatery serves very good bistro food. Don't miss Joe's wild mushroom soup on the menu for both lunch and dinner. Other dinner appetizers may be grilled polenta with bleu cheese and walnuts or oysters pancho rockefeller described as poached oyster Mexican-Polish style. Entrees are suitably comforting: Normandy port, roast chicken with zinfandel sauce and garlic mashed potatoes or filet mignon en croute. Desserts are of the homey variety and include apple upside-down cake and creme caramel. Lunch brings pastas, portabello pizza, crab cakes, and quiche of the day, along with the same dessert choices. Dinner entrees range from $12.50 to $19.50 and lunch from $8.95 to $12.50. The Czarneckis have been serving hand gathered mushrooms for many years, and Jack is the author of several great books on the subject, including *A Cook's Book of Mushrooms* and *Portabello*.

MY FAVORITE RESTAURANTS BY CATEGORY

American: Reflections Fine Food & Haydn Zug's

Breakfast: Glassmyers

Brunch: see page 114

Ethnic: The Taj Mahal, Gallo Rosso & Peking Palace

Family: Dienner's Country Bar-B-Q

Fancy: The Log Cabin Restaurant

French Fancy: Josephine's

French Bistro: J-M's Bistro & Pub

Lunch: Bubbie's Bagels and Nav Jiwan International Tea Room

Neighborhood Restaurant: Lancaster Dispensing Co.

Pub: Lancaster Malt Brewing Co.

Outside Lancaster: Accomac Inn

MOSELEM SPRINGS INN

At Routes 222 & 662

Fleetwood, PA 19522

Mon-Thurs 11:30-9. Fri & Sat 11:30-10. Sun 11:30-8. (610) 944-8213

This handsome inn has been serving hungry travelers since 1852 when it offered food and lodging for Conestoga wagons. The various dining rooms are handsomely decked in colonial era touches, and the food is American country fare with a Pennsylvania Dutch twist. The lunch menu has corn pie, and prices that begin as low as $6.50. Dinner entrees begin at $10.95. This restaurant provides a civilized atmosphere, reasonably priced meal options, and a great place to stop on a country drive.

THE PEANUT BAR & RESTAURANT

332 Penn Street
Reading, PA 19602
Mon-Sat 11-12. (610) 376-8500

The Peanut Bar has something for everyone: a children's menu, simple burgers and sandwiches, more ambitious continental cuisine, and a large selection of beers on tap. An added attraction are the free peanuts which you're encouraged to enjoy, adding your shells to the collection underfoot. Reservations recommended. There is free off-street parking, and the restaurant is located just five minutes from outlet shopping.

> **I believe any cookie not worth stealing is not worth baking, and at my restaurant we judge the quality of our cookies by how many disappear unaccounted for.**
>
> Jasper White,
> *Jasper White's*
> *Cooking from New England*
>
>

OTHER RESTAURANTS TO TRY IN THE READING AREA:

CRAB BARN
Hamden Boulevard
Reading, PA 19605
Lunch: Mon-Fri 11-30-2. Dinner: Mon-Thurs 4:30-9. Fri 4:30-10. Sat 3-10. Sun 3-9. (610) 921-8922

MOM CHAFFE'S CELLARETTE
148 Tulpehocken Avenue
West Reading, PA 19611
Mon-Sat 5 p.m.-9 p.m. Closed on Sunday. (610) 374-5733
1/2 block off the West Reading traffic circle.

PURVEYORS

BAKERIES

BIRD-IN-HAND BAKE SHOP

542 Gibbons Road
Bird-in-Hand, PA 17505
Mon-Sat 9-5. Closed January. (717) 656-7947
Route 340 to Beechdale Road, make a right onto Gibbons Road.

Bird-in-Hand Bake Shop is a small, family owned bakery off the beaten path and definitely worth the finding. Open since 1972, their specialties include excellent sticky buns and my favorite whoopie pies. They sell a full complement of breads, pies, cakes, and cookies.

BIRD-IN-HAND BAKERY

Route 340
Bird-in-Hand, PA 17505
Mon-Sat 6-6. (717) 768-8273

Using Grandma Smucker's recipes, these baked goods are made from scratch. There are wet-bottom shoofly pies, oversized apple dumplings, fresh pumpkin pies, red velvet cakes, and iced raisin cinnamon bread. Not to be confused with the older Bird-in-Hand Bake Shop on Gibbons Road.

FISHER'S PASTRIES

Hess & Newport Roads, (Route 772)
Monterey, PA 17540
Sat 8-4.

This small, family run bakery turns out delicious homemade root beer, Montgomery pie, whoopie pies, and snickerdoodles.

GLEN BROOK BAKE SHOP

96A Glen Brook Road
Leola, PA 17540
Fri 9-6. Sat 8-5.

I have a soft spot in my heart for this small, family bakery. I grew up eating the dry bottom variety of shoofly pie. This doesn't mean it was devoid of the sweet, sticky bottom; it just had a thinner layer. On her trips from her Montgomery County farm, my grandmother would stop by

> As English as apple pie, colonists must have said before America coopted the dish for its own. Settlers had brought apple seeds along with wheat seeds to the colonies.
>
> Betty Fussell,
> *I Hear America Cooking*
>
>

SPELT

Spelt is a grain favored by the Pennsylvania Dutch and is ground into flour for making bread, pastries, and dumplings. It is higher in nutrition than wheat and is perfect for those with flour allergies.

◆◆◆

this bakery for their shoofly pies. My aunt, Geri Sell, began stopping here for a shoofly fix after moving to Lancaster County, and now I am carrying on the family tradition. Today, I buy shoofly pies from a grandchild of the baker my grandmother relied on. They also have delicious fruit pies in season along with breads, cookies, and cakes.

KISSEL VIEW FARM BAKERY
122 West Millport Road
Lititz, PA 17543
Mon-Sat 8-5. (717) 626-4217
From Route 501 head West and go 1 mile. They are on the left.

It is fun to visit this bakery just to see their 14 kinds of old-fashioned cookies. In addition they mold chocolates into a variety of shapes as unique gift ideas: a plate of spaghetti, golf balls and a bag, a hair dryer, false teeth, and all sorts of animals. Along with candies, breads, pies, and cakes, they have a very good selection of grains and flours. There are also picnic tables and rest rooms.

MICHAEL'S HOMESTYLE BREADS
417 Georgetown Road
Strasburg, PA 17579
Mon, Wed-Fri 8-4. (717) 687-6368

Lancaster County bread is a homestyle loaf, featuring a soft crust and tender crumb. Michael's offers the best of its kind. The work of the bakery goes on right behind the cash register, and you can watch and smell the bread coming out of the oven. The iced cinnamon raisin bread is a local favorite and for good reason. It is good toasted or made into French toast for an easy breakfast treat. Other breads are potato or whole wheat. Homemade noodles, jams, and fruit butters are other goodies made in local kitchens and sold here.

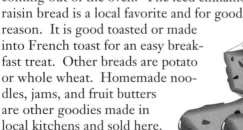

MINNICH'S FARM BAKERY

87 Green Acre Road
Lititz, PA 17543
Thurs 12-6. Fri 8-6. Sat 7-1. (717) 626-7981
From Route 501 go West on Route 772 and make a left onto Green Acre Road.

Minnich's farm kitchen has been supplying the neighborhood with pies, breads, and pastries since 1950. Especially popular is a Moravian sugar cake (breakfast cake) made from a traditional recipe. Their homemade soups and salads, as well, are nothing to sniff at. Minnich's has a stand at the Central Market in Lancaster every Tuesday, Friday, and Saturday.

STOLTZFOOS SISTERS BAKERY

5115 Usner Road
Kinzer, PA 17535
Mon-Sat 8-5
At the corner of Usner Road and Route 772.

This is a very good spot to satisfy your sweet tooth and remind you of home (or just remind you of good home baking). The Stoltzfoos sisters sell bread and cookies Monday through Thursday. On Fridays they splurge with sticky buns, shoofly pies, custard pies, seasonal fruit pies, and a good lemon sponge pie.

OTHER BAKERIES:

BYER'S BUTTERFLAKE BAKERY
36 Keystone Court
Leola, PA 17540
Thurs-Sat 7-5. (717) 656-6803

HERSHEY FARM BAKERY
Route 896
Strasburg, PA 17579
Sun-Thurs 7-8. Fri & Sat 7-9. (717) 687-8635

MILLER'S SMORGASBORD & BAKERY
Route 30 East
Ronks, PA 17572
July 1-Labor Day: Breakfast: 8-12. Dinner: 12-9. Off season hours vary. Call to confirm. (717) 687-6621
2 miles east of Route 896.

BUTCHERS

DIETRICH'S MEATS AND COUNTRY STORE

660 Old 22
Krumsville, PA 19534
Mon-Fri 8-7. Sat 8-6. (610) 756-6344

Welcome to carnivore heaven. Just one step into this country market makes me salivate with its delicious aroma of smoked meats. Dietrich's is famous for its old-fashioned mild or hard smoked hams, picnics, pork loins, and bacon. They also make country sausage, various bolognas, scrapple, puddings, homemade mincemeat, and braunschweiger. Other meats include grain fed beef, hogs, lamb, and custom cut veal, as well as unusual items such as a variety of game, pickled pigs' feet and snouts, tripe and souse pudding, blood and tongue wursts, rocky mountain oysters, and pork, beef, or veal brains. Also worth the trip are the wonderful baked goods made on the premises: old-fashioned coffee cake, funny cake, Amish vanilla pie, shoofly pie, lemon Montgomery pie, cookies, cakes, and fruit pies. Located in Berks County not too far from Fleetwood or Moselem Springs.

EBERLY POULTRY, INC.

1095 Mt. Airy Road
Stevens, PA 17578
Mon-Fri 9-5. Sat 9-3. (717) 336-6440

The Eberly family has been processing quality poultry since 1948. Their chickens and turkeys are free range and organically grown by Amish and Mennonite farmers in Lancaster County. They also offer specialty poultry (not all organically grown) such as Cornish hens, pheasants, quail, squab, Muscovy ducks, and partridge. Not all of these are available year round and some are frozen. Eberly products are sold to butchers and specialty food stores, but the prices at their on-site retail store are quite reasonable. Don't forget to pack a cooler for the ride home.

ABOUT THE PIG

There is no animal who furnishes more variety to the tongue: its meat provides nearly fifty flavors, but that of the other animals only one.

Pliny the Elder

◆◆◆

S. CLYDE WEAVER, INC.

5253 Main Street
East Petersburg, PA 17520
Mon-Thurs 7-6. Fri 7-9. Sat 7-5. (717) 569-0812

S. Clyde Weaver is noted for its smoked meats. They make country style hams, smoked pork chops, Lebanon bologna, bratwurst, bockwurst, and a good variety of country cheeses, smoked and plain. (They also make a mean submarine sandwich to order.) Other treats include specialty food items such as Stash teas, bagel chips, crackers, pretzels, ice cream, jams, fruit butters, olive oils, and vinegars. On Thursday through Saturday at the East Petersburg location, they have a full range of bakery items for sale. They also operate a stand at the Central Market in downtown Lancaster and have a relatively new location in the Lancaster Shopping Center.

SELTZER'S LEBANON BOLOGNA COMPANY

230 North College Street
Palmyra, PA 17078
Retail shop: Mon-Fri 7-5. Sat 7-1. Tour hours: Mon-Fri 8-11:45 & 12:30-3:15.
(800) 282-6336
Three blocks North of Route 422 in Palmyra

Jack and Craig Seltzer are carrying on a family tradition of making Lebanon bologna with lean beef that is coarsely ground, aged for two weeks, finely ground, and smoked over a hardwood fire. The farmers of Lebanon County developed this sausage that is smoked so that it keeps through the summer, thus a summer sausage. The Seltzer family started its business in 1902, and they continue to please customers with their secret recipe.

There are tours that begin with a videotape and feature a visit to the smokehouse where bolognas are smoked for up to three days. The retail store also sells other Pennsylvania Dutch favorites such as smoked hams, turkey, scrapple, and cheeses. The Seltzers have a mail order business and ship their products throughout the country.

STOLTZFUS MEATS

Cross Keys Center
3614 Old Philadelphia Pike, (Route 340)
Intercourse, PA 17534
Tues-Sat 8-6. Fri 8-8. (717) 768-7287
Near the intersection of 772

Stoltzfus Meats has a retail market in Intercourse that is definitely worth a visit. They have been producing smoked meats since 1958, and their specialties include such local favorites as pan pudding (scrapple without the cornmeal), dried beef, ring bologna, country hams, and several varieties of Lebanon bologna. They are also known for their sausages. With the excep-

◆◆◆

tion of some of the lunch meats, all Stoltzfus products are prepared locally. They carry a good selection of baked goods, pickled vegetables, and other small items. If you're interested in bringing some goodies home, the market also displays insulated carriers for sale. The same family owns the Stoltzfus Farm Restaurant where their meat products are prepared and served from May to October.

OTHER BUTCHERS TO VISIT:

WEAVER'S & BAUM'S LEBANON BOLOGNA
15th & Weavertown Roads
Lebanon, PA
Mon-Sat 8-5. (717) 274-6100

CANDY

HERSHEY'S CHOCOLATE WORLD
800 HERSHEYPARK Drive
Hershey, PA 17033
Hours vary with the seasons. Call to verify. (717) 534-4900
Off Route 39.

Hershey's Chocolate World is the official visitors' center of Hershey Foods Corporation. Take a 12-minute tour through a simulation of the chocolate factory and enjoy a sample as your reward. Features a large candy store and two restaurants.

MIESSE CANDIES
60 North Queen Street
Lancaster, PA 17603
Mon-Sat 9-5. (717) 392-6011
One block off the town square.

Someone from the Miesse family ran this candy making business from 1875 until 1981. Frank Taylor, the current owner, still employs 12 of the 14 employees who worked for the last Miesse (Roy Miesse, Jr.). May has been the candymaker at Miesse Candies since 1966, and she learned her trade from a gentleman who started in 1912. That's continuity for you!

Miesse Candies manufactures 95% of its candy centers, and specialties include dark chocolate vanilla buttercream centers, caramels, peanut butter meltaways, and turtles. This store is a center city location, and there are two other locations: Lancaster Shopping Center, between Oregon and Lititz Pike (Route 501), and the village of Intercourse, 3614 Old Philadelphia Pike, (Route 340).

◆◆◆

◆◆

WEAVER CANDY AND COOKIE OUTLETS

1925 West Main Street
Ephrata, PA 17522
Mon-Fri 8:30-8:30. Sat 8:30-5. (717) 738-3337
Between Routes 501 and 272.

With more than 3,600 varieties of candy, dried fruit, nuts, and coffee, this place is a snacker's dream come true. There are fancy, dried fruits like glazed apricots, mangos, dates, cranberries, cherries, and nectarines. Here you will find the latest candies as well as old-fashioned favorites and all sorts of stick candies, toffees, hard candies, and 20 kinds of German gummies. Best of all, prices are barely above wholesale. They also have a store in western Lancaster City.

WEAVER CANDY AND COOKIE OUTLETS

3519 Columbia Avenue
Lancaster, PA 17603
Mon-Fri 8:30-8:30. Sat 8:30-5. (717) 285-3818
West of Centerville Road.

COFFEE & TEA

CROSS KEYS COFFEE AND TEAS

34 North Queen Street
Lancaster, PA 17603
Mon-Fri 7:15-5:30 except Wed 7:15-8:00. Sat 8:30-5. (717) 299-4411

This is a lovely store offering up all sorts of very good coffees and teas, coffee making accouterment, and fresh brewed java to keep you going. Coffee is roasted by First Colony and arrives the next day. A small coffee bar provides a view of passersby.

EDWARD'S COFFEE SHOP

3519 Columbia Avenue
Lancaster, PA 17603
Mon-Fri 6:30-8:30. Sat 6:30-5.
(717) 285-9688

Located in western Lancaster City, this coffee shop is a good place to stop while sightseeing, shopping, or just plain hanging out. It is housed under the same roof as the Weaver Candy and Cookie Outlet. Serving up homemade meals for breakfast, lunch, or

◆◆

supper, Edward's is a nice place to refuel. Along with the coffee, fresh baked pastries, homemade ice cream, soups, hot and cold sandwiches, and salads are the attraction.

SPILL THE BEANS
43 East Main Street
Lititz, PA 17543
Mon-Wed 7-3. Thurs-Fri 7-8. Sat 8-3:30. (717) 627-7827

Spill the Beans is a bright and cheerful spot in downtown Lititz. A stop here makes for a tasty and relaxing respite in your busy schedule whether you need a morning caffeine jolt, a bagel sandwich for lunch, or an afternoon or evening (Friday or Saturday only) espresso. The front of the shop has a cozy sitting area with comfortable stuffed chairs. The rest of the dining room is furnished with a fun mix of cafe tables and yellow decoupaged chairs. Freshly roasted beans come from Philadelphia's New Harmony Roasters, and the bagels are Bubbie's Bagels of Lancaster. In addition to bagel sandwiches, lunch offerings include fresh soups and salads. A nice selection of pastries will tempt you, and the service is friendly and pleasant.

> **Several times every day, food offers each of us the promise of short-term happiness. As a source of satisfaction, joy, discovery, and renewal, few daily rituals have such extraordinary potential as the act of preparing and sharing a good meal.**
>
> Patricia Wells,
> *Simply French*
>
>

COUNTRY STORES
CENTERVILLE BULK FOODS
3501B Scenic Road
Gordonville, PA 17529
Mon-Thurs 7-5. Fri 7-9. Sat 7-4.

Centerville Bulk Foods is an Amish store that specializes in bulk foods such as cereals, baking mixes, spices, cheese, meat, and candy.

THE COUNTRY STORE
906 Mount Joy-Manheim Road, (Route 772)
Mount Joy, PA 17545
Tues-Thurs 9-5. Fri 9-8. Sat 9-12. (717) 653-2652

This Mennonite-run store carries bulk foods, lunchmeat and cheese, and locally made pretzels and potato chips.

ECHO HILL COUNTRY STORE
Fleetwood to Dryville Road
Fleetwood, PA 19522
Mon-Wed 8-5. Thurs & Fri 8-7. Sat 8-4. (215) 944-7858

Located in Berks County, a visit to this store can be scheduled with lunch or dinner at the nearby Moselem Springs Inn (see page 119). Run by Old Order Mennonites just outside the small town of Fleetwood, you'll find health food items, bulk foods, spices, fresh locally prepared meats, and frozen meats and vegetables. There are also large selections of grains, flours, dried beans, teas, candies, dried fruits, and nuts. Prices are reasonable and worth the trip if you stock up. Mail orders are accepted for non-perishable items.

SHADY MAPLE GROCERY
1324 Main Street
East Earl, PA 17519
Mon, Wed, Thurs, Fri 8-9. Tues & Sat 8-5.
On Route 23, at Route 897. (717) 354-4981

Shady Maple Grocery is an appetizing place to wander through. It is so large they offer a map in their sales flyer so you can find your way. A cavernous bakery has all sorts of pastries, pies, and cakes. There are apple fritters, rhubarb pies, raisin pies, oatmeal pies, lemon sponge pies, and much more. The baking supply aisle has locally ground corn meal and interesting flours and grains. They have a very large selection of lunch meats made by favorite local butchers with names like Kunzler and Hatfield. If you're looking for a bargain lunch, they offer Foyer Favorites for $1.69 (plus tax) which could include a pork barbecue sandwich, macaroni salad, chips, and a drink.

FARM STANDS

BEILER'S FRUIT FARM
383 Springville Road (Route 897)
New Holland, PA 17557
Open year round. Oct-June: Mon-Fri 8-8. Sat 8-5. July-Sept: Mon-Fri 8-6. Sat 8-5.
2 1/2 miles North of White Horse. Between Route 340 and 322.

The Beilers grow a wide variety of fruits and vegetables, and they sell only what they've produced themselves. Their peaches are outstanding. During the winter and early spring months, they sell jams, relishes, and potatoes.

BLUE GATE FARM MARKET & BAKE SHOP
Route 30
Ronks, PA 17572
Dec-May: Thurs-Sat 8-5. June-Nov: Mon-Sat 8-5.
Route 30 - 3/4 mile East of Route 896

They sell homemade baked goods, fresh fruits, and vegetables in season. There is also a variety of jams, pickles, canned fruits, and vegetables to choose from.

CHERRY HILL ORCHARDS
2183 New Danville Pike
Lancaster, PA 17603
Mon-Fri 8-7. Sat 8-6. (717) 872-9311

This large farm market sells a large variety of Lancaster County grown vegetables, fruits, herbs, and plants. They also carry pies, maple syrup, honey, crafts, and gifts. Hayrides are scheduled for several weekends in the fall. Call ahead for schedule. Gift boxes of fruit (your choice of ten different kinds of apples) are shipped throughout the United States.

FISHER'S NURSERY AND FARM MARKET
494 White Oak Road
Strasburg, PA 17579
Open year round: Mon-Fri 7 a.m.-Dusk. Sat 7-4:30.

Along with selling the usual complement of produce, flowers, eggs, pies, and honey, Fisher's specializes in old and new fruit trees and other plants. They have 50 varieties of apple trees and 20 varieties of peach trees alone. Also a good source for various types of berry plants, rhubarb, cherry trees, and grape vines.

FUNK'S FARM MARKET & GREENHOUSE
306 South Duke Street
Millersville, PA 17551
Mon-Wed & Sat 9-6. Thurs & Fri 9-8.
(717) 872-8411

More fresh fruit, vegetables, herbs, dairy, meats, eggs, maple, honey, pies, and candy. Come during strawberry season and you can pick your own berries. Children will enjoy the petting zoo and hayrides.

FARMERS' MARKETS

The number of farmers' markets dropped to an all-time low of several hundred by the early 1970s due to the growth of supermarkets. Since then, there has been a tremendous growth of these markets and there are now some 2,000 nationwide.
Urban Land Institute of Washington

◆◆◆

HAMPSHIRE ORCHARD

1813 Camp Road
Manheim, PA 17545
July-Dec: Mon-Fri 9-6. Sat 9-3.
(717) 664-3343
4 miles off PA turnpike exit 20, off Route 72 North.

> The only way to get rid of temptation is to yield to it.
> Oscar Wilde
>

Hampshire Orchard sells fresh produce, plants, apple snitz, and press cider. They also give tours of the farm. Mail and phone orders welcome.

HILLTOP ACRES FARM MARKET

347 Rife Run Road
Manheim, PA 17545
Mon-Wed 8:30-5:30. Thurs-Fri 8:30-8. Sat 8:30-4. (717) 665-7809
2 miles North of Manheim on Route 72.

This is a good place to find seasonal fruit and vegetables; there are strawberry beds where you can pick your own. Hilltop also carries bulk foods, meats, dairy products, groceries, pies, gardening supplies, plants, and a full deli. Telephone orders are accepted.

HODECKER CELERY FARM

1276 Lititz Road
Manheim, PA 17545
Open year round: Tues-Thurs & Sat 8-5. Fri 8-6. (717) 898-8414
5 miles North of Lancaster, 1/4 mile east of Route 72 on Lititz Road.

Hodecker Celery Farm is one of the few growers of bleached celery, a local specialty. They also sell the usual fresh produce, honey, and pies. See page 133 for information about their stand on Central Market, the downtown Lancaster farmers' market.

HOOVER'S FRUIT AND VEGETABLE FARM

30 Erb's Bridge Road
Lititz, PA 17543
Open Apr-Dec: Mon-Fri 8-8. Sat 8-6. (717) 733-1048
From PA 772, turn right onto Picnic Woods Road, and thru covered bridge.

Hoover's features fruits and vegetables from their farm, as well as baked goods and jam. Their garden's offerings are augmented by produce staples such as lemons, grapes, and celery from more conventional food sources. Long hours also add to the attractiveness of this business.

HOTTENSTEIN'S FARM MARKET

1900 State Road

Lancaster, PA 17601

Open May-Dec: Mon-Fri 9-6. Sat 9-5. (717) 898-7021

1/4 mile off Route 283 at the Route 722 exit, corner of State & Colebrook

Another farm stand with farm fresh vegetables, fruit, milk, eggs, pies, honey, and plants.

KREIDER FARMS DAIRY STORES

1461 Lancaster Road

Manheim, PA 17545

Open year round: Mon-Sat 6 a.m.-11 p.m. Sun 7 a.m.-8 p.m. (717) 665-5039

2 miles East of Manheim on Doe Run Road

Kreider Farms features fruit, potatoes, plants, dairy, eggs, maple syrup, honey, gifts, and their own excellent ice cream, along with tours, hayrides, and a petting zoo. The family also owns three family restaurants in the Lancaster area: Lancaster, Manheim, and Hershey (see page 104).

MILLER'S BERRIES

917 Farmingdale Road

Lancaster, PA 17603

Open June-Oct: Mon-Sat 8-6. (717) 393-7452

Off Route 30 between Park City & Rohrerstown, West of Lancaster

During strawberry season, you can pick your own. They also sell other fruits.

PEACH LANE PRODUCE

91 West White Oak Road

Ronks, PA 17572

Open May 1-New Years:

Mon-Sat 7-7.

1 mile West of Route 896 at the corner of Peach Lane.

The usual farm stand offerings of fruit, vegetables, eggs, honey, pies, pick your own strawberries, and canned goods.

RED BARN MARKET

1402 Georgetown Road, (Route 896)

Quarryville, PA 17566

Open May-Oct: Mon-Sat 8-6. (717) 529-6040

Perfect for both the tourist picking up an afternoon snack of juicy peaches and the industrious home cook who orders ahead to have enough corn to freeze for the winter. This large farm stand has a wide variety of produce, beautifully displayed. The staff is friendly and helpful.

STAUFFER FARM MARKET

345 Weaver Road

Lancaster, PA 17603

Open year round: Mon-Fri 9:30-5:30. Sat 9:30-12. (717) 872-5591

Centerville exit off Route 30, go South to Route 462, West to Weaver Road.

Stauffer's sells vegetables, pumpkins, plants, dairy, eggs, pies, honey, and gifts.

A.L. KAUFFMAN'S FRUIT MARKET

3097 Old Philadelphia Pike, (Route 340)

Bird-in-Hand, PA 17505

Mon-Thurs 7-5:30. Fri 7-8:30. Sat 7-5. (717) 768-7112

This is a great market to pick up seasonal fruit and vegetables. They also carry food in bulk, dried fruits and nuts, meats, and groceries.

FARMERS' MARKETS

BIRD-IN-HAND FARMERS' MARKET

Route 340 & Maple Avenue

Bird-in-Hand, PA 17505

Dec-Mar: Fri & Sat 8:30-5:30. Apr, June & Nov: Wed, Fri & Sat 8:30-5:30. July-Oct: Wed-Sat 8:30-5:30. (717) 393-9674

If you are in the area, this small, country market is a fun place to visit. There is a nice assortment of produce, meat, baked goods, and snack counters. Adjacent buildings house The Little Book Shop, Susquehanna Glass Outlet, and Weaver's Shoes.

CENTRAL MARKET

Penn Square

Lancaster, PA 17603

Tues & Fri 6-4:30. Sat 6-2. (717) 291-4723

Lancaster's jewel in the crown is one of the nation's oldest, publicly owned farmers' markets. The current market building was built in 1889 and is on the National Register of Historic Places. Though the building was not in existence when the market began in the 1730s, there has been a market on this site since that time. Named one of America's 63 Great American Public Places, the market is a perfect place to find the best foods of Lancaster County.

Early birds get the worm. The market opens at 6:00 a.m., and shopping before 8:00 gives the added bonus of avoiding the loving crowds. The Central Market is truly a farmers' market with about 80 farmers and specialty food purveyors who have grown or processed the foods they sell. An unusual state of affairs at the typical farmers' markets of the 1990s.

Beautiful, locally grown produce, smoked meats and cheeses, and homestyle sweets are the attraction. Hodecker Celery Farm is one of the few farms that still grows bleached celery. (This means the celery is bleached to remove its slightly bitter taste and stringiness.) Bleached celery is so popular locally that families pass down cut-glass celery trays. Hodecker brings its crisp, sweet celery to Central Market.

Other Lancaster County staples are fresh grated horseradish found at Long's; hot roasted peanuts; or the pan pudding, smoked pork chops, and submarine sandwiches at S. Clyde Weaver's. The German Deli carries salmon paté in a tube, wursts, and imported meats. Nancy's Goodies has some mouthwatering sweets such as black walnut sugar cookies, angel food cupcakes, and old-fashioned molasses cookies. In a nod to the 1990s, the market also has a cappuccino maker and a stand selling Middle Eastern foods.

There are a number of convenient parking lots within a short walk. My choice is the lot at the corner of Prince and King Streets with an entrance on King.

COLUMBIA FARMERS' MARKET
Third & Locust Streets
Columbia, PA 17512
Fri 7-4. Sat 7-2. (717) 684-2468
Columbia Farmers' Market offers seasonal fruits and vegetables.

GREEN DRAGON FARMERS' MARKET & AUCTION
955 North State Street
Ephrata, PA 17522
March-Dec: Fri 8:30-9:30. (717) 738-1117
Take 272 North from Route 322. Make a right onto Garden Spot Road
and another right onto N. State.

Green Dragon is a raucous, rambling market; part farmers' market, part fast food court, and part carnival complete with cotton candy. Their motto is: If you can't buy it at the Green Dragon, it chust ain't fer sale. Vendors hawk a wide variety of items from rare books to gardening tools to the excellent

Lapp Valley Farm ice cream. Especially wonderful are the full-service butchers, and the farmers offering up sparkling fresh fruits and vegetables. Livestock is auctioned weekly. If you are adverse to crowds, I suggest you arrive early in the day.

Shopping for all sorts of goodies at the Green Dragon Farmers' Market.

ROOTS MARKET
AND CONESTOGA AUCTION
705 Graystone Road
Manheim, PA 17545
Open year round: Tues 9-9. (717) 898-7811
7 miles North of Lancaster off Route 72

This market is open only on Tuesdays and makes an excellent country adventure. Besides impeccably fresh produce grown by area farmers, there are meats, baked goods, gifts, and crafts. Throughout the afternoon, there are small auctions for produce, small animals, and household goods. Last but not

least, numerous vendors sell prepared food: pork barbecue, sausage, and other guilty pleasures.

The hustle and bustle at Roots Market.

FLOUR

ROHRER'S MILL
273 Rohrer Mill Road
Ronks, PA 17572
Mon-Sat 7-5. (717) 687-6400

Built in 1852, this traditional flour mill occupies a peaceful corner of the world. Today, fifth generation Rohrer family members raise wheat and corn to be ground by water-powered stone wheels. Preservative-free offerings include wheat germ meal, roasted corn meal (you've got to try this stuff), whole wheat flour, wheat pastry flour, rye flour, buckwheat flour, quick oats, and oat bran. Entry to the mill is from the back, and you go up the steps to the main floor. If no one is around, they have set up a self-service operation. If you would like information or a tour and no one is about, knock at the Landis house and they'll be happy to help.

HERBS

THE HERB SHOP
20 East Main Street
Lititz, PA 17543
Mon-Sat 9-5. Fri 9-7. (717) 626-9206

Barbara Zink opened The Herb Shop in 1978 because of her interest in good food. She supplies traveler and resident alike with a large inventory of herbs, condiments, teas, coffees, cookbooks, and specialty foods. This is a great shop to snoop around in, whether you're a cook or a lover of good food.

HONEY

RAINBOW APIARIES
668 Turkey Hill Road
East Earl, PA 17519
Open year round. Call for hours. (717) 445-6674
Route 625, 2 miles south of Bowmansville.

Bob and Annette Hughes Honey are stewards of a large number of bees. They sell honey candy, beeswax candles, gifts, crafts, and various bee supplies and equipment. A beehive is set up for observation.

ICE CREAM

BOEHRINGER'S ICE CREAM

Route 272

Adamstown, PA 19501

Open Mar-Sept: Mon-Sun 11-8. (717) 484-4227

1/4 mile North of Adamstown's traffic light on the left.

Going on four generations, the Boehringer family has been making rich, homemade ice cream. Opened in 1949, this family store serves up 18 delicious flavors. Other food served includes good old-fashioned drive-in fare: cheese steaks, hamburgers, hot dogs, and shakes. This is not an eat-in restaurant, but picnic tables are strategically placed for maximum contentment by a nearby stream with ducks.

COLEMAN'S ICE CREAM

2195-B Old Philadelphia Pike, (Route 340)

Lancaster, PA 17602

Summer hours: Mon-Thurs 10-9. Fri & Sat 10-10. Sun 12-9. Spring and fall they are closed earlier. (717) 394-8815

When asked how many flavors of ice cream they have, the young woman dipping the homemade ice cream could only say, "Lots." And indeed they do have lots of flavors, including some more, shall we say, unusual taste sensations such as root beer sherbet, lemon chiffon, nutmeg, and bubble gum. There are picnic tables out front so you can enjoy your treat.

LAPP VALLEY FARM

244 Mentzer Road (between Routes 23 and 340)

New Holland, PA 17557

Mon-Thurs 10-Dark. Fri 8-Dark. Sat 8-7. (717) 354-7988

3 miles south of New Holland, take New Holland Road to Mentzler Road.

Lapp Valley Farm is a must-see, particularly for ice cream lovers and families. (Does that leave anyone out?) The Lapp family produces some lusciously, delicious ice cream (16%-19% butterfat) from their herd of 50 Holsteins. They make 20 or more flavors, including peanut butter swirl, cookies and cream, raspberry, and the ever popular vanilla. Besides making your tastebuds happy,

> In *Pennsylfannisch* (**Pennsylvania Dutch**), *Schupf* dumplings are humorously referred to as *Buwweschpitzle* (boys' bits) and are made almost exclusively for such festive occasions as Christmas dinner, weddings, and family reunions.
>
> William Woys Weaver, *Pennsylvania Dutch Country Cooking*
>
>

this is a fun place to walk around the grounds. You can watch a herd of deer in a meadow near the pond or hopefully catch sight of the two peacocks strutting about. The usual farm animals roam about and require petting, and tours of the dairy are available. Lapp Valley also sells its ice cream at the Green Dragon in Ephrata (see page 134) and at Kitchen Kettle Village in Intercourse (see page 139).

PINE VIEW ACRES

2225 New Danville Pike
Lancaster, PA 17603
Mon-Fri 9-9. Sat 9-7. (717) 872-5486

Larry, John, and Janet Hess work this 200-acre dairy farm, one of the few farms that processes milk on site and sells it in their retail store. An added bonus are their 16 flavors of homemade ice cream.

STRASBURG COUNTRY STORE & CREAMERY

Center Square
Strasburg, PA 17579
June-Labor Day: Daily 8-10. Labor Day-June: 9-8. (717) 687-0766
At the intersection of Routes 896 & 741.

Great ice cream sodas and ice cream cones. Inside, there is a charming cafe where you can rest. Outside, there are benches and picnic tables for ice cream licking.

ANOTHER ICE CREAM SPOT TO TRY:

BONNIE'S EXCEPTIONAL ICE CREAM

21 Leaman Road
Paradise, PA 17562
Daily 12-9. (717) 687-9301

IMPORTED FOODS

S. MANDROS IMPORTED FOODS

351 North Charlotte Street
Lancaster, PA 17603
Mon-Sat 8-8, Sun 8:30-7. (717) 397-8926

The Mandros family has been carefully selecting specialty foods to offer the discriminating shopper since 1955. This is *the* place in the Lancaster area for imported cheeses, olive oils, pasta, vinegars, and other gourmet foods.

JAMS AND JELLIES

KITCHEN KETTLE VILLAGE

3529 Old Philadelphia Pike, (Route 340)

Intercourse, PA 17534

Mon-Sat 9-5. During the summer and fall, they are open slightly later. (800) 732-3538

Kitchen Kettle Village is a tourist mecca of 32 shops that grew up around the Kitchen Kettle, a Pennsylvania Dutch jam and jelly making operation. Bob and Pat Burnley began the Kitchen Kettle back in 1954. Today, their business has blossomed into more than 60 varieties of jams, jellies, and relishes which are sold at the Village and through mail order. When you visit, you can watch employees making jams and jellies in kettles bubbling with fruity goodness. A wide variety of special events and festivals are held at the Village throughout the year. Call for dates and times.

Kitchen Kettle Village has numerous specialty shops for your browsing, shopping, and eating pleasure. They include: 1) The Bake Shop, where baked goods, jams, and jellies are sold, along with cookbooks, cooking aprons, and tinware. 2) The Jam and Relish Kitchen, where you can sample an amazing number of jams and jellies and watch them being made. 3) Jim Garrahy's Fudge Kitchen, 4) Kling House Restaurant, 5) Lapp Valley Farms Ice Cream, and 6) the Smokehouse Shop. See pages 199 and 227 for information about non-food shops in the village.

NATURAL FOOD STORES

> Although peopled mainly by descendants of Germans, York is deeply rooted in English tradition. It was named by the Penns, either for the English city of that name, or for the Duke of York, and its older buildings of red brick and white trim follow the architectural style of Georgian England.
>
> An American Guide Series,
> *Pennsylvania:*
> *A Guide to the Keystone State*
>
>

COMMUNITY NATURAL FOODS STORE

1065 West Main Street (Route 23)
New Holland, PA 17557
Mon & Wed 9-5. Tues, Thurs & Fri 9-7.
Sat 10-3. (717) 656-7222

This natural foods store has the area's largest selection of organic produce, a full range of homeopathic remedies, herbs, dietary supplements, personal care products, and healthy foods. Several freezers are stocked with bagels, breads, fruits, and vegetables, as well as an assortment of prepared foods.

IT'S ONLY NATURAL

10 Front Street
Lititz, PA 17543
Mon, Tues & Thurs 10-5:30. Wed & Fri 10-6. Sat 10-4. (717) 627-1174

It's Only Natural is tucked just off Main Street in Lititz. Inside you'll find a good selection of vegetarian foods, vitamins and supplements, grains, beans, natural soft drinks, fresh breads, teas, cashew butter, peanut butter, and fresh organic locally grown produce. They also have books on health and natural foods.

DUTCH SCHOOL NATURAL FOODS

22 N. 7th Street, Suite 2
Akron, PA 17501
Mon, Tues, Thurs, Fri 9-8. Wed & Sat 9-5. (717) 859-4901

Another source for health foods, supplements, grains, and books.

MILLER'S NATURAL FOODS

2888 Miller Lane
Bird-in-Hand, PA 17505
Mon-Fri 7-7. Sat 7-4.

This gaslit, Amish grocery carries very good seasonal produce, bulk foods, health food items, general groceries, and books.

◆◆

WEAVER'S NATURAL FOODS INC.

15 Market Square
Manheim, PA 17545
Mon-Thurs 9-5. Fri 9-8. Sat 9-3. (717) 665-6871

Located in a mansion on Market Square in downtown Manheim, this store has a very large selection of vitamins, mineral supplements, homeopathic products, and books. The food selection is small, but well chosen: bulk grains, beans, cereals, and spices. The homeopathic apothecary is what makes this store, which opened in the 1960s, special. You can shop via mail order also.

PRETZELS

ANDERSON PRETZELS

2060 Old Philadelphia Pike (Route 340)
Lancaster, PA 17602
Store: Mon-Thurs 8:30-5. Fri 7-5. Sat 8:30-3. Tours: Mon-Fri 8:30-4. (717) 299-1616

Started in 1888, Anderson employees hand twisted pretzels for the first 67 years. This large bakery offers an interesting, self-guided tour. You can follow the making of some 100,000 pounds of pretzels, the number generally made in a single, eight-hour shift. Anderson makes a number of pretzel varieties: mini pretzels, sticks, rods, gems, logs, the traditional twist in both the thick, Bavarian Dutch style and the thin version. Flavored pretzels come in whole wheat, oat bran, pizza, cheese flavored, and more. The tour follows the process of mixing the dough, extruding and twisting the pretzel, proofing, salting, baking, and, finally, packaging. Ironically, the soft pretzels sold in the snack shop aren't made by Anderson Pretzels.

AUNTIE ANNE'S SOFT PRETZELS

Central Market Hall, 45 North Market Street
Lancaster, PA 17603
Mon-Fri 10-4. Sat 10-3. (717) 394-6326

1201 Park City Center
Lancaster, PA 17601
Mon-Sat 10-9:30. Sun 12-6. (717) 392-0767

5325 Lincoln Highway, (Route 30)
Gap, PA 17527
Mon-Sat 10-5. (717) 442-4335

Anne Beiler (there is an Auntie Anne!) has come a long way since opening her first pretzel stand in 1988 at the Downingtown Farmers' Market. At press time there are 410 Auntie Anne's Soft Pretzels stores and carts in the United States, Indonesia, Malaysia, and the Philippines. These attractive, blue-and-white tiled franchises draw hungry crowds by hand rolling pretzels in full view. The ten flavors include raisin, garlic, sour cream, and caramel almond pretzels. Whether you take your pretzel flavored or plain, Auntie Anne's pretzels are perfect hot from the oven.

MARTIN'S PRETZELS

1229 Diamond Street
Akron, PA 17501
Mon, Tues & Thurs 8-8 (they close for lunch 11-11:30). Wed & Fri-Sat 8-5:30.
(717) 859-1272

Photograph courtesy of Martin's Pretzels

Watch pretzels being hand twisted the old-fashioned way at this small, family run bakery. Of all the local versions, Martin's regular pretzels are my personal favorites. Pretzels are available for sale.

Twisting the day away at Martin's Pretzels.

STURGIS PRETZEL HOUSE

219 East Main Street
Lititz, PA 17543
Mon-Sat 9-5. (717) 626-4354

Legend has it that in the 1850s, a tramp gave Ambrose Rauch, a bake shop owner, a recipe for hard pretzels in exchange for a meal. The recipe was passed on to Julius Sturgis, an apprentice of Rauch's, who opened his own bakery. This bakery became the first pretzel bakery in America in 1861 and is still owned by descendants of Julius Sturgis. Today for a modest fee, you can watch how the pretzels are made with modern ovens. As a part of the tour, you're given a piece of dough and encouraged to try your hand at pretzel twisting. In the 1860s, the workers who twisted pretzels were paid the second highest wage in Lititz: two cents for every 100 pretzels. The site is on the National Register of Historic Places and has a gift shop with local crafts and antiques, as well as pretzels, for sale. Mail orders for these tasty treats are happily accommodated.

UNCLE HENRY'S PRETZEL BAKERY

1550 Bowmansville Road
Bowmansville, PA 17507
Mon-Fri 9-11:30 & 12-2:30. Call for additional hours. (717) 445-4690
Route 625 North from Route 23. Go through Bowmansville and go under the turnpike overpass. Make first L onto Bowmansville Rd.

This small, family run pretzel bakery still makes pretzels the old-fashioned way. They twist them by hand. Watch this old art, and buy some for the road.

TROUT

SPRING TROUT FISH FARM

637 New Holland Road
New Holland, PA 17557
Fishing: Mar-Sept: Wed & Sat 8-6. To buy fresh fish: Open year round: Mon-Sat 7-6. (717) 355-9947
1.5 miles south of Route 23 in New Holland. Brimmer Road becomes New Holland Road.

James and Selma Martin keep a stocked fish pond where visitors can fish for rainbow or palomino trout from March through September on Wednesdays and Saturdays. No fishing license is required, and there is no limit to the number of fish you can catch. A one dollar admission fee is charged for everyone over twelve years of age. There is also a $2.35 fee for each fish caught. Equipment is available for rental, bait is $1.50 per container, your fish are cleaned upon request (.25 cents each), and picnic tables ring the pond for visitors. Dressed trout are available year round for any sized order. Call ahead, and they'll have your fish cleaned, packed, and ready to go.

WINE AND BEER

CALVARESI WINERY
107 Shartlesville Road
Bernville, PA 19506
Thurs-Fri 1-6. Sat-Sun 12-5. (610) 488-7966

This Berks County, family owned vineyard stresses quality over quantity. To make their wine, they press 30 tons of grapes and 10 tons of fruit varieties, producing 11,000 gallons of wine annually. The wines are fermented in stainless steel tanks at cool temperatures to retain the crisp, fruity, Germanic style of wine making. Their lineup includes a semi-dry Riesling that won a bronze medal at the National Orange Show in San Bernadino, CA. Four other whites, three reds, a blush wine, and six fruit wines are available for tasting.

POACHED PEARS WITH STRAWBERRY SAUCE

4 firm ripe pears
1 cup water
1/2 cup sugar
1 1/2 tablespoons lemon juice
1/4 teaspoon vanilla
Fresh or frozen strawberries

Cut a thin slice from the bottom of each pear so it will stand upright. Core the pears from the bottom, leaving the stems intact. Peel pears. Put in kettle and add the next four ingredients. Bring to boil and poach until the pears are springy when squeezed (about 15 minutes or less for very ripe pears).

When ready to serve, stand pears upright in serving dish. In blender, blend strawberries and drizzle over pears. Garnish with fresh mint.

—Recipe from Ruth Harnish,
Flowers and Thyme Bed & Breakfast
◆◆◆

CHADDSFORD WINERY

Route 1, P.O. Box 229

Chadds Ford, PA 19317

Tues-Sat 10-5:30. (Fri sales until 7). Sun 12-5. (610) 388-6221

Chaddsford Winery is located in Chester County and would be a great place to stop in combination with a visit to the Kennett Square area. They craft premium varietals and table wines which are available for tasting and purchase. See page 177 for more information about sights in Chester County.

MOUNT HOPE ESTATE AND WINERY

Route 72

Cornwall, PA 17016

Apr 1-Dec 31: Mon-Sat 10-5. Sun 12-5. (717) 665-7021

1/2 mile South of exit 20 off the PA turnpike.

The hub of this winery is a sandstone mansion, built by Henry Bates Grubb, a son of one of colonial America's wealthiest iron masters. There are 32 rooms furnished with Victorian elegance. The mansion billiards room serves as the setting for the vineyard's wine tastings, and tours of the house are available. The winery is the site of the Pennsylvania Renaissance Faire, held on weekends from August through September (see page 19)

NAYLOR WINE CELLARS, INC.

Located off Route 24

Stewartstown, PA 17363

Mon-Sat 11-6. Sun 12-5. (717) 993-2431

2 miles North of Stewartstown. Watch for turns on Route 851 in Stewartstown.

This 27-acre vineyard produces award winning wines. There are tours of the winery, wine tastings, and a gazebo for a picnic.

THE NISSLEY VINEYARDS

140 Vintage Drive

Bainbridge, PA 17502

Mon-Sat 10-5. Sun 1-4. (717) 426-3514

Located in western Lancaster County, this lovely, 35-acre vineyard features guided and self-guided tours, as well as wine tastings. During the summer months, a variety of music is played on the lawn for lucky picnickers. Each performance starts at 7:30 p.m. and ends at 10:00. There is an admission fee. Call for details.

STOUDT'S BREWING COMPANY

Route 272
Adamstown, PA 19501
Beer sales and gift shop
hours: Mon-Thurs 9-5.
Fri 9-6. Sat 2-6.
(717) 484-4385

Celebrate life at Stoudt's Brewing Company.

Photograph courtesy of Stoudt's Brewery

There's a whole lot of celebrating going on at this micro-brewery. Beers include an award winning golden lager, pilsener, fest, bock, and many varieties of stoudt. During the months of July, August, and September, the brewery hall becomes home to a Beer Fest each Saturday and Sunday. October brings Oktoberfest, of course. There is music (Steve Huber & the Happy Austrians for example), micro-brews, and munchies. Tours of the brewery are given on Saturdays at 3:00 and Sundays at 1:00.

TWIN BROOK WINERY

5697 Strasburg Road
Route 2, Box 2376
Gap , PA 17525
Jan 1-Mar 31: Tues-Sun 12-5. Apr 1-Dec 31: Mon-Sat 10-6. Sun 12-5. (717) 442-4915
Between Routes 41 and 10 on the North side of Strasburg Road.

This property, once part of a land grant from William Penn's brother to the Religious Society of Friends, became a modern winery in 1989. Approximately half of the 20 acres are planted with the classic European vinifera grapes and half with French hybrid vines. A number of Twin Brook's wines have captured national attention and range from a dry oak aged chardonnay to a semi-dry vidal blanc to the sweet and fruity vignoles. There are tours, wine tastings, a picnic area, outdoor concerts, and other special events. They also sell their wine at Basketville on Route 30 East in Paradise (see page 205).

ANOTHER WINERY TO VISIT:

LANCASTER COUNTY WINERY

799 Rawlinsville Road
Willow Street, PA 17584
Mon-Sat 10-4. Sun 1-4. Closed holidays. (717) 464-3555

PLACES TO SEE & THINGS TO DO

Buggy Rides 149
Covered Bridges 150
Especially for Children 151
For Train Buffs 153
Getting to Know Amish and Mennonites 155
Museums and Historic Sights 157
Recreation 165
That's Entertainment 173
Tours 175
Things to See and Do Outside Lancaster County 176

CHAPTER FOUR: PLACES TO SEE AND THINGS TO DO

As described in Chapter Three, wineries, farm markets, and pretzel and chip factories are fun places to visit in Lancaster County. Or you might choose auctions, antique shops, or country stores as described in Chapter Five. If none of these activities suit your fancy, the sights and activities listed in this chapter are each unique and interesting in themselves.

> **The eye of a Pennsylvania German would be starved by a white, black, and green New England and the gray and white of the lovely stone houses of the English settlers. . . . They love red barns, red cows, red apples, red brick houses, and red geraniums.**
> Frances Lichen,
> *Folk Art of Rural Pennsylvania*
>
>

COVERED BRIDGES

Pennsylvania has the honor of having the most covered bridges in the United States. These bridges were traditionally covered to protect the wooden bases from the elements. The longest covered bridge spanned the Susquehanna River between Columbia in Lancaster County and Wrightsville in York County. It measured over 5,600 feet and was burned down during the Civil War.

In Lancaster County, there are 28 surviving covered bridges, and most are open to traffic. The people of the area prize their bridges and give much care and maintenance to keeping them in good condition. See page 150 for a listing of a few of the bridges you might want to visit.

Be aware that covered bridges are built to accommodate one vehicle at a time. It is important to be sure that it's your turn to go through. Weight limits on the bridges generally prohibit large vehicles, including recreational vehicles such as motor homes.

ESPECIALLY FOR CHILDREN

The County has much to tickle the heart of the youngster in your life. There are chocolate and pretzel museums, factories to tour, and treats to taste. Numerous farm bed and breakfasts (see Chapter Two) encourage children to enjoy the life of the farm. There are trains to ride, model railroads to visit, and buggy rides to take. Dutch Wonderland Family Fun Park offers great rides for children under twelve, and the Hands-on-House north of Lancaster caters to the same age group. In the last section of this chapter on page 165, there is a list of family recreational activities that are perfect for children.

HISTORIC SIGHTS

Lancaster County is steeped in history. Historic sites tell the story of religious freedom, 19th century railroad travel, early American farm life, and the life of Lancaster County society during the 18th century.

RECREATION

Lounging in the backyard of a bed and breakfast or enjoying the peace in one of the many parks are wonderful ways to spend time in Lancaster County. The County also offers one of the best locations in the United States for bicycling. The beautiful countryside, covered bridges, and fairly flat terrain make for lovely riding. In its book *Scenic Tours of Lancaster County*, Lancaster Bicycle Touring, Inc. includes 26 planned tours around the County for those who prefer to ride on their own. They also offer guided tours as described on page 166.

In addition there are plenty of scenic spots for hiking, golfing, and wildlife watching. Hot air ballooning is a great adventure that offers another opportunity to admire the landscape, albeit from a higher vantage point.

Don't miss the last section of this book where I cover interesting things to see and do in other nearby counties.

BUGGY RIDES

ABE'S BUGGY RIDES
On Route 340
Bird-in-Hand, PA 17505
Open year round. Closed Sunday.
1/2 minute West of Bird-in-Hand

This popular buggy ride takes you on a two-mile tour through Amish country in an Amish family carriage. Celebrating their 28th year giving tourists rides, the plain guides are good sources of information about the area and the life of the Amish and Mennonites.

COVERED BRIDGES

HERR'S MILL BRIDGE

Ronks Road

Ronks, PA

From Route 30, go 1/2 mile South on Ronks Road.

Closed to cars, this is the only two-span bridge left in the County. It is currently a part of Mill Bridge Village and for a small fee you can walk across the bridge. Built in 1885, it spans Pequea Creek. A new bridge was built nearby and just about a mile south of Route 30 to carry South Ronks Road.

KAUFFMAN'S DISTILLERY BRIDGE

West Sun Hill Road

Manheim, PA

From Manheim, go West on PA 772. Turn left on West Sun Hill Road.

Built in 1874, this bridge crosses Chickies Creek. Southwest of Manheim on Sun Hill Road, off Route 72 North.

THINGS THAT ARE OPEN ON SUNDAY:

Artworks at Doneckers
Ephrata Cloister
Hands-on-House
Hershey Museum
HERSHEYPARK
Historic Lancaster Walking Tour
Landis Valley Museum
Le Petit Museum of Musical Boxes
Long's Park
Middle Creek Wildlife Management Area
National Toy Train Museum
Rail Road Museum of Pennsylvania
Rock Ford Plantation
Toy Train Museum
Village Green Miniature Golf
Watch & Clock Museum

PINETOWN BRIDGE

Leola, PA

Route 222 North (take Oregon Pike exit) on Pinetown Road.

Built in 1867 over the Conestoga River, this pretty bridge is near Leola.

ZOOK'S MILL BRIDGE

Log Cabin Road

Brownstown, PA

1 mile northwest of Brownstown

This bridge was built in 1849 and crosses the Cocalico Creek. East of Brownstown on Log Cabin Road. Take Route 272 North to Rose Hill Road to Log Cabin Road.

Especially for Children

Dutch Wonderland Entertainment Complex

2249 Route 30 East,
(Lincoln Highway)
Lancaster, PA 17602
Varies by season.
(717) 291-1888

Dutch Wonderland Family Fun Park has 44 acres of rides, shows, and gardens. It is especially enjoyable for families with younger children. The next door Wax Museum of Lancaster County

*Making new friends
at Dutch Wonderland Family Fun Park.*

gives a good introduction to the history of Lancaster County. Admission is $14.50 for children three to five years old and $19 for persons over five.

Hands-on-House

2380 Kissel Hill Road
Lancaster, PA 17601
June 15-Sept 15: Mon-Thurs & Sat 10-5. Fri 10-8. Sun 12-5. Sept 15-June 14: Tues-Thurs 11-4. Fri 11-8. Sat 10-5. Sun 12-5. (717) 569-KIDS

Children learn by playing and Hands-on-House encourages just that. There are eight hands-on exhibits for two- to ten-year-olds and adults to explore together. Admission is $4 per person regardless of age.

Lapp Valley Farm

244 Mentzer Road, (bet. Routes 23 and 340)
New Holland, PA 17557
Mon-Thurs 12-Dark. Fri 8-Dark. Sat 8-7. (717) 354-7988

Lapp Valley Farm is a must-see, particularly for ice cream lovers and families. (Does that leave anyone out?) The Lapp family produces some lusciously, delicious ice cream (16%-19% butterfat) from their herd of 50 Holsteins. They make 20 or more flavors, including peanut butter swirl, cookies and cream, raspberry, and the ever popular vanilla. Besides making your tastebuds happy, this is a fun place to walk around the grounds. You can watch the herd of deer in the meadow near the pond or hopefully catch sight of the two peacocks strutting about. The usual farm animals roam about, requiring petting, and tours of the dairy are available. Lapp Valley also sells its ice cream at the Green Dragon in Ephrata (see page 134) and at Kitchen Kettle Village in Intercourse (see page 139). No admission fee.

STRASBURG RAIL ROAD
Route 741
Strasburg, PA 17579

Mid-Mar thru Nov: Daily. Also the first two weekends in December. Call for train departure times. Reservations are necessary for the dining car. (717) 687-7522

You don't have to be a train buff to have a grand time riding cars pulled by a coal-burning locomotive through the lovely farmland near Strasburg. The rides take 45 minutes. Groff's Picnic Grove is a good spot to enjoy a picnic lunch, and catch the next train back to the station. Boxed picnic lunches can be purchased at the Dining Car Restaurant or the Sweet and Treat Shop. The train station was built at the turn of the century, but the railroad was founded in 1832. It was a shortline that connected Strasburg and Paradise, delivering passengers to the main line of the Pennsylvania Rail Road.

There are various carefully restored coaches to choose from for the nine-mile ride. Lunch is served on the luxurious dining car, the Lee E. Brenner, and dinners are served on Saturdays and Sundays. Reservations are required for dinner. The Marion is a plush parlor car where you can relax, have a beverage and snack, or you can choose an open-air observation car; a perfect spot for warm weather traveling. Admission fee is $4 for children ages three to eleven and $7.75 for persons twelve and above.

Riding through the countryside on the Strasburg Rail Road.

Photograph courtesy of Ron Bowman Visual Communications

THE TEDDY BEAR EMPORIUM

51 North Broad Street

Lititz, PA 17543

Mon-Sat 10-5. (717) 626-TEDI

Across the street from the Wilbur Chocolate Factory just North of the square.

> Both the county and the city of Lancaster were named by John Wright, chief magistrate, for his home shire of Lancashire, England.
>
> ◆◆◆

With its 3,500 different teddy bears, this shop has a bear for everyone. There is the Ty bear which stands three feet high and appears as though it would be very good company. There are bears dressed as proper English golfers, outfitted in chef whites, or decked out for a three alarm fire. Famous brands perfect for hugging include Gund, North American, Mary Meyer, and The Boyd Collection. For the bear collector, this emporium carries a complete line of Steiff collectibles. They ship all over the world. No admission fee.

Children will also enjoy visiting the Landis Valley Museum (page 161), the following section on trains, the pretzel and chocolate factories on pages 141 and 165, and HERSHEYPARK in nearby Dauphin County (page 179).

FOR TRAIN BUFFS

CHOO CHOO BARN

Route 741

Strasburg, PA 17579

Apr-Dec: Daily 10-4:30 for the display. The train store is open until 5. (717) 687-7911

The Choo Choo Barn takes model railroad building to new heights. Children love the animated 1,700 square foot display of Lancaster County, complete with a house on fire and firefighters rushing to the rescue. There is a three-ring circus and 17 continuously operating model trains. Admission fee is $2 for children five to twelve and $4 for persons thirteen and up.

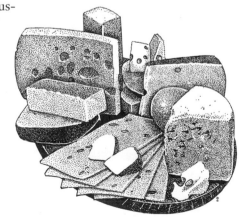

NATIONAL TOY TRAIN MUSEUM

300 Paradise Lane, (off Route 741)
Strasburg, PA 17579
May 1-Oct 31: Daily 10-5.
Call for off-season schedule. (717) 687-8976

The National Toy Train Museum is owned and run by the Train Collectors Association, which is a non-profit organization dedicated to the preservation and history of toy trains. The museum is housed in a replica train station with a shake roof, old-fashioned gaslights, and wooden benches. Inside, there are five working model train layouts of different gauges (the distance between the rails on the track), from HO to Standard. Hundreds of model trains are displayed in cases around the layouts. These trains date from the beginning of railroading back in the 19th century right up to the most modern trains of today. Cost is $3 for adults, $1.50 for kids 5 to 12, and kids 4 and under enter free. Next door is the Red Caboose Lodge (see page 78).

RAILROAD MUSEUM OF PENNSYLVANIA

Route 741
Strasburg, PA 17579
May-Oct: Daily 9-5. July & Aug: Daily 9-5. Sat-Sun 9-7. Nov-Apr: Closed Mon & holidays.
(717) 687-8628

1 mile east of Strasburg.

The Railroad Museum is a fascinating place for train lovers. There are some 150,000 railroading artifacts, including 83 locomotives on exhibit both inside and outside the building, demonstrating the history and technology of the railroad industry. They have the earliest steam locomotives as well as 20th century trains with their much later innovations. Visitors may enter the cab of a steam locomotive, see the state room of a private car, and walk through a Pullman sleeper. Admission is $6 for persons 13 years old to 59, 60 and older are $5.50. Children 6 to 12 are $4 and 5 and younger are free.
See page 152 for information about the Strasburg Rail Road.

Photograph courtesy of the Rail Road Museum of PA/PHMC

*Fine fellows of
the Railroad Museum of Pennsylvania.*

GETTING TO KNOW THE AMISH AND MENNONITES

THE AMISH EXPERIENCE

Plain & Fancy Farm
Route 340
Intercourse, PA 17505
Apr-June: Mon-Sat 8:30-5. July-Oct: Mon-Sat 8:30-8. Nov-Mar: Mon-Sat 10-5. Open Sundays 9:30-5 year round. (717) 768-8400
Between Intercourse and Bird-in-Hand.

Visit the Amish Experience for theater, a recreation of an Amish homestead, or to take a tour of the countryside. If viewing the production of *Jacob's Choice* please be aware that it probably isn't appropriate for children under five because of some noisy special effects. Admission for the theater is $6 for adults and $3.50 for children from ages four to eleven. The homestead admission is $4.50 for adults and $3 for children from ages four to eleven. To take their tour of the countryside, the fee is $17.95 for adults and $10.95 for children ages four to eleven.

MENNONITE INFORMATION CENTER

2209 Millstream Road
Lancaster, PA 17602
Mon-Sat 8-5. (717) 299-0954

The Mennonite Information Center is a good place to start for an introduction to the Plain People of Lancaster County. Features include a regularly shown documentary on the Amish and Mennonites, an exhibit on Mennonite and Amish history and faith, and numerous free brochures for your shopping, lodging, eating, and playing pleasure. This center also offers a tour guide service. For a two-hour minimum tour at $23 an hour, a guide will join you in your own car for a tour of the countryside. Guides will join bus tours for a minimum of three hours at $75. These tours allow you to see the Lancaster County farm country with a guide and to learn about the past, present, and future of the Plain People. Guides who speak French, Spanish, and German can be requested, but prior notice is essential.

> **Lancaster thrived after the Civil War, and by 1880 there were more than 200 industrial plants. Between 1919 and 1929, wages increased 76% compared to a national average of 11%.**
>
>

THE OLD COUNTRY STORE

3510 Old Philadelphia
Pike
Intercourse, PA 17534
Memorial Day to Labor
Day: Mon-Wed & Sat
9:30-5. Thurs & Fri 9:30-8.
9:30-5 the rest of the year.
(717) 768-7171

Photograph courtesy of Roger L. Berger

The Old
Country Store is a good
place to find Amish and
Mennonite handcrafted
gifts. Features include
a large inventory of
quilts, a room with fabrics for quilters, and many other handmade items. Pop
across the street to visit The People's Place also directed by Merle and Phyllis
Good. It offers a good introduction to the Amish and Mennonites.

THE PEOPLE'S PLACE

3513 Old Philadelphia Pike
Intercourse, PA 17534
Memorial Day to Labor Day: Mon-Sat 9:30-8. 9:30-5 the rest of the year. (717) 768-7171

The People's Place and The Old Country Store (across the street) are the
brainchild of co-directors, Merle and Phyllis Good. The People's Place offers an
introduction to the Plain People, housing a combination book store, hands-on
museum, and theater. A documentary film called "Who Are the Amish?" provides
thoughtful information about the Amish and Mennonites.

RED ROSE EXCURSIONS

255 Butler Avenue
Lancaster, PA 17601
Reservations required, best 3-4 days in advance. No Sunday tours. (717) 397-3175

A local plain person (either Amish, Mennonite, or Brethren) will answer
your questions, explain the sights, and give a rare insider view into the plain way
of life. The goal for Red Rose Excursions is to show visitors that: We are real
people who want you, the visitor, to get to know us Plain People in a personal way.
It is our goal to help each visitor get a real glimpse into our way of life while treat-
ing the area's Plain People with the respect and dignity they deserve. This tour
agency has been providing guides and tour packages for groups of all sizes for the
last 17 years. There is a two-hour minimum tour at a cost of $15 per hour. Tours
can be tailored to each group's interests and needs. It is important that you call
ahead to make reservations.

MUSEUMS AND HISTORIC SITES
AMERICAN MILITARY EDGED WEAPONRY MUSEUM
3562 Old Philadelphia Pike, (Route 340)
Intercourse, PA 17534
June 1-October 31: Mon-Sat 10-5:30. (717) 768-7185

This museum houses memorabilia, including bayonets, knives, and swords, from all periods of American military history.

CHARLES DEMUTH HOUSE AND GARDENS
120 East King Street
Lancaster, PA 17602
Mon-Sat 10-4. Sun 12-3. Closed January. (717) 299-9940
One block East of Penn Square in downtown Lancaster.

The Demuth foundation has restored the home of the artist, Charles Demuth (1883-1935), to its early 20th century look when Demuth lived and painted here. He studied in New York and Paris but painted most of his works in a small second floor studio in the rear of the house overlooking his garden. The house was built in the latter part of the 18th century and is one of the oldest in Lancaster. Visit Demuth's Tobacco Shop next door where Charles' family sold tobacco.

EICHER INDIAN MUSEUM
Ephrata Community Park
Cocalico Street
Ephrata, PA 17522
Mon-Sun 11-4. (717) 738-3084

Located in the Eicher Sisters' Cabin, this museum displays hand-crafted, authentic native artifacts from all around the country including dolls, jewelry, puzzles, tapes, mandellas, baskets, ceremonial rattles, and other antiques. One-of-a-kind special order items are available.

THADDEUS STEVENS

Elected to the House of Representatives in 1848 on the Whig ticket for Lancaster, Stevens was an uncompromising foe of slavery. Disillusioned with his party, he used his considerable influence to organize Pennsylvania's Republican Party. The Fourteenth Ammendment to the Constitution, upon which nearly all civil rights legislation is based, is his greatest achievement.

Photograph courtesy of Ron Bowman Visual Communications

Take a step back into the 18th century at Ephrata Cloister.

EPHRATA CLOISTER

632 West Main Street,
(Route 322)
Ephrata, PA 17522
Mon-Sat 9-5. Sun 12-5.
(717) 733-6600

The Ephrata Cloister was one of America's first communal societies. Founded in 1732 by Conrad Beissel, a German Pietist, the followers of this community separated from the Dunkard Church and came to Lancaster County. Housed in a unique collection of medieval style buildings, this group of religious celibates practiced an austere lifestyle that cultivated spiritual goals rather than material ones. The order was known for its papermaking, printing, calligraphic art, and charity. After the Revolutionary War, the Society declined due to a lack of leadership and a loss of interest in the life of self-denial. Ten of the buildings have been restored and interpreted to recreate this unusual 18th century village. I highly recommend that you visit this historic sight.

GAST CLASSIC MOTORCARS

421 Hartman Bridge Road, (Route 896)
Strasburg, PA 17579
May-Oct: Sun-Fri 9-6. Sat 9-7. Call for off season hours. (717) 687-9500
2.5 miles South of the intersection of Routes 30 and 896.

Gast Classic Motorcars has over 50 antique, classic, sports, and high performance cars. The exhibits include a 1948 Tucker, 1899 Roche, a Duesenberg, and a Messerschmitt.

HANS HERR HOUSE

1849 Hans Herr Drive
Willow Street, PA 17584
April 1-Dec 31: Mon-Sat 9-4. (717) 464-4438
South of Lancaster City off 222 South.

Built in 1719 and restored in 1970, the Hans Herr House is the oldest, surviving dwelling in Lancaster County which also served as the earliest meetinghouse for Swiss Mennonite immigrants. Personal tours are given to each party. The tour showcases the house, built in medieval German style, and

Photograph courtesy of Ron Bowman Visual Communications

provides a good introduction to early Mennonite history and culture. The first Saturday in August is Herr House Heritage Day and features demonstrations of rural life such as hearth cooking, gardening, and soap making.

HERITAGE CENTER OF LANCASTER COUNTY

Penn Square at King & Queen Streets
Lancaster, PA 17603
May thru Nov: Tues-Sat 10-4. They also have special holiday hours. (717) 299-6440
Located on Penn Square.

This decorative arts museum is a good introduction to the cultural history of Lancaster with its displays of 18th and 19th century furniture, quilts, silver, fraktur, and other folk art. The museum is housed in the Old City Hall and Masonic Lodge Hall, both dating back to the 1790s. The retail shop sells beautifully made gifts and crafts.

HERITAGE MAP MUSEUM

55 North Water Street
Lititz, PA 17543
Mon-Sat 10-5.
(717) 626-5002
2 blocks East of the square.

The Heritage Map Museum is a combination museum and auction house devoted to historic maps from the 15th to the 19th centuries. The owner, James Hess, has created a world class museum to display his collection of historic maps. Located in a beautifully renovated building that was once a paper box factory, the museum carefully displays 100 or so framed maps at any one time. A visit is an education in geography and history, as well as an aesthetic experience of the first order.

The museum also provides map consultations, appraisal services, and cartographic search services for collectors. A retail store sells antique maps, globes, and other cartographic items. Several times a year, the museum holds a rare map and book auction. See page 191 for information about the map auctions.

THE HISTORICAL SOCIETY OF THE COCALICO VALLEY

249 West Main Street
Ephrata, PA 17522
Mon, Wed & Thurs 9:30-6. Sat 8:30-5. (717) 733-1616

Housed in an impressive, 19th century, Victorian Italianate home, this historical society has a museum and a library. There is a daily $3 fee to use the library.

LANCASTER MENNONITE HISTORICAL SOCIETY

2215 Millstream Road
Lancaster, PA 17602
Tues-Sat 8:30-4:30. (717) 393-9745

Set up by the Lancaster Mennonite Conference in 1958, these research facilities specialize in Amish and Mennonite history. Of the 60,000 volumes, approximately 40,000 are on theology and some 20,000 are historical and genealogical in nature. An excellent resource for those who are doing genealogical, historical, denominational, or cultural research. The daily research fee is $3 for non-members.

In between their times of immigration for religious freedom throughout Europe, to Russia, Canada, and the United States, the Mennonites often found themselves in the enviable position of becoming quite successful. The Swiss Mennonites settled along the Rhine, and the area became known as the garden of Germany until the Thirty Years' War in the early 17th century. The farms of Russian Mennonites helped Ukraine earn the title the bread basket of Europe, interrupted by the Crimean War in 1854 and again by the Bolshevik Revolution in 1917. Today Lancaster County is known as The Garden Spot.

◆◆◆

LANCASTER MUSEUM OF ART

135 North Lime Street
Lancaster, PA 17602
Mon-Sat 10-4. Sun 12-4. (717) 394-3497

Housed in the Grubb Mansion built in 1845 for a noted ironmaster, Clement Bates Grubb, this museum focuses on new and national artists. It is also in the process of building a permanent collection of local artists' work.

LANDIS VALLEY MUSEUM

2451 Kissel Hill Road
Lancaster, PA 17601
Tues-Sat 9-5. Sun 12-5. (717) 569-0401

The Landis Valley Museum is especially enjoyable for families with children. Tour a cluster of 18 historical buildings that portray rural Pennsylvania German life as it was. Bachelor brothers Henry and George Landis began collecting everyday objects as young men. Now their 200,000-some items are part of this village, depicting colonial and federal life. Opened as a museum in 1925, visitors watch activities of bygone days: cooking, weaving, gunsmithing, and blacksmithing. Southern German style kitchen gardens are planted, and the museum sponsors the Heirloom Seed Project which keeps old varieties of fruits and vegetables from disappearing.

There are many interesting workshops and events throughout the year. A sampling is: Harvest Days (lace making, antique engines, and apple butter making), Herb Faire (the largest sale of traditional plants and herbs in Pennsylvania), and Days of Belsnickel (Pennsylvania German Christmas celebration).

The gift shop is open from mid March to December 30, and visitors are given a one-hour tour from November to April. Call for an activities schedule.

Basketmaking
at the Landis Valley Museum Faire.

> Pennsylvania grew more rapidly than any other colony. In 1776 it was third in population among the states but by 1790 it was second.
>
>

LE PETIT MUSEUM OF MUSICAL BOXES
255 West Market Street
Marietta, PA 17547
Mar-Dec: Mon-Sat 10-4. Sun 12-4.
Guided tours each hour. Maximum of 8 people. (717) 426-1154

I highly recommend visiting this museum, particularly if you're staying in the area. If you're not a music box aficionado before touring Le Petit Museum, you will be one by the time you're done! Located in the historic home of George Haddad and David Thompson, music boxes are sprinkled throughout the first floor rooms, among other carefully selected antiques. Mr. Thompson is an enthusiastic tour guide, and visitors are treated to a sampling of sounds from a diverse collection of some 75 music boxes. There is a French coin operated birdcage musical box, circa 1910; a Swiss cylinder musical box, circa 1840-1895; a German musical stein; and the star of the collection, a Regina 10 3/4 disc musical box from 1895. The sounds are beautiful, and Thompson's enthusiasm and thorough knowledge of the subject make a visit to this museum a pure delight. The backyard gazebo set in a pretty garden is open to guests from Memorial Day to Labor Day.

LEONARD & MILDRED ROTHMAN GALLERY
F&M/Steinman College Center (lower level)
Lancaster, PA 17604
Tues-Fri 11-4:30. Sat & Sun 12:30-4:30. (717) 291-3911

This gallery houses an interesting collection of Pennsylvania folk art and American decorative arts.

LITITZ MUSEUM
145 East Main Street
Lititz, PA 17543
Call for hours. (717) 627-4636
Across the street from the Moravian Church Square

The Lititz Historical Foundation operates a museum in the heart of Lititz. It consists of two historic buildings, one filled with museum displays and the other renovated to the way it looked in 1792 when it was occupied by Johannes Mueller and his family. The Muellers, like everyone in Lititz, were members of the religious community of the Moravian Church. Because of this unique heritage, the Lititz Museum has a fascinating story to tell.

MASCOT ROLLER MILL

Stumptown Road at Newport Road, (Route 772)
Bird-in-Hand, PA 17505
May thru Oct: Mon-Sat 9-4.

Built in 1760 by Jacob Becker, this mill was purchased by William Ressler in 1882. The Ressler family were the community millers in Mascot until 1977 when the family formed a foundation to preserve the mill and its family homestead next door. The free tour includes a six minute video about the Ressler family and an interview with W. Franklin Ressler, the last family member to work the mill. The mill is still used to grind corn for the Amish in the area. Mascot Park, across the road, makes a lovely place for a picnic along Mill Creek, see page 172.

NATIONAL WATCH AND CLOCK MUSEUM

514 Poplar Street
Columbia, PA 17512
Tues-Sat 9-4. May-Sept: Also open Sun 12-4. (717) 684-8261
From Route 30 West take Route 441 South to Columbia and make a left onto Poplar Street. Follow the signs.

Established in 1977, this museum is the headquarters of the National Association of Watch and Clock Collectors. Follow the history of timekeeping demonstrated by some 8,000 items from the 1600's to the current time. A library houses 2,500 research volumes, and areas of the museum highlight specific types of timepieces: German musical clocks, American clocks from 1780 to 1880, European pocket watches, American railroad watches, 19th century French clocks, and wristwatches.

Also see page 154 for the Rail Road Museum of Pennsylvania.

Photograph courtesy of The Watch and Clock Museum of the NAWCC

The amazing Engle Clock.

ROCK FORD PLANTATION & KAUFFMAN MUSEUM

881 Rock Ford Road

Lancaster, PA 17603

April 1-Nov 30: Tues-Sat 10-4. Sun 12-4. (717) 392-7223

Built circa 1792, Rock Ford Plantation rests on the wooded banks of the Conestoga River just south of Lancaster. The Georgian style brick mansion, built circa 1792, was home to General Edward Hand, Adjutant General of the Continental Army. It is an authentic example of refined country living during the 18th century.

ROUGH AND TUMBLE MUSEUM

Lincoln Highway East, (Route 30)

Kinzer, PA 17535

Call for hours. (717) 442-4249

They have a large collection of antique steam and gas engines and tractors. The museum sponsers five weekend events between April and October which include tractor pulls, a spring firing up of the engines, and a four day Thresherman's Reunion. Call for dates and times.

SICKMAN'S MILL

Sickman's Mill Road

Conestoga, PA

May-Labor Day: Daily 10-5. (717) 872-5951

South on 324 to Marticville. Make a right onto Frogtown Road for 1.3 miles.

Built on the Pequea Creek in 1793, this four-and-a-half story mill features farm machinery over 100 years old. There is also tubing on the creek.

WHEATLAND

The handsome home of President James Buchanan.

1120 Marietta Avenue, (Route 23 West) Lancaster, PA 17603 April 1-Nov 30: Daily 10-4:15. (717) 392-8721 Peek into the life of an American president in the 19th century. President James Buchanan purchased this house and its 22-acre farm in 1848 while serving as Secretary of State in President Polk's cabinet. He owned Wheatland until his death in 1868. Besides Buchanan's house, the tour includes the carriage house where a video is shown.

WILBUR CHOCOLATES CANDY AMERICANA MUSEUM

48 North Broad Street
Lititz, PA 17543
Mon-Sat 10-5. (717) 626-1131

Wilbur Chocolates is probably best known today for its Ideal Cocoa and Wilbur Chocolate Buds. Started in 1884 as H. O. Wilbur & Sons of Philadelphia, they moved to the present location in 1930 and became part of the Cocoa Division of Cargill, Inc. The factory is not open for tours, but an interesting Americana museum includes antique signs, confectioners' tools, old candy packaging, and a demonstration candy kitchen. If you're interested in how chocolate is made, a video in the back room of the museum explains the process. The plant produces approximately 11,120 million pounds of chocolate and other food ingredients annually. All goodies are for sale.

WRIGHT'S FERRY MANSION

Second & Cherry Streets
Columbia, PA 17512
May-Oct: Tues, Wed, Fri, Sat 10-3. (717) 684-4325

This mansion was built in 1738 for an English Quaker, Susanna Wright. The handsome stone mansion is furnished with an excellent collection of early 18th century Philadelphia furniture and English accessories pre-dating 1750. If you're traveling from a distance, you may want to call ahead to schedule a tour. However, small parties can generally be accommodated with about ten minutes notice.

RECREATION

BALLOONING

LANCASTER BALLOONS, INC.

1085 Manheim Pike, (Route 72)
Lancaster, PA 17601
May-Nov: Daily 2 hours after sunrise or 2 hours prior to sunset. (800) 478-4682

Lancaster Balloons has been giving people breathtaking views of Lancaster County for over 17 years. All pilots are commercially licensed, FAA balloon pilots and are residents of Lancaster County so they are able to point out the sights. There are four different flight packages: a half-hour flight

Photograph courtesy of Ron Bowman Visual Communications

after sunrise with a full breakfast, a one-hour flight with breakfast, a one-hour flight before sunset and dinner, or a one-hour evening flight without dinner. The location chosen for departure depends on the wind on a particular day. Gift certificates are available.

Up, up and away.

FISHING AND BOATING

MUDDY RUN RECREATION PARK

PA 372

Holtwood, PA

Open year-round daylight to dusk. (717) 284-4325

3/4 mile east of the Norman Wood Bridge, south of Holtwood.

Muddy Run Recreation Park is owned by the Philadelphia Electric Company and offers fishing, boating (no gas powered boats), camping, picnicking, ballfields, playground equipment, and an environmental information center.

BICYCLING

BICYCLE TOURING

LANCASTER BICYCLE TOURING, INC.

3 Colt Ridge Lane

Strasburg, PA 17579

(717) 396-0456

Lancaster County is a lovely place for bicycling, and Lancaster Bicycle Touring makes it easy. Tours are available for bicyclists of all experience levels and are led by local guides familiar with the terrain, as well as the sights. Tours are set up as one-, two-, or three-day excursions and include accommodations. There are twelve-speed and mountain bikes for rent. The helmets are free. If you want an unguided tour, the book *Scenic Tours of Lancaster*

County includes 26 planned bicycle tours of the County. Reservations must be made at least two weeks in advance. One-day group rides are normally held on Saturday and Sunday. Call for a brochure and details.

Long's Park in the city of Lancaster also makes a great place for cycling. See page 172 for more information.

BICYCLE SALES, RENTAL, AND REPAIR

BICYCLE WORLD
747 South Broad Street, (Route 501)
Lititz, PA 17543
Mon-Fri 10-8. Sat 10-4. (717) 626-0650

GREEN MOUNTAIN CYCLERY
285 South Reading Road
Ephrata, PA 17522
Mon-Wed 11-6, Thurs & Fri 11-8, Sat 10-4. (717) 859-2422

LANCASTER BICYCLE SHOP
1138 Manheim Pike, (Route 72)
Lancaster, PA 17601
Mon-Thurs 9-7. Fri 9-8. Sat 9-4.
(717) 299-9627

MARTIN'S BIKE SHOP
Route 322
Hinkletown, PA 17522
Mon, Thurs & Fri 9-9. Tues 9-5. Sat 9-4.
Closed Wed. (717) 354-9127

Photograph courtesy of Keith Baum

BOWLING

CLEARVIEW LANES
1990 West Main Street
Mount Joy, PA 17552
Open daily from 9 a.m. until 11 p.m. (717) 653-1818

DUTCH LANES
Route 272
Akron, PA 17501
Mon-Thurs 8 a.m.-12 mid. Fri 12 noon-12:30 a.m. Sat 8 a.m.-1 a.m. Sun 12 noon-11:30 p.m. (717) 859-1616

GARDEN SPOT

226 North Decatur Street

Strasburg, PA 17579

Mon-Thurs 9-12:30. Fri & Sat 9-2. Sun 9-10:30. (717) 687-7648

LEISURE LANES

3440 Columbia Avenue

Lancaster, PA 17603

Open 24 hours all year round except Christmas for bowling. (717) 392-2121

GOLF

FOUR SEASONS

949 Church Street

Landisville, PA 17538

Sunrise to sunset. (717) 898-0104

Has a regulation 18-hole golf course with pro shop and driving range.

FOX CHASE GOLF CLUB

300 Stevens Road

Stevens, PA 17578

Sunrise to sunset. (717) 336-3673

Voted one of the top public courses in the northeast.

HAWK VALLEY

1319 Crestview Drive

Denver, PA 17517

Sunrise to sunset. (717) 445-5445

Regulation 18-hole golf course with pro shop and a bed and breakfast.

LANCASTER HOST RESORT

2300 Lincoln Highway East, (Route 30)

Lancaster, PA 17602

Sunrise to sunset. (717) 299-5500

Hotel amenities include 27 holes of golf, swimming pools, and tennis courts.

Golf is a wonderful exercise.
You can stand on your feet for
hours watching someone else putt.

Will Rogers

OVERLOOK

2040 Lititz Pike

Lancaster, PA 17601

Sunrise to sunset. (717) 569-9551

Regulation 18-hole golf course, a pro shop, and restaurant.

TREE TOP

1624 Creek Road
Manheim, PA 17545
Sunrise to sunset. (717) 665-6262

Regulation 18-hole golf course.

Also see page 178 for information on the Country Club of Hershey.

HIKING

LANCASTER COUNTY CENTRAL PARK

South Duke Street
Lancaster, PA

With more than 500 acres, this park has many miles of hiking trails, a covered bridge, the garden of five senses, and an exhibit farm.

CHICKIES ROCK COUNTY PARK

Route 441
Chickies, PA

A favorite haunt for catching a view, this park over-looks the Susquehanna River and the towns of Wrightsville, Columbia, and Marietta. There are hiking trails that go out to the cliffs lining the river. Chickies is the name of a local Indian tribe.

The view from Chickies Rock.

SUSQUEHANNOCK STATE PARK

PA Dept. of Conservation & Natural Resources
1880 Park Drive
Drumore, PA 17518
(717) 548-3361

From Route 372 West of Buck, PA. Turn South on Susquehannock Drive to Park Drive.

Lovely views of the Susquehanna River are worth the drive to this 224-acre park in southern Lancaster County. Picnicking, horseback riding (bring your own horse), and hiking are other worthy attractions.

◆◆◆

MIDDLE CREEK WILDLIFE MANAGEMENT AREA

Hopeland Road

Kleinfeltersville, PA

Visitors' Center Hours: Mar 1-Nov 30: Tues-Sat 8-4. Sun 12-5. Closed Monday.

(717) 733-1512

PA turmpike exit 21, North 272 and take Route 897 West (left). Follow signs to visitors' center
and make a left onto Hopeland Road.

Middle Creek is a noteworthy bird and wildlife sanctuary. Watch tundra swan, snow geese, eagles, and all manner of water fowl. Check in at the Visitors' Center and pick up a hiking map noting points of interest and six different hiking trails, including a part of the Horseshoe Trail. The Horseshoe Trail originates in Valley Forge and goes for 134 miles to hook up with the Appalachian Trail just north of Hershey. Recreation includes boating (no motors), fishing, hunting, and picnicking. The grounds are open from dawn to dusk.

MINIATURE GOLF

VILLAGE GREEN

Route 741

Strasburg, PA 17579

Open daily Apr-Oct: Mon-Thurs 10-9:30. Sat 10-10:30. Hours vary off season. (717) 687-6933

One mile West of the center of Strasburg.

Miniature golf is played here on two, not so miniature, courses. The orange course is geared to beginners, and the gold course is more challenging.

Both games are played on elegantly, landscaped greens with a waterway that moves thousands of gallons of water in and about the courses. There are waterfalls to play through which adds to the fun, and the gold course also has traps, tunnels, water holes, and bridges to keep one on one's toes. There is a snack bar with hand-dipped ice cream, sandwiches, and soft drinks.

> Of all the great nations of Western Europe . . . Germany alone took no official part in the colonization of the New World. . . Previous to the American Revolution it is estimated that over 100,000 Germans and Swiss settled in Pennsylvania alone.
>
> Oscar Kuhns,
> *The German and Swiss Settlements of Colonial Pennsylvania*
>
> ◆◆◆

◆◆◆

OTHER MINIATURE GOLF COURSES TO VISIT:

HIGH SPORTS MINIATURE GOLF
Route 501
Lititz, PA 17543
Dawn until dusk. (717) 626-8318
1 mile North of Lititz on the East side of Route 501

ZINN'S PARK
Route 272
Denver, PA 17517
(717) 336-3891
North at Exit 21 of the PA Turnpike

PARKS AND GARDENS

EPHRATA COMMUNITY PARK
Oak Street
Ephrata, PA 17522

This park, near the Ephrata Cloister, has a summer theatre playhouse and the Eicher Indian Museum.

LITITZ SPRINGS PARK
North Broad Street
Lititz, PA 17543
Daily 6:00 a.m. until 30 minutes after sunset.
One block north of the intersection of 501 North and 772 East.

A small, peaceful park, in the heart of historic Lititz, this is a lovely place to spend a sunny afternoon. A stone-lined stream runs the length of the park, offering a haven for the many ducks that summer here. All sorts of playground equipment attracts children.

Picnic tables, with or without shelter, attract the hungry. Established in 1843 by the Moravian congregation, the park was given to the town of Lititz in 1956. A highlight of the year's activities is the annual Fourth of July Celebration. It is billed as the oldest, continuing Fourth of July celebration in America.

Life is good in Lititz Springs Park.

LONG'S PARK

1441 Old Harrisburg Pike
Lancaster, PA
Park: Mon-Sun 7-10.
Barn: Mon-Fri 10-3. Sat 10-6. (717) 397-8517
Route 30 bypass to the Harrisburg Pike exit. Watch for signs.

Long's Park is graced by a tree-lined lake populated by duck and geese of various kinds. For children there is a barn with goats, donkeys, pigs, and chickens and a playground for releasing excess energy. Picnic tables ring the lake and pavilions are available with reservations (717) 291-4841. A concession stand offers up standard fast food fare, and the circular drive makes an excellent place to bicycle. During the summer months, there are numerous Sunday concerts at 7:30 p.m. An annual crafts festival, held over the Labor Day weekend, brings nearly 200 artists and crafts people from around the country together. No alcohol is permitted, and dogs must be on a leash.

> **Hans Herr, a Swiss Mennonite, was one of the first settlers of Lancaster County. He acted as an agent to aid in the settlement of his countrymen.**
>
>

MASCOT PARK

Route 772 & Stumptown Road
Bird-in-Hand, PA 17505

Across Route 772 from Mascot Roller Mill. Go north on 772 to the next intersection and pick up a sandwich at Diane's Deli. Return to the picnic site, and enjoy the reservoir of Mill Creek. Touring the nearby mill is also a good way to spend a half hour.

See page 178 for information about Longwood Gardens in Chester County.

SWIMMING

THE LAKE AT MOUNT GRETNA

Route 117
Mt. Gretna, PA 17064
Open Memorial Day to Labor Day: 11:30-6:30. (717) 964-3130
West of PA 72

THAT'S ENTERTAINMENT

CHAMELEON CLUB

223 North Water Street
Lancaster, PA 17603
Wed-Sat nights. Times vary. (717) 393-7133

This hip and happening club offers up artists such as Joan Jett, alternative music, and dance parties. Call and listen to their weekly lineup, and discover why this is one the County's most popular spots for nightclub entertainment.

EPHRATA PLAYHOUSE IN THE PARK

Oak Street
Ephrata, PA 17522
(717) 733-7966

Begun in 1956, the Ephrata Playhouse presents an extensive repertoire of main stage productions. See anything from classic American musical theater to zany off-Broadway camp. Tickets run from $10 to $15.

FULTON OPERA HOUSE

12 North Prince Street
Lancaster, PA 17603
Call for current offerings and show times. (717) 394-7133
On the corner of Prince and King Streets in downtown Lancaster.

The Fulton Opera House is the stage for the Lancaster Symphony Orchestra, the Fulton Academy Theatre, and the Lancaster Opera Company. Highlights for the 1996-1997 season include *Big River*, *DRAGONWINGS*, and *Bye Bye Birdie*.

TIMOTHY DERSTINE'S BAKED OATMEAL (THE AUTHOR'S BROTHER)

1/4 cup butter
1/8 cup oil
1/2 cup brown sugar (or 1/2 cup honey)
1 egg (or 2 eggs, one yolk)
1 cup milk
2 teaspoons baking powder
1 teaspoon salt
1 cup Maypo
2 cups rolled or quick oats

Mix butter, oil, sugar, eggs, and milk. Add other ingredients and mix well. Bake in 8x10-inch pan or individual bowls at 350°F for 30 to 35 minutes. Decrease oven temperature by 25° if honey is used. Three eggs can be used if the recipe is doubled. Other options include using a mixture of quick, rolled, and steel cut oats. Serve with milk, fruit, preserves and/or nuts. Serves 6.

GRETNA THEATRE

P.O. Box 519

Mount Gretna, PA 17604

(717) 964-3627

Summer is the time for music, romance, and comedy at the Mount Gretna Playhouse. A typical lineup might include *Ain't Misbehavin'*, *Arsenic and Old Lace*, or children's theater held on Saturday mornings. Concerts by Broadway stars are also the norm.

ITALIAN VILLA COMEDY CLUB & RESTAURANT

2331 Lincoln Highway, (Route 30)

Lancaster, PA 17602

Fri at 9. Sat at 8 & 10:15. Sun at 8. (Free with dinner.) (717) 397-4973

JUKEBOX NIGHTCLUB

1703 New Holland Pike

Lancaster, PA 17602

Fri & Sat 8 p.m.-2 a.m. (717) 394-9978

1/2 mile East of Route 30.

There is an eclectic mix of dance music from the 50's through the 80's with a $2 cover charge.

LIVING WATERS "ADVENTURE" THEATRE

Route 896

Strasburg, PA 17579

Call for show times. (717) 687-7800

1 mile south of Route 30

Living Waters provides entertainment for the whole family. Seasonal shows include live actors, elaborate waterfalls, computerized lights, and a backdrop of panoramic photography on an 80-foot stage. The shows feature the celebration of America's blessings and biblical dramas. Shows last just under two hours. Tickets for adults are $20

Living Waters "Adventure" Theatre

Photograph courtesy of Sight and Sound Living Waters Theatre

and for children $10 for shows held Monday through Friday. On Saturday nights all seats are $25.

In early 1997, the owners of another Living Waters Theatre suffered the loss of another theatre, due to a fire, which housed Sight and Sound. This theatre held live stage shows with a Christian theme, the most popular one was a show called *Noah*. A larger theatre is being built and the expectation is that they will open in the middle of 1998 with an encore production of *Noah*.

THE VILLAGE

205 North Christian Street

Lancaster, PA 17603

Open Mon, Wed-Sat, beginning most nights at 9. (717) 397-5000

This happening dance club tends toward the alternative music scene with bands like Johnny O and the Classic Dogs of Love, Fuel, or Mint, but there are oldies nights as well. There is a small cover charge.

TOURS

AMISH COUNTRY TOURS

Plain & Fancy Farm

Route 340

Intercourse, PA 17505

Departs at 8:30 a.m. Wed from June-Oct. Returns between 5 & 5:30 p.m.

(717) 768-8400

Between Intercourse and Bird-in-Hand.

> The first gourmets of America were Pennsylvania Dutchmen, and the first dining club in the New World was organized in Philadelphia in 1732, a city which was then a center of good food and has never lost its reputation in this field.
>
> Edwin Valentine Mitchell,
> *It's an Old Pennsylvania Custom*
>
>

Along with tours of the Lancaster countryside, Amish Country Tours provides tours to Philadelphia. The Philadelphia tour includes Independence Hall, Liberty Bell, the Bourse for shopping, U.S. Mint, Ben Franklin's grave, Betsy Ross House, and Christ Church where Ben Franklin attended. Call for reservations to ensure a seat. The fee for adults is $17.95 and $10.95 for children ages four to eleven.

HISTORIC LANCASTER WALKING TOUR

Southern Market Center, Queen & Vine Streets

Lancaster, PA 17603

April thru Oct: Mon-Sat 10 & 1:30. Sun 1:30. (717) 392-1776

If you're interested in the historic highlights of downtown Lancaster city, this 90-minute tour is just the thing.

See the Amish and Mennonite section of this chapter on page 155 for more tours.

Photograph courtesy of Ron Bowman Visual Communications

Historic Lancaster Walking Tour.

THINGS TO SEE AND DO OUTSIDE LANCASTER COUNTY

BERKS COUNTY

CONRAD WEISER HOMESTEAD

Route 422

Womelsdorf, PA 19567

Wed-Sat 9-5. Sun 12-5. (610) 589-2934

Conrad Weiser served as a diplomat, judge, soldier, and one of Pennsylvania's most important Indian treaty makers. His 18th century house, a National Historic Landmark in nearby Berks County, is set on 26 acres of grounds designed by the Olmstead Brothers. A small fee is charged for a guided tour.

CORNWALL IRON FURNACE

Rexmont Road at Boyd Street, (Route 322)

Cornwall, PA 17016

Tues-Sat 9-5. Sun 12-5. During the off season they close at 4. To take the last tour, you must arrive one hour prior to closing time. (717) 272-9711

In operation from 1742 to 1883, Cornwall Furnace is a well-preserved example of a 19th century charcoal ironmaking factory. Its primary products were pig iron, stoves, farm tools, and cast cannon barrels for the Revolutionary and Civil Wars. The town of Cornwall, built as a complete community for the ironworkers, is also a fascinating part of this visit. Its charming, stone houses, built right next to the street, make you feel as though you've fallen into a time warp.

The Pennsylvania German Society

440 Daniel Boone Road
Birdsboro, PA 19508
Tues & Thurs 9-3. (610) 582-1441

Founded in 1891, The Pennsylvania German Society is an educational and literary organization. Its purpose is "to preserve, advance, and disseminate knowledge of the culture of German-speaking immigrants and their descendants." Their library is open two days a week and is located at the Daniel Boone homestead.

Rodale Research Institute

611 Siegfriedale Road
Maxatawny, PA 19538
Farm tours daily: May 1-Oct 15: Mon-Sat at 11 & 2, Sun at 2 only. Store hours: Mon-Sat 9-5, Sun 12-5. (610) 683-6383

Tour this leading facility for organic farming and garden research. On the 333-acre Experimental Farm, the focus is on eliminating agricultural chemicals from soil and water. In addition to tours, Rodale Research Institute offers workshops (for example: Butterfly Gardening or Using Healing Herbs), garden tours, exhibits, nature walks, picnic areas, and a bookstore.

Chester County

Brandywine Battlefield

Route 1
Chadds Ford, PA 19317
Tues-Sat 9-5. Sun 12-5. Last tour is at 4. (610) 459-3342

Tour the battlefield where General Washington fought the British to block their occupation of Philadelphia in September 1777. Visit the houses occupied by Washington and Lafayette and a visitors' center that contains extensive exhibits.

Brandywine River Museum

Route 1 at Route 100
Chadds Ford, PA 19137
Daily 9:30-4:30. (610) 388-2700

This museum specializes in 19th and 20th century American art, including the most comprehensive collection of works by the Wyeth family. Art by Maxfield Parish, Howard Pyle, and Charles Dana Gibson is also featured here.

Lancaster made valuable contributions to the Revolutionary War, including the Kentucky Rifle, a weapon much more accurate than the more commonly used musket. One hundred and fifty Conestoga wagons were purchased for General Braddock and his march against the French in 1755.

LONGWOOD GARDENS

Photograph courtesy of L. Albee/Longwood Gardens

The Orangery at Longwood Gardens.

Route 1
Kennett Square, PA 19348-0501
Open 365 days a year. The grounds open at 9 and the conservatory at 10. Call for closing times. (610) 388-1000, ext. 711
Approximately 3 miles Northeast of Kennett Square.

If you're into gardens or even if you're not, Longwood Gardens is worth a drive. Consisting of 1,050 outdoor acres and 20 indoor gardens, Longwood offers beautiful blooms throughout the year. Founded by Pierre S. DuPont, the gardens boast 11,000 different kinds of plants, illuminated fountains, an indoor children's garden, outdoor theatre, and The Terrace Restaurant and Cafe.

MUSHROOM MUSEUM AT PHILLIPS PLACE

909 E. Baltimore Pike, (Route 1)
Kennett Square, PA 19348
Open Daily 10-6. (610) 388-6082

The United States is one of the world's top mushroom growing countries. Phillips Place has been at the forefront of growing wild mushrooms commercially. With its movies, exhibits, and slide presentations, this museum is a great place for mushroom lovers to learn the history and lore of this delicacy. It is especially fun to see mushrooms at various stages of development.

DAUPHIN COUNTY

COUNTRY CLUB OF HERSHEY

600 West Derry Road
Hershey, PA 17033
(717) 534-3450

Founded in 1930 by Milton S. Hershey, Country Club of Hershey boasts one of Pennsylvania's best public golf courses and also offers a pro shop, lodging, and candlelight dining. There are courses for the amateur as well as the champion golfer. Certified PGA teachers are on hand to help perfect your game. Facilities include tennis courts, locker rooms, sauna, and banquet rooms, and the clubhouse has 18 guest rooms with views of the golf course.

HERSHEY GARDENS

Hotel Road

Hershey, PA 17033

Open daily Apr-Dec. (717) 534-3492

Across from The Hotel Hershey.

Hershey Gardens has 23 acres of botanical gardens that are open spring, summer, and fall. There are guided and unguided tours for visitors.

HERSHEY MUSEUM

170 West HERSHEYPARK Drive

Hershey, PA 17033

Daily 10-5. Memorial Day-Labor Day: Open until 6. (717) 534-3439

A visit to this museum is particularly intriguing for those interested in the story of Milton Hershey and his chocolate making empire. There is also an outstanding Pennsylvania German collection, including original furniture, ceramics, textiles, and folk art, along with a significant collection of Native American artifacts, clothing, and ceremonial objects.

HERSHEYPARK

100 West HERSHEYPARK Drive

Hershey, PA 17033

Open daily from the end of May until Labor Day. The park opens at 10:30 and the closing time varies. (800) HERSHEY

Kids of all ages love HERSHEYPARK. The newest ride is the Wildcat, a state-of-the-art wooden roller coaster that careens over two acres. Going on its 91st season, this theme park also has 50 other rides, many games of skill, and, of course, food. Entertainers take the stage with acts that range from

Photograph courtesy of HERSHEYPARK

The Wild Cat at HERSHEYPARK.

dance revues to a dolphin show. Included in your admission to HERSHEY-PARK is a visit to the adjacent ZooAmerica with its 200 animals native to North America.

MONTGOMERY COUNTY

BARNES FOUNDATION MUSEUM AND ARBORETUM

300 North Latch's Lane

Merion, PA 19066

Thurs 12:30-5. Fri-Sat 9:30-5. First come, first served basis. Reservations for groups of 10 or more. (610) 667-0290

Take the Schulykill Expressway (76) to City Line Avenue (Route 1) South. Make a right onto Merion and a right onto Latch's Lane.

The Barnes Foundation houses one of the finest collections of early French modern and post-modern impressionist paintings in the entire world. The Foundation was established in 1922 by Dr. Albert Coombs Barnes to "promote advancement of education and appreciation of the fine arts." The art gallery contains more than 2,500 art objects, including more than 800 paintings. Dr. Barnes has died, leaving an unusual will which has made this very special collection rather inaccessible. I recommend that you call ahead to make sure they are open on the Thursday or Friday of your choice and verify the procedures for viewing this collection.

> And I must tell you that there is a breathing, hungering, seeking people, solitarily scattered up and down the great land of Germany, where the Lord hath sent me.
>
> William Penn,
> *Works, London, 1726*
>
>

The Barnes Foundation's land had an existing arboretum established by a previous owner, Captain Joseph Lapsley Willson in 1887. Dr. and Mrs. Barnes purchased the 13-acre property with the understanding that they would maintain the arboretum. The collection has a great diversity of species, including rare and mature plants, and annual and formal gardens.

BOYERTOWN MUSEUM OF HISTORIC VEHICLES

28 Warwick Street

Boyertown, PA 19512

Tues-Sun 9:30-4:30. (610) 367-2090

You don't have to be a car lover to enjoy this museum. Not only are there 75 rare vehicles, but you are taken through the evolution of road transportation from the horseless carriage to an electric vehicle exhibit. There are custom cars by Fleetwood, high wheel bicycles, children's vehicles, and craftsman's tools.

◆◆◆

YORK COUNTY

HARLEY DAVIDSON MUSEUM

1425 Eden Road, (Route 30)

York, PA 17402

Mon-Fri 10 a.m.-1:30 p.m. (Museum tour only. 12:30 p.m.)

Sat Museum Tours 10, 11, 1-2. No plant tours. (717) 848-1177 (press 1, then ext. 5900)

1 mile East of Exit 9E of Interstate 83.

Harley Davidson has the distinction of being the only American-based motorcycle manufacturer. The York plant, their largest facility, covers 200 acres and employs 2,400 employees. Tour the plant and museum, and learn about America's favorite motorcycles. Plant tours show the final assembly of these bikes. Admission is free, but call ahead to make sure tours are scheduled during the time of your visit.

SHOPPING

5

Antiques 188
Auctions 191
Books 193
Country Stores 196
Galleries 197
General 198
Handcrafted Furniture 199
Handcrafted Gifts 205
Knives 213
Outlets 213
Quilts 218
Quilting Materials 221
Consignment Shops 222

CHAPTER FIVE: SHOPPING

> **Pennsylvania was the first state to pull itself out of the mud. In 1792, it authorized a private company to construct a macadamized road from Philadelphia to Lancaster, a distance of 62 miles, and this turnpike, completed in 1794 at a cost of $465,000, was the first hard-surfaced road of any consequence in America.**
>
> Edwin Valentine Mitchell,
> *It's an Old Pennsylvania Custom*
>
>

Unfortunately, there are far too many mass production shops capitalizing on the Pennsylvania Dutch, all with designs on the unsuspecting traveler's cash. Staying at an area bed and breakfast and tapping the owner's knowledge of interesting, small, off-the-beaten-path businesses is one way to avoid mass produced goods. There truly is something for everyone when it comes to shopping in Lancaster County. Bargain hunters may choose from a number of large outlets, plentiful antique stores, and frequent auctions.

Lancaster County is full of serendipitous moments, whether chatting with an Amish woman about her quilts or shopping at a gaslit, country store. I've found that the further you stray from the major highways, the more rewarding the experiences and the finds.

ANTIQUES

Whether you are a seasoned antique buyer looking for an investment, a homeowner needing to furnish a house, or simply shopping for fun, Lancaster County has an antique spot for you. If your time is limited and you want to make one stop, weekends in Adamstown, also known as "Antiques Capital U.S.A.," might be the place for you. On most weekends, the town has over 3,000 dealers of 18th and 19th century collectibles and antiques. Three times a year (see Calendar of Events on pages 17 and 20) an antiques extravaganza adds another 4,800 dealers from across the country. An unbelievable array of antiques draws some of America's top collectors.

AUCTIONS

I am particularly fond of auctions. Whether or not you're interested in buying, auctions are a great way to glimpse the lives of Lancaster area residents. Country food beckons, plain folks gossip among themselves, and bargains abound. There are still many people in this area who make their living by farming, and the auctions often involve items such as livestock, farming equipment, lumber, and produce.

The local newspaper is a good source for auction information. A number of the larger towns have a weekly paper that will prove useful, but the two largest newspapers covering the County are the *Lancaster New Era* and the *Intelligencer Journal*. Friday's edition is especially good for checking auction listings.

FOLK ART

Pennsylvania German folk art motifs can be found on fraktur (pronounced frock-tur), fabric samplers, painted furniture, or pottery. Images of the sun, stars, birds, flowers, and the tree of life are commonplace. Most of these decorative items were traditionally made or commissioned by the Pennsylvania Germans, many of whom were not plain, and brought their love of bright colors from Germany.

Fraktur is a combination of words and colorful artwork sometimes used to beautify religious writing or to record important family milestones such as births, baptisms, or marriages. For the Pennsylvania Germans, this decorative calligraphy, was something they brought with them to the colonies and was a continuation of the practice of manuscript illumination begun in medieval times. Many of the motifs have meanings and were selected by the artist for their appropriateness to the occasion or their significance to the family. In answer to my question, "did the Amish and Mennonites both practice fraktur?" my Amish born editor Louise Stoltzfus made the following comments, "yes, and very prolifically. Some of the finest surviving examples were done by Mennonite artists, and there are numerous Mennonite fraktur artists still plying the trade. The Amish practiced a much more restrained version, creating a clear genre of Amish style fraktur."

Scherenschnitte, cutting paper to make intricate, lacy patterns, is another method of making decorative birth and marriage certificates. These certificates were often framed and displayed in the home.

Other decorative and practical handmade items included lace, redware pottery, tinware, woven coverlets, and baskets. A number of Lancaster County residents still make a living creating redware pottery. This was pottery used in the kitchen during the 18th and

A fraktur.

early 19th centuries. It was called redware because the clay was red. Basic redware for daily use was made with little or no decoration.

Highly decorated redware is called slipware and appears in the form of decorative plates, jars, and other tableware. Like fraktur, decorative plates were used to commemorate special occasions and sometimes featured elaborate designs and text. Sgraffito is the method of producing a design on ceramics by incising the outer coating of slip or glaze to expose the underlying clay, thereby adding color and design. Sgraffito appears on many redware pieces.

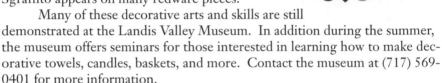

Many of these decorative arts and skills are still demonstrated at the Landis Valley Museum. In addition during the summer, the museum offers seminars for those interested in learning how to make decorative towels, candles, baskets, and more. Contact the museum at (717) 569-0401 for more information.

HANDCRAFTS

Furniture making, for the Amish and Mennonites in particular, is an acceptable alternative to farming. Many small, local businesses make good, solid, and very reasonably priced furniture. Thankfully, there are also families continuing the tradition of fine cabinetmaking in Lancaster County. You can find beautifully made intricate Victorian lowboys, 17th century Chippendale and Queen Anne reproductions, and many examples of the simple, but elegant, 18th century Lancaster County furniture. Many of these businesses are accustomed to shipping furniture throughout the United States.

OUTLETS

Outlet shopping is plentiful in and around Lancaster County. Tanger Factory Outlet Center and Rockvale Square Outlets are great bargain hunting destinations. Reading, slightly north of Lancaster County, boasts one of America's most popular outlet destinations, drawing some eight million shoppers annually. Housed in restored, turn of the century, textile buildings, Reading's VF Factory Outlet is billed as the "Outlet Capital of the World."

> Until late in the eighteenth century very little tinware was used in the colonies, and what there was was very expensive and highly regarded. . . To please their country clientele, they [the tinsmiths] devised, besides the coffeepots and teapots, brightly colored stencilled trays and other quaintly decorated objects in the pale metal which have a distinctly peasant quality.
>
> Frances Lichen,
> *Folk Art of Rural Pennsylvania*
>
>

QUILTS

For women throughout the world, quilting has been an activity engaged in not just for "pretty," but also to use scraps of material and worn-out clothing. Amish women began quilting in earnest during the middle of the 19th century after the sewing machine was invented. Amish quilts generally are not hand pieced but are hand quilted. For many of us, an appreciation for the beauty and creativity that goes into a quilt has replaced the strictly functional use of quilts. Though many quilts are still used to keep us warm, many are also hung as decoration.

Traditional Amish quilts were made from dark, jewel-tone colors. While quilting was once done primarily for the family, many Amish women today are not only making quilts to sell, but they have also opened retail quilt shops with regular business hours. This allows these women to augment the family income and stay at home at the same time. Many non-Amish quilt lovers like lighter colors, and this preference is reflected in the quilts available for sale today. Contemporary quilt patterns often also tend to be more intricate, using smaller pieces, than those made primarily from scraps of fabrics.

Some things to keep in mind when looking for a quilt:

- ◆ Buy from a reputable shop.
- ◆ Make sure the quilt is made by hand.
- ◆ The smaller the stitches, the more valuable the quilt.
- ◆ A quilt made by one person is also more valuable because the stitches will be uniform.
- ◆ The more intricate the pattern and the better the color combinations, the better and more valuable the quilt.

When shopping in Lancaster County, please keep in mind that many businesses are closed on Sundays, particularly those owned and operated by the Amish and Mennonites.

ANTIQUES

ANTIQUES SHOWCASE AT THE BLACKHORSE
Route 272
Denver, PA 17517
Mon 9-5. Tues-Thurs 10-5. Fri-Sat 9-6. (717) 335-3300
PA turnpike exit 21, Route 272 North.

Featuring some 200 dealers with fine antiques and collectibles that fit into a showcase. There are also gallery pieces here and there.

CLOCK TOWER ANTIQUES
Route 272
Adamstown, PA 19501
Thurs 10-5. Fri & Sat 10-6. Sun 7:30-5. Mon-10-5.
(717) 484-4385
1 1/2 miles North of PA turnpike exit 21.
Half a mile North on 272.

Located next to Stoudt's Antique Mall, Clock Tower Antiques has 100 showcases and ten individual shops and is an excellent place to stop.

FREY'S ANTIQUES
209 West Main Street
Strasburg, PA 17579
Mon-Sat 9-5. (717) 687-6722

At Frey's you'll find quality 18th and 19th century furniture, stoneware, redware, china, glass, primitives, and folk art.

HONEYBROOK CLASSICS INC.
Route 10
Honeybrook, PA 19344
Showroom hours by appointment only. (610) 273-2445
On Route 10 just south of 322

Shopping for a '64 Mustang or a '58 Studebaker Lark? If so, you'll probably be surprised to learn that an excellent dealer is located out in the country near the Lancaster County and Delaware County border. Honeybrook Classics specializes in antique cars that have been fully renovated. The day I went by they had a 1969

> **I base most of my fashion taste on what doesn't itch.**
> Gilda Radner
>
>

HEX SIGNS

Part of the Pennsylvania Dutch habit of decoration, hex signs are native to the counties surrounding Lancaster: Lehigh, Berks, and Montgomery. Lancaster barns generally do not display these colorful signs.

Mustang Boss 429 and a 1965 Shelby Cobra 427 (very nice!). Also, a 1956 Corvette convertible, an MG sports coupe, a Rambler Nash sedan, a 1937 Ford roadster, and a 1964 Corvette fastback. If you're in the market for cars such as these, Honeybrook Classics is the place to go.

LANCASTER COUNTY ANTIQUES & COLLECTIBLE MARKET

Route 272
Denver, PA 17517
Daily: Mon-Thurs 9-5. Fri & Sat 9-9. Sun 9-8:30. (717) 336-2701
PA turnpike exit 21. Half a mile North on 272.

Lancaster County Antiques is the County's oldest co-op featuring more than 70 dealers.

OAK FURNITURE AND ANTIQUES

Georgetown Road, (Route 896)
Georgetown, PA 17503
Mon-Sat 8-6. (717) 786-7852
5 miles South of Strasburg.

This Amish owned store is a bargain hunter's paradise. Spread out between three buildings that straddle Route 896, there are rooms where oak reigns; they are chock-full of new and used country furniture and antiques. This is a must-see if you're furniture hunting. Please note that they list their address as Bart which is the same as Georgetown.

RENNINGER'S

Route 272
Adamstown , PA 19501
Sunday 7:30-5. (717) 336-2177
1/2 mile north of PA turnpike exit #21.

Sunday is the day for Renninger's Antique & Collectors Market with 375 dealers indoors. During the spring, summer, and fall there are up to 400 dealers displaying their wares outdoors as well.

RENNINGER'S ANTIQUE & FLEA MARKET
Noble Street
Kutztown, PA 19530
Saturday 8:30-5. (717) 385-0104
1 mile South of the center of Kutztown. Between Allentown and Reading off Route 222.

Located in Berks County, this location has 250 indoor booths and several large, outdoor pavilions to offer bargain hunters shelter from the weather throughout the summer. Special events such as craft shows and antique extravaganzas featuring 1,200 dealers from around the country are held periodically. Call for dates.

RICE ANTIQUES
At Stoudt's Antique Mall
Route 272
Adamstown, PA 19501
Sun & Mon 1-5 or by appointment. (717) 627-3780

One of Pennsylvania's leading dealers in quality 19th and 20th century furniture, tall clocks, music boxes, and accessories. Authenticity is guaranteed. They also have a location in Brickerville.

RICE ANTIQUES
Route 272
Brickerville, PA 17522
Sun & Mon 1-5 or by appointment. (717) 627-3780

SHUPP'S GROVE
Route 897
Adamstown, PA 19501
Apr-Oct: Sat & Sun 7 a.m.-5 p.m. (717) 484-4115
PA Turnpike exit 21, right onto Route 272, right onto 897 for 1 mile.

Shupp's Grove is an outdoor flea market that covers several acres. Vendors sell a wide variety of treasures and have a wide spread in quality.

SOUTH POINTE ANTIQUES
Route 272
Adamstown, PA 19501
Thurs 9-5. Fri 9-8. Sat & Sun 9-6. Mon 9-5. (717) 484-1026
PA turnpike exit 21. One block south on 272.

South Pointe is just two miles south on Route 272 from Stoudt's Antique Mall. There are 135 dealers featuring quality antiques. Especially strong in art deco and art pottery.

STOUDT'S ANTIQUE MALL
Route 272
Adamstown, PA 19501
Sunday 8-5. (717) 484-4385
1 1/2 miles North of PA turnpike exit 21.

With 400 dealers selling everything from the high end to the high kitsch, this is my choice (when I have time for only one stop) for antique shopping. Especially exciting are the Antiques Extravaganzas held on the last Saturdays and Sundays of April, June, and September. The number of dealers swells by the hundreds. (Also almost universally known as Black Angus because of the restaurant on site).

AUCTIONS

GORDONVILLE FIRE COMPANY AUCTION
Old Leacock Road between Route 30 and 340
Gordonville, PA 17529
(717) 768-3869

This auction is held twice a year on the second Saturday of March and the fourth Saturday of September. The spring event includes the sale of quilts, farm machinery, livestock, furnishings, antiques, and crafts. Quilts, buggies, sleighs, wagons, and building materials are under the gavel in September.

HERITAGE MAP MUSEUM
55 North Water Street
Lititz, PA 17543
Mon-Sat 10-5. (717) 626-5002

The Heritage Map Museum is a combination museum and auction house devoted to historic maps from the 15th to the 19th centuries. The owner, James Hess, has created a world class museum to display his collection of historic maps. Several times a year, the museum holds a rare map and book auction. People come from all over the world to watch the sale of maps such as the Ptolemy map of 1535 or the Map Atlas for the Official Records of the Civil War. Call for auction dates. See page 159 for more information about the museum.

HORST AUCTION CENTER
Corner of Route 322 and Durlach Road
Ephrata, PA 17522
Wed, Sat, and some holidays. (717) 738-3080

Visiting a good, old-fashioned country auction is a great way to while away a morning, especially when fortified by a mid morning snack of chicken corn soup and possibly even a slice of lemon meringue pie. It's a great place to rub shoulders with the locals and pick up a bargain or two. Horst Auction Center sells real estate, farms, coins, antiques, and household goods.

LEOLA PRODUCE AUCTION

Brethren Church Road
Leola, PA 17540
Apr-Dec. Mon-Fri 9-until done. (717) 656-9592

Leola Produce Auction is wholesale food auction for farmers, supermarkets and locals when there are smaller lots.

NEW HOLLAND SALES STABLES

Fulton Street
New Holland, PA
17557
Open Mon, Wed &
Thurs. See text for
schedule.
(717) 354-4341
From Route 23, take
Custer Avenue south,
make a left onto Fulton.

Buying and selling livestock at New Holland Sales Stable.

If you love auctions, animals, and local color, you'll be in hog heaven. Farmers bring their livestock here to be sold to the packing companies. The weekly schedule is as follows:

Monday:	7:30 a.m. Market hogs, sows and boars. 10:00 a.m. Horses 1:30 beef sales: Bulls, steers, cows, veal, and calves.
Wednesday:	11:00 a.m. Heifers, bulls, and dairy cows. 1:30 p.m. Feeder pigs
Thursday:	10:00 a.m. Fat bulls, steers, and beef cows. 1:30 p.m. Sheep, goats, veal, and calves.

Also see the Roots Market and Green Dragon Farmers' Market and Auction on pages 135 and 134.

BOOKS

B. DALTON BOOKSELLER
Park City Shopping Center
Lancaster, PA 17601
Daily 10-9:30. Holiday hours vary. (717) 295-4618

B. Dalton sells a large number of new books and magazines.

BOOK BIN BOOKSTORE
14 West Orange Street
Lancaster, PA 17603
Mon-Tues, Thurs-Fri 10-6. Wed 10-9. Sat 10-5. Sun 12-5. (717) 392-6434

Browse this store's inventory of 30,000 used books on general subjects, out-of-print, used, and rare hardbacks or paperbacks. There are also one-of-a-kind books spanning four centuries.

THE BOOK HAVEN
146 North Prince Street
Lancaster , PA 17603
Mon-Tues, Thurs-Fri 10-5. Wed 10-9. Sat 10-4. (717) 393-0920

The Book Haven stocks some 125,000 used books on subjects such as children's illustrated books, early American imprints, German-Americana, Pennsylvania and local history.

BORDERS BOOK SHOP
940 Plaza Boulevard
Lancaster, PA 17601
Mon-Sat 9-11. Sun 9-9. (The coffee shop closes 30 minutes before the store.)
(717) 293-8022
Across from Park City Mall.

> **Reading all the good books is like a conversation with the finest men of past centuries.**
> René Descartes,
> *Discourse on Method*
>
>

Borders Book Shop is the largest bookstore (for new books) in the Lancaster area with over 100,000 titles. Their books cover a wide selection of general topics with local customer interest driving their specialties. Local interest books and Civil War books are unusually well covered. Borders hosts eight Civil War roundtables which meet monthly. This is also a great place to meet authors, listen to music, or just hang out in the café, visiting, having a snack, or drinking espresso.

CHESTNUT STREET BOOKS

11 West Chestnut Street

Lancaster, PA 17603

Mon-Sat 10-6. (717) 393-3773

One block from Book Bin and Book Haven.

This store stocks some 20,000 used books on history, biography, religion, literature, poetry, and baseball. Also offers a fast, free, out-of-print search service.

CLAY BOOKSTORE

2450 West Main Street

Ephrata, PA 17522-9731

Mon, Thurs-Fri 8-9. Tues-Wed & Sat 8-5. (717) 733-7253

Clay Bookstore is an interesting bookstore to browse through. They have an unusual mix of old school readers, topographic maps, genealogy books, Bibles, and old and new books in both German and English.

CML BOOKS

The Market Place

Morgantown, PA 19543

Mon, Wed-Fri 10-5. Sat 10-6. Sun 11-3. (610) 286-7297

CML carries 18,000 used volumes on literature, the military, and the Roman Catholic faith.

THE LITTLE BOOK SHOP

2710 Old Philadelphia Pike, (Route 340)

Bird-in-Hand, PA 17505

Varies with the season. (717) 295-7580

Right beside the Bird-in-Hand Farmers Market.

The Little Book Shop carries used paperbacks and new local books.

MASTHOF BOOKSTORE

Mill Road

Morgantown, PA 19543-9701

Mon-Sat 9-5. (610) 286-0258

PA turnpike exit 22, left onto Route 23 and an immediate right onto Mill Road. Go one mile and the store is on the left.

This marvelous bookstore is a great place for people doing genealogical research, studying Anabaptist (Brethren and Mennonite) history, or looking for books on Amish and Mennonite quilting and cooking traditions. There are also maps, European reference sources, biographies, and novels, as well as American folk toys. A catalog is available. The bookstore is next to the Masthof Press, which among other things, prints the *Mennonite Family History*. This is a quarterly periodical featuring Amish, Mennonite, and Brethren genealogy and family history.

MOYER'S BOOK BARN
1419 Village Road, (Route 741 West)
Strasburg, PA 17579
Mon-Fri 10-5. Sat 10-3. (717) 687-7459

The Book Barn was founded in 1985 in a renovated barn. There are no remainders here and no piles of beat up paperbacks. Instead, there are thousands of hardbacks, all neatly arranged in Dewey Decimal format. The Book Barn has two floors of books, over 35,000 titles in all, and is very strong in early children's books, popular authors from the 30's and 40's, local books, and local authors. The Book Barn has a full range of book categories, and the titles are well selected. They receive new books weekly and also provide book locating services.

PROVIDENT BOOKSTORES
Lancaster Shopping Center
1625 Lititz Pike Lancaster, PA 17601
Mon-Sat 9-9. (717) 397-3517

Park City Shopping Center
Lancaster, PA 17601
Mon-Sat 9-9. (717) 397-2702

Pharmhouse
Mon-Sat 9-9. Ephrata, PA 17522
Mon-Sat 9-9 (717) 733-2098

16 South Tower Road
New Holland, PA 17557
Mon-Sat 9-9. (717) 354-5258

Open since 1895, this Christian bookstore carries over 30,000 books for the family and church. This chain of stores is owned and operated by the Mennonite Church.

WALDENBOOKS
Park City Shopping Center
Lancaster, PA 17601
Mon-Sat 10-9:30. Sun 12-6. (717) 299-0905

Waldenbooks carries 50,000-plus titles with an emphasis on new releases.

WALTER AMOS BOOKSELLER
The Marketplace
Morgantown, PA 19543
Mon-Thurs & Sat 10-5. Fri 10-6. Closed Sun. (610) 286-0510
At the south end of Route 176.

With over 72,000 books covering literature, religion, biography, cooking, and history, this store is worth any book hound's attention.

COUNTRY STORES

COUNTRY HOUSEWARES STORE

601 Musser School Road

Leola, PA 17540

Mon & Wed 8-5. Tues, Thurs-Fri 8-8. Sat 8-4. (717) 656-9733

Before arriving at this country store, you travel down a long lane festooned with all sorts of farm implements looking for a buyer. Lit by gaslight and skylights you can shop for anything from Noritake china, Corelle, Melmac (remember Melmac?), silverware, and Farberware to Amish clothes, sewing notions, bedspreads, games, toys, and hardware.

GOOD'S STORE

On Route 23 at 897

East Earl, PA 17519

Mon & Wed-Fri 9-9. Tues 9-5. Sat 9-5. (717) 354-4026

You'll find the usual wide variety of household goods, clothing, and hardware items. For sewers there are good prices on fabric and patterns. You'll also see everything from conservative Mennonite suitcoats in black fabrics to candy that will tempt small children of every persuasion. This store is located next to Shady Maple Smorgasbord.

KAUFFMAN'S HARDWARE

Route 23

New Holland, PA 17557

Mon & Thurs 6:30-8. Tues & Wed 6:30-5:30. Fri 6:30-9. Sat 6:30-5. (717) 354-4606

Kauffman's Hardware first opened in 1779 as a small store, selling its wares to the neighboring country folk. In addition to supplies for cooks, gardeners, gift givers, and amateur or professional carpenters, they have an interesting inventory of antique hardware, old documents, and tools.

Drawing courtesy of Kauffman's Hardware

Kauffman's Hardware has been selling country wares for generations.

ZIMMERMAN HARDWARE & FARM SUPPLIES

50 Woodcorner Road

Lititz, PA 17543

Mon, Thurs & Fri 7-8:30. Tues & Wed 7-5:30. Sat 7-4. (717) 738-7350

Just South of Route 322, 1 mile West of Ephrata.

This is a fascinating hardware store that caters to local farmers, professional tradesmen, and the do-it-yourselfer. It isn't very often that you see hog and cattle watering fountains at your local hardware store! There are electric fence chargers, rows of welding and plumbing supplies, tractor and tiller parts, and tools of all sizes, shapes, and functions.

> **One of the most important pieces of furniture for the early German settlers was a schrank or very large wardrobe made either of highly polished walnut or colorfully painted soft woods. This furniture varied little from 18th century European painted peasant furniture.**
>
>

ZIMMERMAN'S STORE

3601 Old Philadelphia Pike

(Route 340)

Intercourse, PA 17534

Mon-Sat 7-9. (717) 768-8291

Entering Zimmerman's Store is like walking back in time. It's a simple, country, grocery store with a feeling of the 1940's. Along with the usual items you find in a grocery store, Zimmerman's carries bulk grains, cereals, dried fruit, nuts, chocolate, and items for baking. They also stock garden seeds, local produce, and locally produced apple butter.

GALLERIES

CENTRAL MARKET ART COMPANY

15 West King Street

Lancaster, PA 17603

Mon-Fri 10-5. Sat 10-3. (717) 392-4466

Around the corner from the Central Market.

Central Market Art Company features local artists and offers custom framing, personal home portraits, scenes of Lancaster, pottery, and more.

LANCASTER GALLERIES

34 North Water Street

Lancaster, PA 17603

Mon-Fri 9-6. Sat 9-5. (717) 397-5552

This gallery carries still lifes, florals, landscapes, etchings, and original work by local artists. Popular are the posters of local scenes, including the work of P. Buckley Moss.

GENERAL

BAREVILLE FURNITURE
295 East Main Street
Leola, PA 17540
Mon-Fri 9-9. Sat 9-5. (717) 656-9913

You will find well priced, good quality furniture here with plenty of pleasant service. Shipping is available.

BOWMAN'S STOVE & PATIO, INC.
906 East Main Street
Ephrata, PA 17522
Mon-Wed 10-6. Thurs-Fri 10-8. Sat 10-4. (717) 733-4973

Are you renovating your kitchen and looking for an old-fashioned oven? Need new patio furniture? Bowman's has a large selection of Samsonite patio furniture, Hatteras hammocks, Ducane gas grills, and more. They carry woodstoves made by The Earth Stove and Vermont Castings, gas grills, and a good selection of hearth products.

DEMUTH'S TOBACCO SHOP
114 East King Street
Lancaster, PA 17602
Mon-Fri 9-5. Sat 9-3. (717) 397-6613
One block East of Penn Square in downtown Lancaster.

Established in 1770, Demuth's Tobacco Shop is the oldest tobacco shop in America. Opened by Christopher Demuth, this shop has been passed down through the family for over 200 years. Owned and operated by the Demuth Foundation, the shop continues to sell tobacco products and supplies. To add to the shop's old-fashioned charm, a collection of old fire helmets lines the cabinets around the perimeter of the ceiling. A glass case displays decorative ceramic tobacco jars from the early 1900s.

PARK CITY
Park City Shopping Center
Lancaster, PA 17601
Mon-Sat 10-9:30. Sun 12-5.
(717) 299-0010
Harrisburg Pike Exit off Route 30.

Park City is the largest mall in the area with department stores such as Boscovs, The Bon-Ton, JC Penney, Woolworth, Sears, and Clover.

> **In 1748 the town of Reading was laid out under the supervision of Thomas Penn, one of William Penn's sons, and named for the seat of Berkshire, England. Though settled by English, this area rapidly became known for its German citizens and is so today.**
>
>

THE SHOPS AT DONECKERS

**409 North State Street
Ephrata, PA 17522**
Mon-Tues & Thurs-Fri
11-9. Sat 9-5. Closed
Wed (except Dec) and
Sun. (717) 738-9500
Exit 21 from the PA turn-
pike and take Route 322
West. Make a right onto
N. State Street for three
blocks.

The Shops at Doneckers.

The Shops at Doneckers feature fine home furnishings and clothing for the whole family presented with old-fashioned service. They feature special events such as trunk shows and personal appearances by designers. A personalized shopper service is available.

TIE ONE ON

**Central Market Mall
44 North Queen Street
Lancaster, PA 17603**
Mon-Fri -10-5. Sat 10-4. (717) 291-6875
Just off the square.

This is an excellent place to go tie shopping. They stock a wide variety of well-made silk ties at very good prices.

HANDCRAFTED FURNITURE

BRATTON'S WOODCRAFT

**At the Kitchen Kettle Village
Intercourse, PA 17534**
Mon-Fri 9-5:30. Sat 9-6. (717) 768-3214

Bratton's Woodcraft carries a large selection of country furniture, early American furniture, and children's furniture in either solid oak or cherry. Most of the furniture is made on the premises but some pieces are made by local craftsmen. Prices are reasonable and custom orders are taken.

BYERSTOWN WOODWORK

5019 Newport Road, (Route 772)
Kinzers, PA 17535
Mon-Fri 7-4:30. Sat 9-2. (717) 442-8586

Handcrafted chests, made with oak, cherry, cedar, and walnut, are the specialty here. They also have delightful children's rocking horses, toy chests, small tables and chairs, and miniature rocking chairs. Byerstown also builds entertainment centers, wardrobes, tables, and chairs. Custom orders are taken and can be shipped anywhere in the United States. The telephone number listed above is an answering service.

DUANE L. MENDENHALL, WOODCARVER

Lancaster, PA 17602
By appointment. (717) 393-0692
Call for directions.

Duane Mendenhall's interest in woodcarving began in VoTech cabinet-making classes. Through the years, he has developed a passion for carving by studying 18th century furniture, and apprenticing for a well-regarded local company. Several years ago he started his own business. Mendenhall specializes in carvings and furniture influenced by the 18th century, but he works equally well with Victorian and Empire styles. Much of his work is architectural carving: mantles, pediments over doors, and carved stairways. If you're looking for an elegant humidor for the cigar lover in your life, Mendenhall has just the thing: a rococo mahogany humidor with cedar lining and beautiful carvings.

Photograph courtesy of Duane L. Mendenhall

*For the cigar lover in your life:
a hand carved humidor by Duane Mendenhall.*

FISHER'S QUALITY FURNITURE

3061 Newport Road, (Route 772)

Ronks, PA 17572

Mon-Fri 8-5. Sat 9:30-3:30. (717) 656-4423

Sold from a gaslit showroom, this handsome, early American furniture is made by Amishman Levi Fisher and his craftsmen. The workshop is located on the Fisher farm, not far from the showroom. The furniture is well designed, well constructed, and very reasonably priced. For example, a Queen Anne table, in cherry with four leaves, is $795. The same quality table would cost several hundred dollars more if purchased from a nationally known store. In addition to tables, the Fishers also sell chairs, bed frames, dry sinks, armoires, china cabinets, desks, and entertainment centers. Most are available in either oak or cherry. Inventory is limited so most items are made to order, with a four- to five-month wait. This store is off the beaten path, but worth the time it takes to find it.

> The Conestoga wagon was originally built and used by German farmers to haul supplies to and from the market. These sturdy wagons could easily accommodate 2,000 to 3,000 pounds of produce or farm equipment.
>
>

FISHERCRAFT CUSTOM-BUILT FURNITURE

123 Groffdale Church Road

Leola, PA 17540

Mon-Fri 7-5. Sat 7-3. (717) 656-8728

If you're looking for kitchen and dining room tables that measure only 42 x 42 when closed, but will seat four to twenty-four people when fully extended, Merv and Calvin Stoltzfus are the men to see. They custom build tables in styles ranging from round pedestal, trestle, dropleaf, oval, or rectangular with oak, maple, or cherry woods. Their prices range from $398 for a table that seats four to six to $717 for a dropleaf table measuring 14 feet that seats 18 to 20. Shipping is available throughout the United States.

HARVEY MARTIN

230 South Fairmount

Ephrata, PA 17522

Mon-Fri 7-5. Sat 7-3. (717) 354-5657

This is not just another furniture crafter. Three generations of the Martin family oversee the making of beautifully, handcrafted, custom-made furniture. Their mainstay is early American, but they can work from photographs or even hand drawings of the desired design. Typical woods used are cherry, oak, and walnut with a variety of finishes and hardware to choose from. The prices are a bargain. There is a twelve-month wait. They do arrange for shipping within the United States.

JAY BRUBAKER, CABINETMAKER
723 Sixth Street
Lancaster, PA 17603
By appointment. (717) 397-5034, 0523

Jay Brubaker comes by his ability to work with wood honestly. Both his father and grandfather made wooden toys. Returning to the area after completing college, Brubaker took a job with cabinetmaker Stephen Van Ormer and worked with him for seven years. In 1990, having learned cabinetmaking, he felt he was ready to start his own business. Brubaker specializes in custom reproduction 18th century furniture. He particularly enjoys making Chippendale or Queen Anne chairs and lowboys or dressing tables. Customers learn about Jay's work primarily through word-of-mouth, and his home features his work. There is a twelve-month wait on most commissions.

KING'S WOODCRAFT
35 South Groffdale Road
Leola, PA 17540
Mon-Sat 7-5. (717) 656-8015

Mr. King makes very good quality custom furniture in oak, cherry, and maple. Walnut is available upon request but is not normally used because of the cost. He handcrafts furniture in a variety of styles. Prices are reasonable, though the wait can be seven to twelve months. Definitely worth a visit if you're in the market for furniture and want to support local craftsmen.

L. B. EBERSOL & SONS, INC.
146 Butter Road
Leola, PA 17540
Mon-Fri 7-5. Sat 7-3. (717) 656-9230

Located a half mile northeast of Bareville, this family shop specializes in handpainted children's furniture. The Ebersol family has been making furniture since the Depression. It is said painted furniture originated with the need immigrants had to cheer up their humble homes. Thus, they decorated and painted chairs, cradles, and chests. The Ebersol family has kept this tradition alive. They make an adorable children's table with two chairs ($165), stools, a small deacon's bench ($145), a rocking chair ($112), and a plain varnished toy box ($45).

MARTIN'S CHAIRS INC.

124 King Court
New Holland, PA 17557
Mon-Fri 9-5. Sat 10-4. (717) 355-2177
From Route 23, go 1.3 miles South on Diller Avenue in New Holland.

Since 1962, John E. Martin, Jr. and his family have been handcrafting wood furniture, using traditional 18th century techniques. They feature fine furniture crafted on the premises in traditional and antique reproduction styles. There are some 20 different styles of chairs alone, including the elegant Philadelphia Combback Chair, a Lancaster County Arm Chair, and a Windsor Lowback Settee. The chairs are made of oak, maple, and cherry. Martin's also produces a full range of tables, hutches, and sideboards, as well as bedroom and office furniture.

R. TODD HOBDAY, CABINETMAKER

239 Poplar Street, (At the corner of S. 441)
Columbia, PA 17512
By appointment. (717) 684-7233
Route 30 West to the Columbia/Marietta exit. Take Route 441 South. Make a right onto Poplar and park.

You'll find no factory-made furniture in R. Todd Hobday's gallery. As the youngest student to be accepted to the North Bennett Street School for cabinetmaking in Boston, Todd had a distinguished start. He specializes in custom-built, fine furniture from contemporary pieces to 18th century historical reproductions. The gallery has several of Todd's pieces on display and there is a portfolio of his work to choose from. Calling for an appointment is the best way to ensure that the gallery is open.

STEPHEN VAN ORMER

10 Miller Street, (Route 741)
Strasburg, PA 17579
Mon-Fri 9-5. Call ahead. (717) 687-8331

Stephen Van Ormer's focus is on 17th and 18th century reproductions with Chippendale and Queen Anne carvings as his specialty. He also makes primitive furniture of this period with distressed paint so his range is broad. His furniture is all custom made, and potential clients can look at his large portfolio as well as tour his home next to the shop to see samples of his work. Van Ormer operates a one-man shop so it's wise to call ahead to make sure he's open. Evening and Saturday appointments are available.

STEVEN CHERRY, CABINETMAKER

1214 Goshen Mill Road
Peach Bottom, PA 17563
By appointment. (717) 548-3254 or (717) 392-2217

Steve Cherry started his own cabinetmaking business in 1987. Working on commission, he does a wide range of work, including restoration of 18th and 19th century furniture, fancy architectural millwork, custom framing, reproduction early and contemporary American furniture, and interior design. If pressed for an area of specialty, Cherry mentions painted furniture, such as blanket chests and chairs, of all the periods.

In late 1997, Cherry plans to open a showroom in the city of Lancaster. He will sell antiques in addition to his own work.

THOMAS B. MORTON CABINETMAKERS

30 South Hershey Avenue
Leola, PA 17540
Mon-Fri 9-5 and by appointment. (717) 656-3799

Thomas Morton opened this furniture shop in 1989. His handcrafted furniture is an eclectic mix of styles: Mission, Shaker, and 17th and 18th century Lancaster County. The Lancaster County versions show a heavy

Photograph courtesy of Thomas B. Morton Cabinetmakers

German influence, almost a combination Shaker and early American with good proportions. The common thread in all the furniture is its graceful, clean lines highlighting carefully selected wood. Most pieces are made from Pennsylvania cherry, allowing for beautiful broad grains. Morton's furniture is finished with natural oil and wax, again highlighting the wood's true grain and color. Particularly eye-catching are the elegant pencil post beds that come with a choice of six different headboards. The beds are constructed with an old-fashioned method using solid posts which will provide years of use. Custom work is

*The beautiful clean lines
of Thomas B. Morton Cabinetmakers.*

a significant part of the business especially for entertainment centers and built-in work. This is furniture that gives years of happiness. While not inexpensive, the prices are comparable to, if not less than, what you would pay at better home furnishing stores. They deliver.

They also sell their work at The Artworks at Doneckers. See below for hours.

HANDCRAFTED GIFTS

THE ARTWORKS AT DONECKERS

100 North State Street

Ephrata, PA 17522

Mon-Tues & Thurs-Fri 11:45-5. Sat 10-5. Closed Wed and Sun. (717) 738-9503

Exit 21 from the PA turnpike and take Route 322 West. Make a right onto N. State Street & a left onto Duke St.

A refurbished shoe factory now serves as a showplace for working artists and crafts people selling art, jewelry, pottery, fine furniture, crafts, contemporary and traditional quilts, and collectibles. A cafe serves lunch and snacks. Admission is free.

ABC WOODCRAFT

1698 Georgetown Road

Christiana, PA 17509

Mon-Thurs 7:30-6. Fri 7:30-8. Sat 7:30-4. (717) 529-3285

ABC Woodcraft is an Amish business and has all sorts of furnishings, children's toys, and gifts. Their inventory includes some amazing swing sets and playhouse combinations elaborate enough to warrant their $1,200 price tags. Children's furniture and toys in stock include cradles, doll rockers, children's clothes trees, hobby horses, musical train penny banks, various sizes of red wagons, and three sizes of rocking horses. Handsome outdoor furniture, good quality oak reproduction furniture, and many gift items round out the store. Call the number above between 8:30 and 9:00 a.m. or leave a message.

BASKETVILLE

Route 30 East

Paradise, PA 17562

Open 9-9 daily. (717) 442-9444

7 miles East of Lancaster

This large chain store carries all sorts of baskets from the traditional American ash splint baskets made by Basketville to baskets made in Chinese communes, Philippine villages, Mexican pueblos, and Polish workshops. Other items include woven outdoor furniture, bathroom furnishings, and wicker furniture. They ship worldwide. Also on the premises is a retail outlet for the nearby Twin Brook Winery, featuring a good selection of wines.

◆◆

THE CLAY DISTELFINK

2246 Old Philadelphia Pike, (Route 340)

Lancaster, PA 17602

Primarily Mon-Sat 9-5. Call to confirm hours. (717) 399-1994

1 mile East from the intersection of Route 30 and 340.

Photograph courtesy of The Clay Distelfink

Marilyn Stoltzfus White has been practicing the traditional art of sgraffito, the scratching of patterns on plates, for 16 years. Her redware plates are decorated with Pennsylvania Dutch flowers, tulips that symbolize love, distelfinks (the German bird of happiness that wishes newlyweds a long lasting marriage), and pomegranates,

*Commemorate an occasion
with Marilyn White's decorative plates.*

which are said to bring farmers a good harvest. White specializes in custom made plates to commemorate weddings, births, and other special occasions. It is fascinating to watch her work so call ahead if you want to be sure she has a plate in progress.

COUNTRY ROAD FLOWERS

3546 West Newport Road, (Route 772)

Intercourse, PA 17572

Mon-Sat 9-5. (717) 768-8478

1/2 mile North of Route 340 on the West side of the street.

This attractive, Amish-owned shop has all kinds of dried flower arrangements, Yankee candles, locally made handcrafts, and painted furniture.

ELDRETH POTTERY

Route 896

Strasburg, PA 17579

July 1-Sept 1: Mon-Wed 9:30-6. Thurs & Fri 9:30-8. Sat 9:30-5. Sun 1-5. Call for other hours. (717) 687-8445

Just North of Strasburg and the intersection of Routes 896 and 741.

◆◆

Eldreth pottery continues a 500-year-old German tradition of making salt-glazed stoneware. Most early American stoneware was glazed with salt. When the kiln temperature reaches 2,250 degrees F, salt is thrown into the kiln. The salt changes from a solid to a vapor and adheres to the clay, forming a glass coating on the pots. No lead or toxic chemicals are used, making the pottery food safe, oven-proof, and microwaveable. Besides functional pottery, Eldreth also produces lovely, handpainted clay sculptures from original castings. The first weekend in December, they host an open house featuring one-of-a-kind gifts, including Santas and manger figurines. Eldreth Pottery also produces the traditional Pennsylvania German redware.

FOLTZ POTTERY

225 North Peartown Road
Reinholds, PA 17569
Mon-Fri & most Sat 10-4. (717) 336-2676
Go 6 miles West of Intersection of Route 272 and 897 on 897.
Make a right onto Peartown Road.

Ned Foltz carries on a 200-year-old tradition of making redware pottery. In 1962 Foltz began to experiment with local clay. He developed a passion for redware, mastering old forms and techniques such as sgraffito and

Photograph courtesy of C. Ned Foltz

slipware. Foltz makes his pottery in an 1840 stone building, formerly a one-room school. Each piece is hand-made, signed, and can be used safely with food. December is an especially good time to visit the shop because of the special Christmas show, featuring many prized Foltz collectibles. Call the studio in advance if you want to see the artist working.

Ned Foltz working on redware pottery.

KAREN DUNWOODY

972 Valley Rd., Route 372
Quarryville, PA 17566
Varies. Please call to verify. (717) 786-8249

Karen Dunwoody makes museum quality handmade tinware. Her emphasis is on traditional lighting fixtures such as lanterns, chandeliers, and sconces, but she also makes cookie cutters and decorative items. She has a small retail shop, but since the hours are irregular, it is important to call for an appointment.

KAUFFMAN'S HANDCRAFTED CLOCKS

3019 West Newport Road, (Route 772)
Ronks, PA 17572
Mon-Fri 8-5. Sat 9-4. (717) 656-6857
On 772 between Intercourse and Leola

Isaac Kauffman has been making handcrafted clocks for over 15 years, specializing in grandmother and grandfather clocks in cherry, walnut, oak, and mahogany. He imports his clock movements from Germany and offers a wide variety of clock faces, some handpainted. Visitors may see finished clocks in a showroom next to the shop. You may purchase from in-stock items, or place a special order. Kauffman also repairs and services clocks.

KING'S HOMESTEAD

3518 West Newport Road, (Route 772)
Ronks, PA 17572
Mon-Sat 8-5. (717) 768-7688
1/2 mile or so north of 340 on 772 on the left hand side of the road.

The King's Homestead is a large two-story building crammed with collectibles, knickknacks, and beautifully made handcrafted items. The lawns surrounding the building display exceptional lawn furniture, gazebos, life-sized playhouses complete with shutters and wood shingles, and adorable bird feeders. Inside are locally made baskets of all shapes and sizes, children's wooden toys and dolls, pine and oak furniture, pottery, birdhouses, and many (many!) more things. They ship but do not accept credit cards.

LAPP'S COACH SHOP

3572 West Newport Road (Route 772)
Intercourse, PA 17534
Summer: Mon-Sat 8-6. Winter: Mon-Sat 8-5. (717) 768-8712
Half block North of Route 340.

Lapp's Coach Shop has some of the best kid's toys I've seen. I never knew such a variety of wagons existed until I visited this delightful shop in Intercourse. They have old-fashioned red wagons in a variety of sizes, from simple and small four-wheelers to large double tandem eight-wheelers. They have trail-along wagons to be towed by other wagons. All are well built and durable. In addition they have a large assortment of well-designed wooden furniture in oak and cedar; rocking horses in many shapes and sizes; rocking chairs made from cherry, oak, and hickory; as well as bird feeders and other items. I was impressed with the Amish Scooter and Dirt King tri-cycles. They are well-made and fun.

Photograph courtesy of Lapp's Coach Shop

Children will find it hard to leave without one of Lapp's adorable wagons.

LAPP'S WOODEN TOYS

3006 Irishtown Road
Ronks, PA 17572
Mon-Fri 7-5. Sat 7-3. (717) 354-2278

This a great place to find children's furniture, including tables and chairs, ovens, refrigerators, ironing boards, dolls and doll beds, and toy chests. There are also wooden trucks, trains, doll houses, and high chairs. Prices are very reasonable.

MANNIE'S WOOD SHOP

58 Queen Road
Intercourse, PA 17534
Mon-Fri 8-5. Sat 8-12. (717) 354-4374
1/4 mile south of Intercourse

Mannie's offers up beautifully crafted copper and brass weather vanes (over 50 to choose from), custom built redwood cupolas, and redwood bird feeders with wood shingle roofs. Leave a message at the number above or write for a price sheet and order form.

MAPLE CROFT INTERIORS AND UNIQUE CRAFTS

701 Penn Grant Road

Lancaster, PA 17602

Tues-Thurs 10-5. Fri 10-7. Sat 10-4. (717) 464-4895

Corner of 222 and Penn Grant Road, 7 miles South of Lancaster

Maple Croft carries all sorts of gifts and decorative items.

MOSES F. STOLTZFUS

39 Pequea Valley Road

Kinzer, PA 17535

Mon-Fri 7-5. Sat 8-4.

This Stoltzfus family weaves thick country rugs and carpet. They accept custom requests. Also take a look at their homemade brooms, old-fashioned cake testers, placemats, and table runners.

THE OLD CANDLE BARN

340 at the corner of 772

Intercourse, PA 17534

Mon-Sat 8-5:30.

(717) 768-8926

The Old Candle Barn is located next door to Kitchen Kettle Village. The building's Quonset hut shape holds every type of candle imaginable: scented and unscented, old-fashioned and newfangled, functional and decorative. You name it, it's probably here. They also stock a wide variety of craft materials, local crafts, local cookbooks, quilts, doilies, stationary, Americana, and silk flower arrangements.

SOUR CREAM PEACH MUFFINS

2 eggs
1/2 cup melted butter
1 cup sugar
1 cup sour cream
2 cups flour
1 teaspoon baking powder
1/2 teaspoon baking soda
1/2 teaspoon salt
1 cup fresh peaches, pitted and coarsely chopped

Mix together eggs, melted butter, sugar, and sour cream. Sift together dry ingredients and add peaches. Fold peaches and flour mixture into egg mixture just until blended. Line muffin tins with paper liners, spoon in mixture. Bake in a preheated 350°F oven for 20 to 25 minutes or until it tests done. Sprinkle with sugar. Makes 1 dozen.

—Recipe from Heidi and Tim Soberick, *The Candlelight Inn Bed & Breakfast*

THE OLDE MILLHOUSE SHOPPES

105 Strasburg Pike
Lancaster, PA 17602
Mon, Wed, Thurs & Sat: 10-5:30. Tues & Fri: 10-9. Oct 10 to Dec 24: Open daily 10-9 & Sat
10-5. (717) 299-0678
From Route 462, turn South onto Strasburg Pike. Go 1/2 mile.

This is a good place to gift hunt for someone near and dear to you or, better yet, for yourself. Housed in an old barn, this shop is full of decorative items, furnishings, and lamps (made of tin, brass, wrought iron, and wood). Handmade wreaths, pottery, folk art, and framed prints will keep you browsing for some time.

SHARP JEWELERS

21 West King Street
Lancaster, PA 17603
Mon-Tues, Thurs-Fri 9:30-5:30. Wed 9:30-8. Sat 9:30-5. (717) 291-1611

Sharp Jewelers focuses on various styles at this gallery and studio. Works from 30 designers are featured, and custom requests are welcome.

TEN THOUSAND VILLAGES

240 North Reading Road, (Route 272)
Ephrata, PA 17522
Mon-Sat 10-5:30. Fri 10-9. (717) 738-1101
1/4 mile North of the intersection of Route 272 and 322.

An excellent place to search for gifts, shop for rugs, or look for household furnishings. This Ephrata store is the largest in the chain of 116 Ten Thousand Villages stores which highlight the work of artisans from over 30 countries. For more than 50 years, Ten Thousand Villages has provided fair income to people of the developing countries for their handcrafted items. It is a nonprofit program of Mennonite Central Committee, the relief and development agency of the Mennonite and Brethren in Christ churches in Canada

Photograph courtesy of Ten Thousand Villages

*Help out a neighbor near and far
by purchasing handmade items from Ten Thousand Villages.*

and the United States. The company's wholesale craft purchases provide the equivalent of more than 12,000 full-time jobs in a single year. Items include jewelry, carvings, folk art, stationary, collectibles, toys, holiday decorations, and heirloom-quality, handknotted Persian, Bokhara, Kilim, and Afghani tribal rugs. The Nav Jiwan International Tea Room housed in the same building is an excellent place for lunch. Please see page 101 for more information.

THE TIN BIN
20 Valley Road
Neffsville, PA 17601
Mon-Sat 10-5. Wed 10-8. (717) 569-6210

This charming shop is housed in a converted barn and specializes in 18th and 19th century lights and accessories, handcrafted in tin, copper, and brass. The work of eight tinsmiths offers varied styles of post and wall lights, sconces, window lights, chandeliers, and lanterns. In addition there are handcrafted wooden chandeliers, wrought iron floor and table lamps, pottery lamps, and solid brass and pewter lighting fixtures for a more formal look. A catalog is available for $2.

WILL CHAR THE HEX PLACE
3056 Old Lincoln Highway, (Route 30)
Paradise, PA 17562
Mon-Sat 9-6. Sun 9-5. (717) 687-8329

Hex signs are not superstitious symbols, but designs handed down by German immigrants who loved to use bright patterns and geometric forms as decorations. Birth certificates, furniture, pottery, and textiles all were graced with bright colors. Two typical patterns are the Sun and Tree of Life. This shop carries a large selection of hex signs, crafts from area artisans, and lawn ornaments.

WILTON ARMETALE STORE
Plumb & Square Streets
Mount Joy, PA 17552-0600
Mon-Sat 9:30-5:30. Sun 12-5. Call for extended hours in season. (717) 653-5595
One block South of Route 230.

Durable Armetale metal is an alloy of ten different metals produced with a combination of contemporary technology and traditional hand casting techniques. Wilton Armetale carries gifts, table serviceware, and decorative accessories.

KNIVES

COUNTRY KNIVES

4134 Old Philadelphia Pike, (Route 340)
Intercourse, PA 17534
Mon-Sat 9-6. Sun 12-5. (717) 768-3818

Country Knives has more knives than I ever knew existed. Brian Huegel presides over one of the best cutlery stores in the country. Knives of all kinds are displayed with great care. There are pocket knives of endless variety, daggers, military knives, custom-made knives, kitchen knives, antique reproductions, limited edition collector knives, Samurai swords, scissors, and more. All told, there are more than 7,000 different cutlery items on display, made by 275 manufacturers from 22 countries. These manufacturers have one thing in common; they produce the best quality knives. Huegel has customers from all over the world who shop by mail or phone, as well as drop-in traffic, including local Amish farmers. This is a store not to miss, and an ideal place for a truly unique gift.

> **When using your knives, use a cutting board that is soft enough to yield slightly so that the edge of the knife is not damaged or dulled as it works against the board.**
>
>

OUTLETS

DOMAKI LEATHER OUTLET

85 New Holland Pike, (Route 23)
Leola, PA 17540
Mon-Fri 9:30-5:30. Sat 9:30-4:30. (717) 656-3201
5 1/2 miles East of Route 30

Domaki Leathers stocks one of the largest inventories of leather coats for men and women in the area. Alterations are done on the premises. Leather goods are made on site and include handbags, vests, belts, chaps, hats, briefcases, and wallets.

THE FABRIC STORE

625 Locust Street
Columbia, PA 17512
Mon-Fri 10-6. Wed 10-8. Sat 9-4. (717) 684-2306

Brothers Dave and Charlie Platkin have shepherded this store from its prior focus as the Columbia Garment Company to the large fabric and lace business it is today. They have the largest selection of ribbons and lace almost anywhere, and they make most of their gathered laces on old machines, which are slow but make a fine product. Where a normal fabric store might have a representative sampling of cotton lace, The Fabric Store has 20 to choose from. The prices are unbeatable.

Their bridal department has the latest styles of fabric, lace, custom headpiece designs, and flowers. Sewing notions, a wide variety of fabrics, clothing, and craft patterns are also well represented. The sales people are notable for also being accomplished seamstresses. They spend as much time as the customer needs.

HOME FURNISHINGS FACTORY OUTLET

Route 10, 1/2 mile north of Route 23

Morgantown, PA 19543

Mon-Sat 10-9. Sun 12-5. (800) 226-8011

This outlet bills itself as: Acres of furniture and accessories under one roof. You will find the factory outlets for Drexel Heritage, Flexsteel, and Pennsylvania House as well as smaller home furnishing stores.

LANCASTER POTTERY & GLASS

2335 Lincoln Highway East, (Route 30)

Lancaster, PA 17602

Mon-Sat 9-9. Sat 9-6. (717) 299-6835

This store is a good source for kitchen glass made by Pyrex, Farberware, Corningware, and Anchor Hocking. There are also various kitchen gadgets, Bulova watches and clocks, candles, and t-shirts.

LEATHER WEARHOUSE

Lincoln Highway East, (Route 30)

Across from Tanger Outlet Center

Lancaster, PA 17602

Mon-Thurs 10-6. Fri & Sat 9-8. Sun 1-5. (717) 299-3049

Clothing for the whole family (big and tall sizes), shearlings, motorcycle jackets, wallets, belts, purses, and fanny packs.

OUTLETS ON HIESTERS LANE

755 Hiesters Lane

Reading, PA 19612

Mon-Sat 9:30-9. Sun 10-5. (610) 921-8130

Outlets on Hiesters Lane is actually a collection of three stores. Luxury Linens: featuring Martex, Fieldcrest, Royal Family, Utica, Springfield, Croscill, Waverly, and other brand names. Burlington Coat Factory: a large inventory of coats for the whole family, along with sportswear, suits, dresses, and accessories. Kids & Baby Depot: Clothes and furnishings for babies and kids.

QUALITY OUTLET CENTER

Routes 30 and 896
Lancaster, PA 17602
Jan 1-March 31: Mon-Sat 9:30-6. Sun 12-5. April 1-December 31: Mon-Sat 9:30-9. Sun 11-5. (717) 299-1949

The family apparel, shoe, and specialty stores are: Christmas Etc., The Comic Store, Delta Hosiery, Gold Exchange, Red Wing Shoes, The Stitch Dimension, and Totes. The home furnishings stores are: Fieldcrest Cannon, Mikasa, Shady Lamp Workshop, Sony, and Villeroy & Boch.

QVC OUTLET

Rockvale Square Outlets
35 South Willowdale Drive
Lancaster , PA 17601
Off Route 30 East of Lancaster City.
Mon-Sat 9:30-9. Sun 12-5. Call for winter hours. (717) 392-4330

QVCer's alert. Here is your opportunity to shop for items sold on air. A wide range of items from jewelry, collectibles, dolls, kitchen appliances, electronics, exercise equipment, toys, and craftsmen tools are for sale. Product selection varies and comes from returns of on-air purchases, unsold stock, and discontinued items. Clothing and accessories will be available at a nearby store sometime in 1997.

READING OUTLET CENTER

801 North Ninth Street
Reading, PA 19601
Mon-Sat 9:30-8. Sun 11-5. Jan 1-March 31: Mon-Thurs 9:30-6. Fri 9:30-8. Sat 9:30-6. Sun 11-5. (800) 5-OUTLET

This collection of over 100 stores certainly has something for everyone. The stores range from Laura Ashley to Vitamin World and Burberrys to Casual Corner.

READING STATION OUTLET CENTER

951 North Sixth Street
Reading, PA 19601
Mon-Thurs, & Sat 9:30-7. Fri 9:30-9. Sun 11-5. (610) 478-7000
Between Spring and 6th Streets.

Reading Station Outlet Center is heavy on footwear: Allen Edwards for men's shoes, Cole-Haan for men's and women's shoes, Johnston & Murphy for men's shoes, Nine West for women's shoes and handbags, and Sox Market for socks for the whole family.

Center stores also carry clothes for men and women at Brooks Brothers and Calvin Klein. The He-Ro Group sells Oleg Cassini, Bob Mackie, and

Bill Blass formal and day wear. Robert Scott & David Brooks and Maidenform feature clothes for women. The Book Warehouse, Napier (women's fashion jewelry), Perfumania, and West Point Stevens, which sells linens, round out the offerings here.

ROCKVALE SQUARE OUTLETS
Routes 30 and 896
Lancaster , PA 17602
Regular hours: Mon-Sat 9:30-9, Sun 12-6. Call for winter hours. (717) 293-9595

Rockvale Square Outlets is located in the center of Lancaster County. Well represented in the 120 stores are apparel shops (47 stores), footwear, children's apparel, books, cosmetics, lingerie, and home and electronics supplies.

Some of my favorites are: The Book Warehouse (295-7535), Gap Outlet (391-7841), Bose Factory Store (290-6060), and Reading, China & Glass (393-9747).

SUSQUEHANNA GLASS
Avenue H
Columbia, PA 17512
Mon-Sat 9-5. (717) 684-2155
Take Route 30 West of Lancaster. Columbia exit and follow the yellow signs to Avenue H.

This factory store has been selling glassware since 1910. Susquehanna Glass does not manufacture glass; they specialize in decorative handcutting. This is a good place to pick up inexpensive glass kitchenware: canisters, covered bowls, water pitchers, candleholders, and tableware. They also have another location in Bird-in-Hand beside the farmers' market along Route 340.

TANGER FACTORY OUTLET CENTER
Route 30 East, 4 miles East of Lancaster
Lancaster, PA 17602
(717) 392-7202
Mon-Sat 9:30-9, Sun 11-6

Looking for clothing from some the best clothing manufacturers? This center as 53 factory outlets. The highlights include: Polo Ralph Lauren, Anne Taylor, Jones New York, Coach, Brooks Brothers, Reebok, OshKosh B'Gosh, and London Fog.

VF FACTORY OUTLET VILLAGE
801 Hill Avenue
Reading, PA 19610
Jan-Feb: Mon-Thurs 9-7. Fri 9-9. Sat 9-7. Sun 10-5. Mar-July: Mon-Fri 9-9. Sat 9-7. Sun 10-5. Aug-Dec: Mon-Fri 9-9. Sat 7-9. Sun 10-5. (800) 772-8336

VF has a separate building called The Designers' Place: Anne Klein, Benetton, Carol Little, Coach, Designer Forum, Designer Fragrances, Ellen Tracy, Etienne Aigner, G-III Outerwear, JH Collectibles, Jones N.Y., Donna Karan, Mark Cross, Perry Ellis, Reading China & Glass, Sunglass Station, and Tommy Hilfiger.

In addition there are 50-some stores with discount prices for family and home.

ROAST TURKEY AND FILLING

8-10 pound turkey or chicken
2 pkgs. soft bread cubes
1/2 cup butter
1 cup finely chopped celery
3 eggs
10 3/4-oz. can chicken broth
1 tablespoon celery seed
salt and pepper to taste

1. Prepare turkey or chicken according to directions.
2. Saute celery in butter until light and clear.
3. In large bowl, pour celery and butter over bread cubes and mix thoroughly by hand. Add eggs, chicken broth and seasonings and work into bread mixture by hand. (I like a moist filling so sometimes I add a bit of water until it feels right to me.)
4. Remove meat from bones. Tear into bite-sized pieces. Put all dark meat in bottom of large roasting pan. (I prefer my agate roaster.) Take about 1/2 cup of broth from baking the turkey or chicken. Pour over meat in bottom of roaster and stir lightly.
5. Layer filling on top of meat. Do not stir! Cover and bake at 350° F for about 45 minutes. Baste filling occasionally with fat from chicken broth.
6. Remove from oven and stir filling and meat thoroughly. Return to oven and bake uncovered for 30 minutes, stirring occasionally.
7. Slice and serve white meat on a separate platter.

Note: My husband says this roast filling (as my family calls it) is best when served piping hot from the oven. I always wait until everyone is seated and the blessing has been offered on the meal before putting it on serving platters.

—Recipe submitted by Miriam M. Stoltzfus,
Ronks, Pennsylvania

QUILTS

BEILER'S QUILTS & CRAFTS

110 Hartman Bridge Road (Route 896)

Ronks, PA 17572

Mon-Fri 8-5. Sat 8-4.

This is a good place to shop for genuine, Amish-made quilts. Located just south of Rockvale Square Outlet Center, the store has a variety of sizes and patterns to chose from. Custom orders are welcome and take four to six months, depending on the size. Beiler's also carries some adorable dresses for little girls.

LAUNDRY INSTRUCTIONS FOR QUILTS

The first time you wash a quilt, add one cup of salt to warm water to set print into the fabric.

COUNTRY LANE QUILTS

211 South Groffdale Road

Leola, PA 17540

Mon-Sat 8-5. (717) 656-8476

Country Lane Quilts offers very good quilts for sale, all locally made. When calling, please let the phone ring.

HANNAH STOLTZFOOS QUILTS AND HOMEMADES

216 Witmer Road

Lancaster, PA 17602

Mon-Sat 9-5.

6 miles East of Lancaster at the corner of Witmer Road and Route 340.

Hannah Stoltzfoos oversees the production of a large selection of quilts with traditional patterns. There are also smaller gifts to choose from. Mail orders are welcome.

J & B QUILTS AND CRAFTS

157 North Star Road

Ronks, PA 17572

Mon-Sat 8-5.

Take Route 896 S to North Star Road. East past a one-room school.

The farm is the second on the left.

From a store located in their home, this family assists visitors in finding the perfect, Amish-made quilt. They also sell crafts, aprons, quillows, hand-bags, pot holders, kitchen towels, placemats, pillows, wall hangings, and Amish dolls.

◆◆◆

LAPP'S QUILTS AND CRAFTS

206 North Star Road
Ronks, PA 17572
Open Mon-Sat.

The Lapp family sells ready made and custom made quilts from the basement shop of their home. All their merchandise is made by the Lapp family or their Amish and Mennonite neighbors. Quilts can be ordered in any size and color.

LOVINA'S STITCHERY

826 May Post Office Road
Strasburg, PA 17579
Mon-Sat 9-5. (717) 687-8868
2 1/4 miles South of Strasburg. Take South Decatur which becomes May Post Office Road.

Open since 1982, Lovina Beiler's quilt shop is a reliable place to find beautifully handmade quilts. All are made by Amish women, and quilts can be made to order.

MARIAN STOLTZFUS QUILTS

3068-3070 Irishtown Road
Ronks, PA 17572
Mon-Sat 9-5. (May be closed in Jan & Feb). (717) 768-8690

Visiting Marian Stoltzfus's quilt shop is a delightful treat. You are welcomed by a gas lamp and Marian's obvious pleasure in greeting her visitors.

The quilts, which are designed by Marian (or her customers if custom made) and sewn by Amish neighbors, come in a wide variety of beautiful patterns. Custom orders are welcome. These orders generally take six months and can be shipped. If you would like to reach her by mail, write to Marian Stoltzfus Quilts, 3066 Irishtown Road, Ronks, PA 17572.

Active participation in congregational life locally, or active involvement in study and service opportunities elsewhere, are assumed as part of committee, voluntary, and adult membership. The ideals of being peacemakers in a broken world, and servants to one another, help Mennonites to seek constructive work in a world of destruction, to minister to the needs of the most disadvantaged.

Cornelius J. Dyck,
An Introduction to Mennonite History

◆◆◆

◆◆◆

OMAR & SYLVIA PETERSHEIM
QUILTS AND CRAFTS

2544 Old Philadelphia
Pike, (Route 340)
Bird-in-Hand, PA
17505
Summer hours: Mon-
Sat 8:30-5. Winter
hours: 8:30-4:30.
(717) 392-6404

This basement shop offers handmade quilts, pillows, wall hangings, and small crafts.

*Find beautifully made quilts
at Petersheim's Quilts and Crafts.*

RIEHL'S QUILTS AND CRAFTS

247 East Eby Road
Leola, PA 17540
Mon-Fri 7-5. Sat 7-3. (717) 656-0697

Another choice for custom made quilts and quillow blankets. UPS service is available.

SMUCKER'S QUILT SHOP

117 North Groffdale Road
New Holland, PA 17557
Mon-Sat 8-8. (717) 656-8730

Smucker's Quilt Shop is on a working farm. They carry a wide variety of quilts and handcrafts. Their quilts are special for their colors, designs, and craftsmanship.

◆◆◆

WITMER QUILT SHOP

1070 West Main Street

New Holland, PA 17557

Mon & Fri 8-8. Tues, Wed, Thurs & Sat 8-6. (717) 656-9526

The Witmer Quilt Shop is stocked with over 150 new quilts and 50 antique quilts. Gift certificates available.

ZOOK'S HANDMADE QUILTS AND CRAFTS

209 Gap Road, (Route 741 East)

Strasburg, PA 17579

Mon-Sat 9-5. (717) 687-0689

Route 741 East of the light in the middle of Strasburg. Left side of 741 after 896 Y's south.

In addition to ready made or custom quilts, the Zooks also carry pine and oak country furniture, handmade brooms, and loom rugs. All items for sale are made by the family or their neighbors.

QUILTING MATERIALS

BURKHOLDER'S FABRICS

2155 West Route 897

Denver, PA 17517

Mon, Tues & Fri 8:30-8:30. Wed, Thurs & Sat 8:30-5. (717) 336-6692

Located on Route 897 between Schaefferstown and Reinholds.

CEDAR LANE DRY GOODS

204 Orlan Road

New Holland, PA 17557

Mon, Thurs, & Fri 8-8. Tues, Wed & Sat 8-5. (717) 354-0030

A good destination for dress materials, quilting supplies, stuffing, batting, and quilt tops.

LAPP'S DRY GOODS

3137 Old Philadelphia Pike, (Route 340)

Bird-in-Hand, PA 17505

Mon, Tues, & Thurs 8-5. Wed 8-12 noon. Fri 8-8. Sat 8-4.

In addition to fabrics, stencils, notions, and patterns for quilters, this Amish shop carries a good selection of quilts.

SAUDER'S FABRICS

681 South Muddy Creek Road

Denver, PA 17517

Mon, Tues, Thurs & Fri 8-8:30. Wed & Sat 8-5. (717) 336-2664

You'll find a large inventory of fabrics in virtually every imaginable

◆◆◆

print and material, as well as a full range of sewing and quilting notions. Sauder's slogan is "If we don't have it, you may not be able to find it!"

WEAVER'S DRY GOODS
108 West Brubaker Valley Road
Lititz, PA 17543
Mon, Thurs & Fri 8-9. Tues, Wed & Sat 8-5. (717) 627-1724

Whether you're a quilter or not, this old-fashioned country fabric store is sure to charm you. A large portion of their inventory is displayed by color and arranged along the wall so you can page through the fabric bolts. Weaver's carries a line of cotton prints with the tradename "Aunt Grace's." These prints are especially lovely reproductions of fabrics from the 1800's. In the Weaver's store, they are displayed with a color chart so the prints not in stock from the line can be ordered. Weaver's also has craft supplies, sewing notions, and quilting supplies. Their prices are very reasonable.

CONSIGNMENT SHOPS

A SECOND GLANCE
903 Nissley Road
Lancaster, PA 17601
Mon-Wed & Fri 10-4:30. Thurs 10-8. Sat 10-4. (717) 898-1994

A Second Glance specializes in fine apparel and accessories for women and children, including maternity clothing and plus sizes. They accept merchandise by appointment only.

BEV'S CONSIGNMENT SHOPPE
Towns Edge Shopping Village
Routes 372 & 222
Quarryville, PA 17566
Mon-Wed 9-6. Thurs & Fri 9-8. Sat 9-5. (717) 786-0190

Carrying a broad range of items, Bev's Consignment Shoppe offers clothing for the whole family, household goods, children's furniture and equipment, and formal attire.

DÉJÀ VU
2831 Columbia Avenue
Lancaster, PA 17603
Tues 10-8. Wed-Sat 10-4. (717) 291-4481
Near Park City-just east of Centerville Road

Shop here for women's and children's clothing and accessories. They feature clothing by Limited, Express, Gap, and other designer labels.

JAYNE'S

27 East State Street

Quarryville, PA 17566

Tues-Wed 9:30-3. Fri 9:30-7. Sat 9:30-4. (717) 786-8028

In addition to clothing for women, children, and infants, Jayne's carries antiques and collectibles.

NEXT TO NEW FINE CLOTHING

1920 Lincoln Highway East, (Route 30)

Lancaster , PA 17602

Mon-Wed & Sat 10-5. Thurs & Fri 10-8. (717) 299-2924

This shop is a quality consignment shop for women and children.

NEXT TO NEW FINE FURNITURE

1886 Lincoln Highway East, (Route 30)

Lancaster , PA 17602

Mon-Wed 10-6. Thurs 10-8. Fri & Sat 10-5. (717) 392-0106

Next to New sells fine furniture and accessories on consignment.

SUSAN WITMAN CONSIGNMENTS

2119 Marta Avenue

Lancaster, PA 17602

Mon-Tues & Thurs 10-4. Wed & Fri 10-9. Sat 9-5. (717) 397-2119

403 West Lexington Road

Lititz, PA 17543

Mon-Thurs 10-4. Reopens Tues -6-9. Fri 10-9. Sat 9-5. (717) 626-0381

1601 Oregon Pike

Lancaster, PA 17603

Mon-Wed 10-4. Thurs & Fri 10-9. Sat 9-5. (717) 299-6242

A favorite Lancaster County destination for good quality clothing going on a second round of wear.

INTRIGUING TOWNS
OF
LANCASTER COUNTY

Map 226
Ephrata 227
Intercourse 227
Lancaster City 228
Lititz 229
Marietta and Columbia 229
Strasburg 230
Trips Outside Lancaster County 231
Resources 233

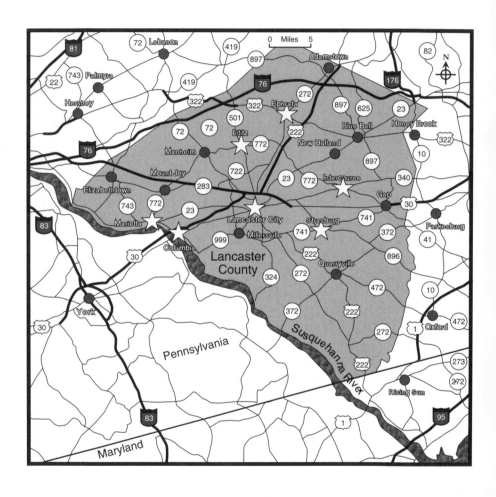

CHAPTER SIX: THE INTRIGUING TOWNS OF LANCASTER COUNTY

EPHRATA

> The name Ephrata means fruitful or plentiful and was picked by the founder of the Ephrata Cloister, Johann Konrad Beissel, from the Book of Ruth.
>
>

Ephrata is located in relatively quiet northern Lancaster County along Route 322. The name Ephrata, aptly originates from the word "fertile" because the local economy is primarily agricultural. There is also some light industry.

One of the earliest settlements in the County, Ephrata is best known for a communal society founded in 1732 by Conrad Beissel, a German Pietist. The Ephrata Cloister is an historic site with a unique collection of medieval style buildings. I highly recommend taking their tour.

Other notable places to visit are The Artworks at Doneckers with its collection of art and handcrafted items; the Green Dragon Farmers' Market & Auction (the mothers of all farmers' markets) which is only open on Fridays; Ten Thousand Villages with its collection of handmade items from around the world; and nearby Adamstown, the ultimate antique hunter's destination.

INTERCOURSE

Speculation about the origin of this village's unusual name has yielded many legends. Some are more believable than others. One story maintains the village was once home to a race course with a sign at the entrance reading "enter course." What we do know is the village was originally called Cross Keys after an old tavern. It was founded in 1754.

Intersected by the Old Philadelpia Pike (Route 340), Intercourse is in eastern Lancaster County in the middle of Amish territory. Surrounded by farmland, this village is a good place to park the car and wander. Some of my favorite places are Stoltzfus Meats, a good old-fashioned butcher shop; The People's Place, an excellent source for information about the Amish and Mennonites; The Old Country Store, filled with quilts and other handcrafted gifts; Zimmerman's Store, a great old hardware store; Kitchen Kettle Village, lined with all sorts of shops; and Lapp's Coach Shop with its handmade children's wagons. East of town on Route 340 is Country Knives, not to be missed for its kitchen knives, pocket knives, and scissors.

LANCASTER CITY

In 1730 the city of Lancaster was laid out as the seat of Lancaster County. John Wright, as chief magistrate, named the city and the county after his home in Lancashire, England. The city's red rose symbol also originates from the house of Lancashire. During the late 18th century, Lancaster was the largest inland city in the United States.

No visit to Lancaster would be complete without browsing through the Central Market, one of our country's oldest publicly owned farmers' market. It is a perfect place to find the best foods of Lancaster County. Next door is the Heritage Center of Lancaster County, fascinating for its introduction to the cultural history of Lancaster and its displays of 18th and 19th century furnishings and folk art. Take the Historic Lancaster Walking Tour of downtown Lancaster for an introduction to the city's history and the early 18th century buildings in and around Penn Square.

Just west of the square on King Street is the Central Market Art Company, displaying the work of local artists. Also just off the square, but on Queen Street, you'll find Miesse Candies, a place to stock up on caramels or peanut butter meltaways; a fun tie shop, called Tie One On; and Cross Keys Coffee and Teas, a place to get a hit of caffeine after all the walking.

East King Street is the location of the Charles Demuth House and

Garden and Demuth's Tobacco Shop next door. Operated by the Demuth Foundation, these two destinations are interesting Lancaster historical sites. The Demuth house was home to the painter, Charles Demuth. The family's tobacco shop is the oldest tobacco shop in America.

Photograph courtesy of Ron Bowman Visual Communications

A must-see destination just north of the city is the Landis Valley Museum with its historical buildings and depiction of life during the colonial and federal eras. The Landis Valley Museum hosts many special events and demonstrations of skills, such as candlemaking, basketweaving, quilting, gunsmithing, blacksmithing, and farming, practiced by the families who settled here during the 17th and 18th centuries. An enjoyable stop for the whole family.

LITITZ

Though I enjoy much of Lancaster County, I find Lititz to be one of the County's most charming spots. Settled by Moravians fleeing Bohemia (present-day Czechoslovakia) because of religious persecution in 1749, Lititz still has the feel of an 18th century village.

Highlights of a self-guided walking tour of this town can include a walk around the building complex that formed the beginning of Lititz. The Moravian congregation built its church in 1787 and the nearby schoolhouse in 1746. The schoolhouse was later expanded to become Linden Hall, the first residence school for girls in the United States. Nearby, the Heritage Map Museum has an impressive collection of 15th to 19th century rare maps. The Lititz Museum is a good place to learn about the history of Lititz, and a stop at Sturgis Pretzel House, the first commercial pretzel bakery in America, is fun for the whole family.

On the other end of Main Street is Wilbur Chocolates, another fun family destination with its Candy Americana Museum and requisite tastings. During good weather, a visit to Lititz Springs Park can be the perfect way to spend an afternoon. The beautiful old trees, a stone-lined stream, and the resident ducks all make for a peaceful respite.

Religious holidays still bring traditional celebrations for the local Moravian residents, events enjoyed by the whole community as well. The Christmas story is celebrated with lights, greens, and nativity scenes. This tradition, with roots in colonial times, is called "putz" or to decorate. Easter is ushered in by the Lititz Moravian Trombone Choir.

MARIETTA AND COLUMBIA

Marietta was originally known as Anderson's Ferry and served as a river crossing during the colonial era. Between the flourishing river trade and the Pennsylvania Rail Road built in the 1850's, Marietta became a prosperous town. It was also a center for lumbering and iron smelting. After the river trade disappeared, this little town hit hard times. Today, 45% of the town is declared a National Historic District. Many of the grand homes of yesteryear have been restored, and some house delightful bed and breakfasts. Marietta is an appealing town to explore with its numerous small shops and casual and fine dining places. Le Petit Museum of Musical Boxes is a museum not to be missed.

Also a Susquehanna River town, Columbia was established by John Wright, an English Quaker who felt called to preach to the natives living along the river. In 1726 Wrights Ferry began carrying people and goods across the river, and the town benefited from all the hustle and bustle. The industrial trade which sustained both Columbia and Marietta around the turn of the century fell into decline as water transport switched to railroads. During the Civil War, Columbia housed a stop on the Underground Rail Road to assist the safe passage of runaway slaves.

The people of Columbia have worked together to make this riverside town an inviting destination. There are various museums, art galleries, antique shops, and the best views of the Susquehanna from nearby Chickies Rock County Park. The river also offers fishing, canoeing, and boating. Do not miss the National Watch and Clock Museum located near downtown Columbia.

> ## PRESIDENT JAMES BUCHANAN
>
> **Nicknamed Old Buck, James Buchanan was the 15th president of the United States, holding the office from 1857 to 1861. He was the only bachelor president, and the only president to hail from Pennsylvania. Visit his home in Lancaster called Wheatland.**
>
>

STRASBURG

Named for Strasbourg, France, by the French Huguenots who founded this village in the early 18th century, Strasburg today is a truly charming village with beautiful old stone and log homes and tree-lined streets. Located in the southern part of Lancaster County along Route 741, it boasts the longest historic district in the United States.

A destination for train lovers, Strasburg offers model train layouts at the Choo Choo Barn and the National Toy Train Museum, retired old locomotives from days gone by at the Rail Road Museum of Pennsylvania, and rides through Amish country in restored railroad cars at the Strasburg Rail Road.

Strasburg Country Store and Creamery, built as a country store circa 1788 in the center of town, makes an delicious destination, with or without children, for an ice cream treat. Families also enjoy the Village Green for miniature golfing. For handcrafted items, head for Eldreth Pottery or Lovina's Stitchery.

TRIPS OUTSIDE LANCASTER COUNTY

CHADDS FORD AND KENNETT SQUARE

> **The original owner of the land where Columbia stands today was George Beale of Surrey, England. In 1701 William Penn transferred 3,000 acres to him at a rental fee of one penny a year for each 100 acres.**
>
>

This area is definitely worth the 45-minute trip from the city of Lancaster. In Kennett Square, visit Longwood Gardens, founded by Pierre S. DuPont and featuring year round displays of flowers. If you're interested in mushroom lore, you'll find the Mushroom Museum at Phillips Place a half mile south of Longwood on Route 1.

The Brandywine Valley also has Chadds Ford, site of the Brandywine Battlefield, where General Washington fought the British in 1777. The most comprehensive collection of Wyeth family artwork is housed at Brandywine River Museum, along with other 19th and 20th century American art. Top your visit with a stop at Chaddsford Winery where they offer tastings of their popular, premium wines.

HERSHEY

Many of the attractions in the town of Hershey owe their existence to Milton S. Hershey, the founder of Hershey's Chocolate. Hershey's Chocolate World offers a short tour of a simulated chocolate factory with samples, of course. The children's choice destination is HERSHEYPARK complete with the Wildcat, a two-acre wooden roller coaster. There are 50-some other rides, ZooAmerica, games, entertainers, and food.

Hershey Gardens, with its 23 acres of botanical gardens, and the Hershey Museum, with its outstanding collection of Pennsylvania German furniture, folk art, textiles, and ceramics, are worthy places to visit.

Kreider Dairy Farms Family Restaurant is perfect for family dining at any time of day. For slightly more serious dining the Hershey Pantry is a good choice.

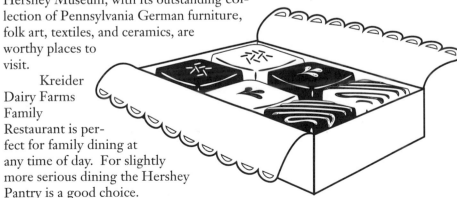

READING (RED-ING)

Founded by two of William Penn's sons, Richard and Thomas, Reading's settlers were primarily German. The area's economy relied on heavy industry until recently when it turned to high technology to stay healthy. Because of the eight million visitors who come to shop its outlet stores, this city is billed the "Outlet Capital of the World."

The largest outlets include VF Factory Outlet Village, with a separate building called The Designers' Place filled with upscale shops; Reading Station Outlet Center; Reading Outlet Center; and Outlets on Hiesters Lane. Sprinkled throughout the town of Reading are other single store outlets selling anything from children's furniture to furs.

Jack and Heidi Czarnecki's restaurant, Joe's Bistro 614, is my choice for refueling when strenuous shopping leaves your energy at a low ebb.

RESOURCES

AIRPORT

LANCASTER AIRPORT
Airport Road
Lititz, PA 17543
(717) 569-1221

AUTO RENTAL

AVIS RENT A CAR
Lancaster County Airport
Lititz, PA 17543
(717) 569-3185

ENTERPRISE RENT-A-CAR
1573 Manheim Pike
Lancaster, PA 17601
(800) 325-8007

HERTZ RENT A CAR
Lancaster County Airport
Lititz, PA 17543
(800) 654-3131

HERTZ RENT A CAR
625 East Orange Street
Lancaster, PA 17603
(717) 569-4345

LANDIS RENT-A-CAR
RD 3
Lititz, PA 17543
(717) 569-9401

NATIONAL CAR RENTAL
INTERRENT
Liberty Street & Lititz Pike
Lancaster, PA 17602
(800) 227-7368

MEDICAL SERVICES

FAMILY PHYSICIAN

DR. DAVID J. SILVERSTEIN, ASSOCIATES
2920 Marietta Avenue
Lancaster, PA 17601
(717) 898-2356

HOSPITALS

COMMUNITY HOSPITAL OF LANCASTER
1100 East Orange Street
Lancaster, PA 17602
(717) 397-3711

LANCASTER GENERAL HOSPITAL
555 North Duke Street
Lancaster, PA 17603
(717) 290-5511

MEDICAL CENTER

COMMUNITY WAY MEDICAL CENTER
1950 Marietta Avenue
Lancaster, PA 17603
(717) 392-7986

PET LODGING

GOCHENAUER KENNELS
995 Fruitville Pike
Lititz, PA 17543
Mon-Fri 8-6. Sat 8-12. Sun 4-6.
(717) 569-6151
This is a good place to board your pet.
All pets must be up-to-date with yearly
vaccines. Accommodations are climate-
controlled, and pets have indoor and outdoor runs.

SMOKETOWN VETERINARY HOSPITAL
2497 Old Philadelphia Pike, (Route 340)
Smoketown, PA 17576
Mon-Thurs 8-7:30. Fri 8-5:30. Sat 8-11:30.
Sun 9 a.m.-9:30 a.m. & 5 p.m.-6 p.m. for
pick up. (717) 394-5542
Indoor and outdoor runs for your furry
friend. Shots and vaccinations must be
up-to-date. Bring vaccination records
along.

PHARMACIES

RED ROSE PHARMACY
333 North Water Street
Lancaster, PA 17603
Mon-Fri 9-5. Sat 9-12. (717) 291-1326

WILLIAMS APOTHECARY, INC.
201 East Chestnut Street
Lancaster, PA 17603
Mon-Fri 8:30-9. Sat 8:30-3.
(717) 393-3814

SERVICE STATIONS

CONESTOGA VALLEY GARAGE
2008-D Horseshoe Road
Lancaster, PA 17602
Mon-Fri 7-5. (717) 299-2137

HEMPSTEAD TEXACO
1741 Hempstead Road
Lancaster, PA 17601
Mon-Fri 7:30-5. (717) 291-2020

LANCASTER FLEET & AUTO
625 East Orange Street
Lancaster, PA 17603
Mon-Sat 8-5. (717) 295-4444
Corner of Prince and Orange Streets.
Lancaster Fleet and Auto is a AAA-
approved auto repair center and offers
24-hour towing. Next door is Hertz
RentACar if the worst happens.

PEP BOYS AUTOMOTIVE SUPERCENTERS
2080 Lincoln Highway, (Route 30)
Lancaster, PA 17602
Mon-Fri 8-9. Sat 8-8. Sun 9-6.
(717) 299-3335

TRANSPORTATION

FRIENDLY TAXI SERVICE
625 East Orange Street
Lancaster, PA 17603
24 hours. (717) 392-2222

RED ROSE TRANSIT AUTHORITY (RRTA)
45 Erick Road
Lancaster, PA 17603
(717) 397-4246
Transit bus and shared ride service throughout Lancaster city
and county.

RECOMMENDED READING

AMISH AND MENNONITES

Dyck, Cornelius J. *An Introduction to Mennonite History*. Scottdale, Pa.: Herald Press, 1993.

Friesen, Steve. *A Modest Mennonite Home*. Intercourse, Pa.: Good Books, 1990. The story of the 1719 Hans Herr House in Willow Street, Lancaster County.

Gingerich, Melvin. *Mennonite Attire Through Four Centuries*. Breiningsville, Pa.: The Pennsylvania German Society, 1970.

Hostetler, John A. *Amish Society*. 4th ed. Baltimore: The Johns Hopkins University Press, 1993.

Keim, Albert N. *Compulsory Education and the Amish: The Right Not to Be Modern*. Boston: Beacon Press, 1975.

Kraybill, Donald B. and Steven M. Nolt. *Amish Enterprise: From Plows to Profits*. Baltimore: The Johns Hopkins University Press, 1995.

Kraybill, Donald B. *The Puzzles of Amish Life*. Intercourse, Pa.: Good Books, 1990.

Leahy, Donna and photographs by Robert Leahy. *Wisdom of the Plain Folk: Songs and Prayers from the Amish and Mennonites*. New York: Penguin Studio, 1997.

Ruth, John L. *Maintaining the Right Fellowship*. Scottdale, Pa.: Herald Press, 1984.

Ruth, John L. *A Quiet and Peaceable Life*. Intercourse, Pa.: Good Books, 1979.

Scott, Stephen. *Why Do They Dress That Way?* Intercourse, Pa.: Good Books, 1986.

Seitz, Ruth Hoover with photography by Blair Seitz. *Amish Country*. New York: Crescent Books, 1987.

Stoltzfus, Louise. *Amish Women: Lives and Stories*. Intercourse, Pa.: Good Books, 1986.

van Braght, Thieleman J. *The Bloody Theater or Martyrs Mirror of the Defenseless Christians*. Translated by Joseph F. Sohm in 1886. Scottdale, Pa.: Herald Press, 1950.

FOOD

Czarnecki, Jack. *A Cook's Book of Mushrooms*. New York: Artisan, 1995.

Good, Phyllis Pellman and Louise Stoltzfus. *The Central Market Cookbook*. Intercourse, Pa.: Good Books, 1989.

Longacre, Doris Janzen. *More-with-Less Cookbook*. Scottdale, Pa.: Herald Press, 1976.

Showalter, Emma. *The Mennonite Community Cookbook*. Scottdale, Pa.: Herald Press, 1978,

Stoltzfus, Louise. *Favorite Recipes From Quilters*. Intercourse, Pa.: Good Books, 1994.

Weaver, William Woys. *Pennsylvania Dutch Country Cooking*. New York: Abbeville Press Publishers, 1993.

Weaver, William Woys. *Sauerkraut Yankees*. Philadelphia: University of Pennsylvania Press, 1983.

GENERAL LANCASTER COUNTY

Alexander, Edwin P. *On the Main Line: The Pennsylvania Rail Road in the 19th Century*. New York: Clarkson N. Potter, 1971.

Doll, Eugene E. *The Ephrata Cloister: An Introduction*. Ephrata, Pa.: Ephrata Cloister Associates, 1958.

Evans, Benjamin D. and June R. *Pennsylvania's Covered Bridges: A Complete Guide*. Pittsburgh: University of Pittsburgh Press,1994.

Gerstell, Vivian S. *Silversmiths of Lancaster, Pennsylvania, 1730-1850*. Lancaster, Pa.: Lancaster County Historical Society, 1972.

Long, Amos Jr. *The Pennsylvania German Family Farm*. Breinigsville, Pa.: The Pennsylvania German Society, 1972.

Seitz, Ruth Hoover with photography by Blair Seitz. *Pennsylvania's Historic Places*. Intercourse, Pa.: Good Books, 1989.

Soderlund, Jean R. Ed. *William Penn and the Founding of Pennsylvania, 1680-1684: A Documentary History*. Philadelphia: University of Pennsylvania Press, 1983.

Swank, Scott T. et. al. *Arts of the Pennsylvania Germans*. New York: W. W. Norton, 1983.

Wood, Jr., Stacy B. C. *Clockmakers and Watchmakers of Lancaster County, Pennsylvania*. Lancaster, Pa.: Lancaster County Historical Society, 1995.

QUILTING

Granick, Eve Wheatcroft. *The Amish Quilt.* Intercourse, Pa.: Good Books, 1989.

Hughes, Robert text, plate commentary by Julie Silber. *Amish The Art of the Quilt.* New York: Alfred A. Knopf, 1993.

Kraybill, Donald B., Patricia T. Herr, and Jonathan Holstein. *A Quiet Spirit: Amish Quilts from the Collection of Cindy Tietze & Stuart Hodosh.* Los Angeles: UCLA Fowler Museum of Cultural History, 1996.

Pellman, Rachel and Kenneth *The World of Amish Quilts.* Intercourse, Pa.: Good Books, 1984.

Pellman, Rachel and Kenneth *A Treasury of Amish Quilts.* Intercourse, Pa.: Good Books, 1990.

INDEX

A

ABC Woodcraft, 205
A. L. Kauffman's, 133
Abe's Buggy Ride, 149
Accomac Inn, 108, 114, 117, 119
Adamstown Inn, 44
Agricultural Preserve Board, 31
Airport, 233
Akron Restaurant, 102, 114, 117
Alden House Bed, 44
Alex Austin Steakhouse, 89
Alois Bube, 114
American Military Edged Weaponry Museum, 157
Amish,
 Enterprise, 32-33, 235
 Society, 31-40, 149, 160, 194, 235-236
Amish Country Tours, 175, 239
Amish Experience, The, 155
Amish Mennonite Information Center, 39
Ammann, Jakob, 34
Anabaptists, 33-34, 194
Anderson Pretzels, 141
Antique Airplane Restaurant, 118
Antiques, 16-18, 20, 44, 158, 160, 162, 184, 188-191
Antiques Extravaganza, 17-18, 20, 191
Antiques Showcase at the Blackhorse, 188
Apple Bin Inn, The, 44
Artworks at Doneckers, 17-18, 21, 62, 150, 205, 227
Auctions, 16-18, 20, 134-135, 160, 184, 191-192
Auntie Anne's Soft Pretzels, 142
Authentic Bed & Breakfast of Lancaster County, 43
Automobiles,
 Antique, 158, 180
 Rental, 233
 Repair, 234
Avis Rent A Car, 233

B

B. Dalton Bookseller, 193
Ballooning, 20, 165
Bareville Furniture, 198
Barnes Foundation Museum, 180
Basketville, 146, 205
Beer, 98, 114-117, 144, 146
Beiler's Fruit Farm, 129
Beiler's Quilts & Crafts, 218
Bella Vista Bed & Breakfast, The, 45, 94
Ben-Mar Guest Home, 73
Berks County, 15, 124, 129, 144, 176-177, 190
Berks County Visitors' Center, 15
Best Western, 80
Bev's Consignment Shoppe, 222
Bickles Chips, 106
Bicylces,
      Rentals & Sales, 167
      Touring, 149, 166
Bicycle World, 167
Bird-in-Hand Bake Shop, 106, 121
Bird-in-Hand Bakery, 121
Bird-in-Hand Family Inn, 78
Bird-in-Hand Family Restaurant, 107
Bird-in-Hand Farmers' Market, 53, 78, 133, 194
Black Horse Lodge, The, 80
Black Horse Restaurant, The, 94
Blue Gate Farm Market, 130
Boating, 75, 166, 170
Boehringer's Ice Cream, 137
Bon-Ton, 198
Bonnie's Exceptional Ice Cream, 138
Book Bin Bookstore, 193
Book Haven, 193-194
Book Warehouse, 216
Borders Book Shop, 193
Boscovs, 198
Bowling, 167-168
Bowman's Stove & Patio, 198
Boxwood Inn Bed & Breakfast, 45
Boyertown Museum of Historic Vehicles, 180
Brandywine Battlefield, 177, 231

Brandywine River Museum, 177, 231
Bratton's Woodcraft, 199
Bridge Bust, 21
Bridge, 148, 150
Brubaker, Jay, 202
Brunch, 91-94, 99, 103, 108, 110, 114
Bubbie's Bagels, 95, 119, 128
Bube's Brewery, 114
Buchanan, James, 22, 93, 164, 230
Buggy Rides, 149
Burkholder's Fabrics, 221
Byer's Butterflake Bakery, 123
Byerstown Woodwork, 200

C

Calvaresi Winery, 144
Cameron Estate Inn, 61
Camping, 74, 74-76, 166
Candlelight Inn Bed, The, 46, 210
Candy, 126-127, 165
Candy Americana Museum, 165, 229
Carlos and Charlie's, 101
Cedar Hill Farm Bed & Breakfast, 46
Cedar Lane Dry Goods, 221
Centerville Bulk Foods, 128
Central Market, 133-134, 236
Central Market Art Company, 197
Central Market Cookbook, 236
Chadds Ford, 231
Chaddsford Winery, 145, 231
Chameleon Club, 173
Char The Hex Place, 212
Charles Demuth House and Gardens, 157, 228
Cherry Hill Orchards, 130
Cherry, Steven, 204
Chester County, 20, 23, 145, 177-178
Chestnut Street Books, 194
Chickies Rock County Park, 169, 230
Choo Choo Barn, 153, 230
Churchtown Inn, 61
Clay Bookstore, 194
Clay Distelfink, The, 206
Clearview Farm Bed & Breakfast, 47

Clearview Lanes, 167
Clearwood Farm, 69
Clock Tower Antiques, 188
CML Books, 194
Coleman's Ice Cream, 137
Columbia, 229-230
Columbia Farmers' Market, 134
Columbia Garment Company, 213
Columbian Bed & Breakfast, The, 47
Comfort Inn, 80
Community Hospital of Lancaster, 233
Community Natural Foods Store, 140
Community Way Medical Center, 233
Conestoga Auction, 135
Conestoga Valley Garage, 234
Conrad Weiser Homestead, 176
Continental Inn, 68
Cornwall Iron Furnace, 176
Country Club of Hershey, 178
Country Gardens Farm Bed & Breakfast, 48, 103
Country Haven Campground, 74
Country Housewares Store, 196
Country Knives, 213, 227
Country Lane Quilts, 218
Country Living Inn, 62
Country Pines Farm, 48-49
Country Road Flowers, 206
Country Stores, 124, 128-129, 156, 196-197
Country Table Restaurant, 102, 106
Crab Barn, 120
Creekside Inn Bed & Breakfast, 49
Cricket Hollow Bed & Breakfast, 49
Cross Keys Coffee and Teas, 127, 228

D

D & S Brasserie, 94
Dauphin County, 178, 180
Days Inn of Lancaster, 80
Decoy Bed & Breakfast, The, 60
Delaware County, 188
Demuth's Tobacco Shop, 157, 198
Déjà Vu, 222
Derstine, Timothy, 5, 173

Dienner's Country Bar-B-Q, 102, 106, 119
Dietrich's Meats and Country Store, 124
Dining Car Restaurant, 89, 152
Dining Car at the Strasburg Rail Road, 89
Distillery Bridge, 150
Doc Hollidays, 90, 117
Doctors, 233
Domaki Leather Outlet, 213
Doneckers Fashion Stores, 62
Doneckers-The Gerhart House, 64
Doneckers-The Homestead, 63
Downtown Visitors' Center, 15
Duane L. Mendenhall, 200
Dunwoody, Karen, 208
Dutch Lanes, 167
Dutch School Natural Foods, 140
Dutch Wonderland Entertainment Complex, 151
Dyck, Cornelius J., 219

E

East of Eden Pub, 98
Eberly Poultry, 124
Ebersol, L. B. & Sons, Inc., 202
Echo Hill Country Store, 129
Edward's Coffee Shop, 127
Ed Stoudt's Black Angus, 94
Eicher Indian Museum, 157, 171
Eldreth Pottery, 206-207, 230
Enterprise Rent-A-Car, 233
Ephrata, 227
Ephrata Cloister, 18, 150, 158, 227, 236
Ephrata Community Park, 157, 171
Ephrata Playhouse, 173

F

Fabric, 156, 213-214, 218, 221-222
Fabric Store, The 213
Family Time Restaurants, 107
Farm Supplies, 197
Farm Vacations, 43
Farm View Guest House, 73
Farmers' Markets, 129-135
Favorite Foods, 86, 106
Favorite Restaurants, 119

Fisher's Nursery and Farm Market, 130
Fisher's Pastries, 121
Fishercraft Custom-Built Furniture, 201
Fishers Quality Furniture,
Fishing, 51, 57-58, 60, 74, 83, 143, 166, 170, 230
Flowers & Thyme Bed & Breakfast, 50, 144
Flory's Camping and Cottages, 74
Folk Art, 159, 162, 179, 185, 188, 211-212, 231
Foltz Pottery, 207
Foltz, Ned, 207
Four Seasons, 168
Fox Chase Golf Club, 168
Fraktur, 159, 185-186
Franklin and Marshall College, 19, 162
Frey's Antiques, 188
Friendly Taxi Service, 234
Frogtown Acres Bed & Breakfast, 50
Fulton Academy Theatre, 173
Fulton Opera House, 173
Fulton Steamboat Inn, 64
Funk's Farm Market, 130

G

Gallo Rosso, 109, 119
Garden Spot, 168
Gardens of Eden Bed & Breakfast, The, 51, 112
Gast Classic Motorcars, 158
General Sutter Inn, 65
George Zahn House, The, 60
German,
General, 20, 34, 37, 58, 67, 86, 98, 127, 144, 155, 158, 163, 170, 197, 207, 212, 235
Pennsylvania, 18, 21, 31-32, 86, 161, 177, 179, 185, 194, 198, 201, 204, 206, 232, 236
Germantown, 34
Glassmyer's Restaurant, 95, 119
Glen Brook Bake Shop, 106, 121
Gochenauer Kennels, 234
Golf, 79, 82-83, 168-169, 178-179
Good'n Plenty Family Style Eating, 103
Good's Store, 196
Gordonville Fire Company Auction, 16, 191
Goschenhoppen Historians Annual Folk Festival, 19

Green Acres, 69

Green Dragon Farmers' Market, 12, 134-135, 138, 227

Green Hills Inn, 118

Green Mountain Cyclery, 167

Greystone Manor, 60

Groff's Picnic Grove, 89, 152

Groff Farm Home, 70

Groff's Farm Restaurant, 104

H

Hampshire Orchard, 131

Hampton Inn, 80

Handcrafted, 156-157, 185-186, 199-212, 218-223

Hands-on-House, 148, 150-151

Hannah Stoltzfoos Quilts, 218

Hans Herr House, 19, 21-22, 158, 172, 235

Harley Davidson Museum, 181

Harvest Drive Motel, 81

Harvey Martin, 201

Hawk Valley, 168

Haydn Zug's, 109, 119

Hayrides, 130, 132

Heirloom Seed Project, 161

Hempstead Texaco, 234

Herb Shop, The, 136

Heritage Center of Lancaster County, 159, 228

Heritage Map Museum, 159, 191, 229

Herr's Mill Bridge, 150

Hershey, 178-180

HERSHEYPARK, 23, 83, 150, 179-180, 231

Hershey Bed & Breakfast Reservation Service, 60

Hershey Farm Bakery, 123

Hershey Farm Motor Inn, 78

Hershey Farm Restaurant, 107

Hershey Gardens, 179, 231

Hershey Lodge, 82

Hershey Museum, 150, 179, 231

Hershey Pantry, 118, 231

Hershey's Chocolate World, 126, 231

Hertz Rent A Car, 233

Hex, 33, 189, 212

High Sports Miniature Golf, 171

Hiking, 51, 58, 169-170

Hilltop Acres Farm Market, 131
Hinkle's Restaurant, 96
Historic Lancaster Walking Tour, 21, 150, 176, 228
Historic Revere Tavern, 94
Historic Strasburg Inn, The, 15, 20-21, 65, 94
Historical Society of Cocalico Valley, The, 160
Hobday, R. Todd, 203
Hodecker Celery Farm, 131, 134
Holiday Inn Lancaster Host Resort, 16-17, 80, 168
Home Furnishings Factory Outlet, 214
Honeybrook Classics Inc, 188
Hong Kong Garden, 101
Hoover's Fruit and Vegetable Farm, 131
Horse Inn, 94
Horses, 192, 200, 205, 209
Horseshoe Trail, 170
Horst Auction Center, 191-192
Hospitals, 233
Hotel Brunswick, 81
Hotel Hershey, 82, 179
Hottenstein's Farm Market, 132
House on The Canal Bed, The, 83
Howard Johnson, 81

I

Ice Cream, 102, 104, 106,132, 135, 137-139, 151-152
Indian, American, 49, 157, 169, 176
Information Centers, 15, 39
Inn at Mt. Hope, 52
Intelligencer Journal, 185
Intercourse, 227
Intercourse Village Restaurant, 104
Isaac's Restaurant and Deli, 113, 208
Italian Villa Comedy Club, 174
It's Only Natural, 140

J

J & B Quilts and Crafts, 218
J-M's Bistro & Pub, 90, 117, 119
Jams and Jellies, 139
Jay Brubaker, Cabinetmaker, 202
Jayne's, 223
JC Penney, 198

Jennie's Diner, 96
Joe's Bistro 614, 119
Josephine's, 110, 119
Jukebox Nightclub, 174

K

Karen Dunwoody, 208
Kauffman's Distillery Bridge, 150
Kauffman's Handcrafted Clock, 208
Kauffman's Hardware, 196
Kauffman Museum, 164,
Keen, Martin & Carol, 40, 87
Kegel's Seafood Restaurant, 91,
Kennett Square, 20, 23, 145, 178, 231
King's Cottage, The, 43, 52, 77
Kings Homestead, 208
King's Woodcraft, 202
Kissel View Farm Bakery, 122
Kitchen Kettle, 17-18, 20, 139, 152, 199, 227
Kling House Restaurant, 139
Kraybill, Donald B., 32-33, 235, 237
Kreider Dairy Farms Family Restaurant, 104, 118, 231
Kreider Farms Dairy Stores, 132
Kutztown University, 18

L

L. B. Ebersol & Sons, Inc., 202
Lake at Mount Gretna, 172
Lancaster Balloons Inc., 165
Lancaster Bicycle Shop, 167
Lancaster Bicycle Touring, 149, 166
Lancaster City, 228
Lancaster County Antiques, 189
Lancaster County Central Park, 169
Lancaster County Winery, 146
Lancaster Dispensing Company, 115, 117
Lancaster Farmland Trust, 31
Lancaster Fleet, 234
Lancaster Galleries, 197
Lancaster General Hospital, 233
Lancaster Hilton Garden Inn, 81
Lancaster Host Resort, 16, 168
Lancaster Malt Brewing Company, 114-115, 119
Lancaster Mennonite Historical Society, 160

Lancaster Museum of Art, 161
Lancaster New Era, 185
Lancaster Pottery & Glass, 214
Lancaster Opera Company, 173
Lancaster Symphony Orchestra, 173
Lancaster Travelodge, 81
Landis Farm Guest Home, 70
Landis Rent-A-Car, 233
Landis Valley Museum, 21-22, 87, 150, 161, 186, 228
Lapp's Coach Shop, 208-209,227
Lapp's Dry Goods, 221
Lapp's Family Restaurant, 105
Lapp's Quilts and Crafts, 219
Lapp's Wooden Toys, 209
Lapp Valley Farm's Ice Cream, 106, 135, 137-139, 151
Le Petit Museum of Musical Boxes, 150, 162, 230
Leahy, Donna, 235
Leahy, Robert, 4, 235
Leather Wearhouse, 214
Lebanon Bologna Company, 125
Lebanon County, 19, 125
Lebanon Valley Tourist Visitors' Bureau, 15
Lee E. Brenner Dining Car, 89
Leisure Lanes, 168
Lemon Grass Thai Restaurant, 100
Leola Family Restaurant, 105
Leola Produce Auction, 192
Leonard & Mildred Rothman Gallery, 162
Limestone Inn, 67
Lincoln Haus Inn, 60
Lititz, 229
Lititz Historical Foundation, 162
Lititz Museum, 65, 162, 229
Lititz Springs Park, 171, 229
Little Book Shop, The, 133, 194
Living Waters Theatre, 174-175
Loft Restaurant, The, 112
Log Cabin Restaurant, The, 111, 117, 119
Lombardo's Italian American Restaurant, 101
Long's Park, 19, 150, 172
Longwood Gardens, 20, 23, 178, 231
Loreto's Ristorante, 99

Lovina's Stitchery, 219
Luthy, David, 35

M

M & J Greider Farm, 40, 87
Manheim Manor Bed & Breakfast, 53
Mannie's Wood Shop, 209
Manor, The, 60
Maps, 23-27, 226
Maple Croft Interiors and Unique Crafts, 210
Maple Lane Farm Guest House, 71
Marian Stoltzfus Quilts, 219
Marietta, 229-230
Marion Court Room, 114
Market Fare Restaurant, 91, 114
Martin, Harvey, 201
Martin's of Akron, 106, 142
Martin's Bike Shop, 167
Martin's Chairs Inc., 203
Martyrs Mirror, The, 235
Mascot Park, 163, 172
Mascot Roller Mill, 163,
Masthof Bookstore, 194
McIntosh Inn, 68
Medical Assistance, 233
Mendenhall, Duane L., 200
Mennonite,
       History, 30, 33-34, 155-156, 158-160, 235
       of Lancaster, 17, 31-34, 34, 38, 62, 102, 104, 149. 155-156, 185,
       187, 235
Michael's Homestyle Bread, 122
Middle Creek Wildlife Management Area, 150, 170
Miesse Candies, 126, 228
Mill Bridge Village, 150
Mill Creek Homestead Bed & Breakfast, 53
Mill Stream Motor Lodge, 81
Miller's Smorgasbord & Bakery, 123
Miniature golf, 74, 76, 82, 150, 170-171
Minnich's Farm Bakery, 123
Molly's Pub, 116
Mom Chaffe's Cellarette, 120
Montgomery County, 180
Morning Meadows Farm, 71

Morton, Thomas B., 204
Moselem Springs Inn, 119, 129
Mount Gretna Inn, 54
Mount Gretna Playhouse, 174
Mount Hope Estate and Winery, 19, 145
Moyer's Book Barn, 195
Muddy Run Recreation Park, 166
Museums, 150-151, 153-154, 157-166, 177-181, 186, 191
Mushroom Museum at Phillips Place, 178, 231

N

National Car Rental, 233
National Toy Train Museum, 79, 150, 154, 230
National Watch and Clock Museum, 163, 230
Nav Jiwan International Tea Room, 101, 119, 212
Naylor Wine Cellars, 145
Neffdale Farm of Paradise, 71
Next to New Fine Clothing, 223
Next to New Fine Furniture, 223
New Harmony Roasters, 128
New Holland Sales Stables, 192
New Life Homestead, 60
Nissley Vineyards, The, 18, 145
Noble House Bed & Breakfast, 54
Nolt, Steven M., 32-33, 235

O

O'Flaherty's Dingeldein House B & B, 54, 55
O'Halloran's Irish Pub, 117
Oak Creek Campground, 74
Oak Furniture and Antiques, 189
Oktoberfest, 20, 146
Old Candle Barn, The, 210
Old Country Store, 156, 227
Old Mill Stream Camping Manor, 74
Olde Country Log House Farm, 72
Olde Fogie Farm, 72
Olde Greenfield Inn, 110, 114
Olde Lincoln House, The, 94
Olde Millhouse Shoppes, The, 211
Olde Square Inn, The, 55
Omar & Sylvia Petersheim Quilts & Crafts, 220
Osceola Mill House, 56
Outlets, 44, 120, 186, 205, 213-217

Outlets on Hiesters Lane, 214, 232
Overlook, 168

P

Park City, 193, 195, 198
Parks, 12, 149, 171
Prudhomme's Lost Cajun Kitchen, 96, 114
Peach Lane Produce, 132
Peanut Bar & Restaurant, The, 120
Peking Palace, 97, 117, 119
Penn, William, 30, 34, 140, 180, 198, 228, 231-232, 236
Pennsylvania Dutch Balloon & Craft Festival, 20
Pennsylvania Dutch Convention & Visitors' Bureau, 39
Pennsylvania Dutch Food, 18, 86- 88, 102-107, 137, 236
Pennsylvania Dutch, see Pennsylvania Germans
Pennsylvania Farm Show, 16
Pennsylvania German Society, 177, 235-236
Pennsylvania Relief Sale, 17,
Pennsylvania Renaissance Faire, 19, 145
Pennsylvania State Craft Show, 19
People's Place, The, 156
Peoples Restaurant, 105
Pep Boys Automotive Supercenters, 234
Peppers, 91
Petersheim, 220
Pets, 42, 65, 68, 76, 83, 234
Pharmacies, 234
Picnicking, 89, 145-146, 152, 163, 166, 169-172
Pinch Pond Family Campground, 77
Pine View Acres, 138
Pinehurst Inn Hershey, 83
Pinetown Bridge, 150
Plain & Fancy Farm Restaurant, 106
Portofino, 99-100
Pressroom, The, 116
Pretzels, 106, 141-143, 153
Provident Bookstores, 195

Q

Quality Outlet Center, 215
Quilts,
        Auctions, 17, 20
        General, 16, 18, 156, 187, 218-221
        Material, 156, 221-222

Quips Pub, 116
QVC Outlet, 215

R

R. Todd Hobday, 203
Rail Road House Bed & Breakfast, The, 56, 92
Railroad Museum of Pennsylvania, 154
Rainbow Apiaries, 136
Ramada Inn, 81
Reading, 232
Reading China, 216-217
Reading Outlet Center, 215, 232
Reading Station Outlet Center, 215, 232
Recipes, 37, 40 55, 56, 77, 82, 94, 103, 112, 144, 173, 210, 217
Red Barn Market, 133
Red Caboose Lodge, 78-79, 154
Red Rose Excursions, 40, 156
Red Rose Pharmacy, 234
Red Rose Transit Authority, 234
Red Run Campground, 75
Reflections Fine Food & Spirits, 92, 114, 117, 119
Renninger's, 189-190
Restaurant at Doneckers, The, 111-112, 114
Rice Antiques, 190
Riehl's Quilts & Crafts, 220
Rising Sun Hotel, 96
River Inn Bed & Breakfast, The, 39, 57
Roamer's Retreat Campground, 75
Rock Ford Plantation, 22, 150, 164
Rockvale Square Outlets, 186, 215-216
Rocky Acre Farm, 72
Rodale Research Institute, 177
Rohrer's Mill, 71, 136
Roots Market, 135, 192
Rose Manor English, 60
Rough and Tumble Museum, 164
Ruth, John L., 30-31

S

S. Clyde Weaver, 106, 125, 134
S. Mandros Imported Foods, 138
Sauder's Fabrics, 221-222
Sears, 198

Second Glance,A, 222
Sell, Geri, 122
Seltzer's Lebanon Bologna Company, 125
Service Stations, 234
Shady Maple Grocery, 129
Shady Maple Smorgasbord, 106, 196
Shank's Tavern, 117
Sharp Jewelers, 211
Shops at Doneckers, The, 199
Shupp's Grove, 190
Sickman's Mill, 164
Sight and Sound, 174-175
Sill's Family Campground, 76
Silverstein, Dr. David J., 233
Simons, Menno, 33-34
Smithton Inn, 67
Smokehouse Shop, 139
Smoketown Veterinary Hospital, 234
Smoketown Village Guest House, 73
Smokin Jake's, 114
Smucker's Quilt Shop, 220
Soudersburg Motel, 81
South Pointe Antiques, 190
Speedwell Forge Lake, 58
Spill the Beans, 106, 128
Spring Gulch Resort Campground, 76
Spring Trout Fish Farm, 143
Springhouse Inn Bed & Breakfast, 57
Starlite Camping Resort, 76
Stauffer Farm Market, 133
Stephen van Ormer, 202-203
Steven Cherry, 204
Stockyard Inn, The, 93, 116
Stoltzfoos Sisters Bakery, 123
Stoltzfus Farm Restaurant, 107, 126
Stoltzfus, Louise, 4, 185, 236
Stoltzfus, Miriam M., 217
Stoltzfus Meats, 106, 125, 227
Stoltzfus, Moses F., 210
Stone Haus Farm Bed & Breakfast, 73
Stoudt's Antique Mail, 17-18, 20, 191
Strasburg, 230

Strasburg Country Store, 138, 230
Strasburg Rail Road, 21-22, 67, 79, 89, 152, 154, 230
Strasburg Visitors' Information Center, 15
Sturgis Pretzel House, 143, 229
Sun Valley Campground, 77
Susan Witman Consignments, 223
Susquehanna Glass Outlet, 133
Susquehanna Heritage Tourist Information Center, 15
Susquehanna River, 48, 57, 108, 148, 169, 230
Susquehannock State Park, 169
Swimming, 53, 65, 75-76, 168, 172
Swiss Woods Bed & Breakfast, 58

T

Taj Mahal, 98, 114, 117, 119
Tanger Factory Outlet Center, 186, 216
Teddy Bear Emporium, 153
Ten Thousand Villages, 16, 18-19, 21, 101, 211, 227
Thomas B. Morton Cabinetmakers, 204
Tie One On, 199, 228
Tin Bin, The, 212
Tobias S. Frogg, 93
Tony Wang's Chinese Restaurant, 97
Top Honeymoon Hideaways, 43
Touch of Taste, 113
Tours, 40, 175-176
Toy Train Museum, 79, 150, 154, 230
Trains, 21-22, 89, 150, 152-154
Transportation, 234
Travelers Rest Motel, 81
Tree Top, 169
Trips Outside Lancaster, 11, 225, 231
Twin Brook Winery, 146, 205
Inn at Twin Linden, The, 43, 66

V

Uncle Henry's Pretzel Bakery, 143

W

VF Factory Outlet Village, 216, 232
van Ormer, Stephen, 202-203
Village Green Miniature Golf, 150
Village Inn of Bird-in-Hand, 68
Village of Dutch Delights, 102
Visitors' Centers, 15, 39

Vogt Farm Bed, 58
Waldenbooks, 195
Walkabout Inn, The, 60
Walnut Hill Farm Bed & Breakfast, 59
Walter Amos Bookseller, 195
Washington House Restaurant, 94
Waterford House Bed & Breakfast, 59
Wax Museum of Lancaster County, 151
Weaver Candy and Cookie Outlets, 127
Weaver, William Woys, 86, 137, 236
Weaver's Dry Goods, 222
Weaver's Natural Foods Inc., 1414
West Ridge Guest House, 60
Wheatland, 17, 21-22, 164-165, 230
White Oak Campground, 77
Wilbur Chocolates Candy Americana Museum, 165
Williams Apothecary, 234
Willow Valley Family Resort, 79
Willow Valley Family Restaurant, 107, 117
Wilton Armetale Store, 212
Wineries, 144-146
Witmer Quilt Shop, 221
Wright, John, 153, 165, 228, 230
Wright's Ferry Mansion, 165

Y

Yang's Restaurant, 101Yangs Restaurant,
York County, 108, 148, 181

Z

Zimmerman Hardware & Farm Supplies, 197
Zimmerman's Store, 197
Zinn's Diner, 107
Zinn's Park, 171
ZooAmerica, 180, 231
Zook's Mill Bridge, 150
Zook's Handmade Quilts & Crafts, 221

LANCASTER COUNTY:
The Best Fun, Food, Lodging, Shopping, and Sights
Mail Order Form

Use this form if:

◆ you would like to order this book through the mail. For information on quanity discounts, call the Food Companion Press sales and distribution number at (215) 844-3850.

◆ you would like to communicate with the author about any special place or activity that was not included in this book that you think should have been.

◆ you would like to communicate with the author about entries that were included in this book that you think should not have been included.

◆ you have any other thoughts, comments, compliments, or criticisms.

FOOD COMPANION PRESS
P.O. Box 27266
Philadelphia, PA 19118-0266

❏ I would like to order ___ book(s). I have included a check for $11.60 ($10.95, tax, shipping is free) for each book. The total amount included is $_____. Please give your address below.

❏ I would like to recommend _____
I think it is a marvelous place because _____
_____

If I agree with you and include your recommendation in the next edition, would you like to be mentioned in the review? (Eg. Sam Smith of Ephrata told me about XYZ, where he is a regular.) If so, how would you like to be mentioned? _____
_____

❏ Other comments: _____
_____

Name: _____
Address: _____
City: _____
State: _____ Zip: _____
Phone: _____

255